Context
Starter

Niedersachsen

Cornelsen

Context · Starter Niedersachsen

Im Auftrag des Verlages herausgegeben von
Prof. Hellmut Schwarz, Mannheim, und Dr. Annette Leithner-Brauns, Dresden

erarbeitet von
Dr. Paul Maloney, Hildesheim; Carl Bamber, Kloster Lehnin; Irene Bartscherer, Bonn; Ingrid Becker-Ross, Krefeld; Friederike von Bremen, Hannover; Dr. Angelika Czekay, Berlin; Dr. Peter Hohwiller, Landau; Marcel Sprunkel, Köln; Sabine Struß, Verden; Michael Thürwächter, Heidelberg

unter beratender Mitwirkung von
Martina Baasner, Berlin; Dr. Sabine Buchholz, Hürth; Bernd Koch, Marburg; Gunthild Porteous-Schwier, Moers; Thomas Wöhlke, Weinheim

in Zusammenarbeit mit der Englischredaktion
Cornelia Hansch und Elke Lehmann *(Projektleitung)*; Dr. Marion Kiffe und Hartmut Tschepe *(koordinierende Redakteure)*; Neil Porter, Dr. Christian v. Raumer, Ingrid-Maria Sauer, Ralph Williams sowie Dr. Ilka Soennecken

Layout und technische Umsetzung
zweiband.media, Berlin *(Gesamtausgabe)*; designcollective, Berlin

Umschlaggestaltung
axeptDESIGN, Berlin

Weitere Bestandteile des Lehrwerks
- Schülerbuch als E-Book 978-3-06-036179-3
- Lehrerfassung des Schülerbuchs 978-3-06-036177-9
- Lehrerfassung des Schülerbuchs als E-Book 978-3-06-036180-9
- Workbook: Language, Skills and Exam Trainer (mit Lösungen 978-3-06-033464-3, ohne Lösungen 978-3-06-033460-5)
- Active Vocabulary (Vokabeltaschenbuch) 978-3-06-036178-6
- Vokabeltrainer-App 978-3-06-036181-6
- Audio-CDs (+ MP3) 978-3-06-033459-9
- Video-DVD 978-3-06-033461-2
- Handreichungen für den Unterricht 978-3-06-036176-2
- UMA und Begleitmaterialien auf USB-Stick 978-3-06-036354-4
- Vorschläge zur Leistungsmessung 978-3-06-033588-6
- Speaking Practice (Rollen- und Bildkarten) 978-3-06-033587-9

Website zum Lehrwerk:
www.cornelsen.de/context-starter

Die Links zu externen Webseiten Dritter, die in diesem Lehrwerk angegeben sind, wurden vor Drucklegung sorgfältig auf ihre Aktualität geprüft. Der Verlag übernimmt keine Gewähr für die Aktualität und den Inhalt dieser Seiten oder solcher, die mit ihnen verlinkt sind.

1. Auflage, 1. Druck 2018

Alle Drucke dieser Auflage sind inhaltlich unverändert und können im Unterricht nebeneinander verwendet werden.

© 2018 Cornelsen Verlag GmbH, Berlin

Das Werk und seine Teile sind urheberrechtlich geschützt. Jede Nutzung in anderen als den gesetzlich zugelassenen Fällen bedarf der vorherigen schriftlichen Einwilligung des Verlages. Hinweis zu §§ 60 a, 60 b UrhG: Weder das Werk noch seine Teile dürfen ohne eine solche Einwilligung an Schulen oder in Unterrichts- und Lehrmedien (§ 60 b Abs. 3 UrhG) vervielfältigt, insbesondere kopiert oder eingescannt, verbreitet oder in ein Netzwerk eingestellt oder sonst öffentlich zugänglich gemacht oder wiedergegeben werden. Dies gilt auch für Intranets von Schulen.

Druck: Mohn Media Mohndruck, Gütersloh

ISBN 978-3-06-031691-5 – broschiert
ISBN 978-3-06-036175-5 – gebunden

PEFC zertifiziert
Dieses Produkt stammt aus nachhaltig bewirtschafteten Wäldern und kontrollierten Quellen.
www.pefc.de
PEFC/04-31-1033

Welcome to *Context Starter*

Context Starter will help you prepare for the 'Oberstufe'. It will introduce you to new content, texts, methods and intercultural topics. It will also offer support as you improve your language competence and the skills you have already practised in the last few years.

Each of the four **chapters** is centred around one or more of the key skills: listening, viewing, speaking, reading, writing and mediation. Additionally, there are optional literature modules **Focus on Literature** between the chapters, each of which focuses on a different literary genre. These modules show you how to work with and analyse different text types, but they also give you the opportunity to read for fun.

The four chapters and literature modules can be done in any order, which means you don't have to start with Chapter 1. There is no vocabulary progression in this book.

Each chapter has **Support and Partner Pages**, and is divided into these sections:

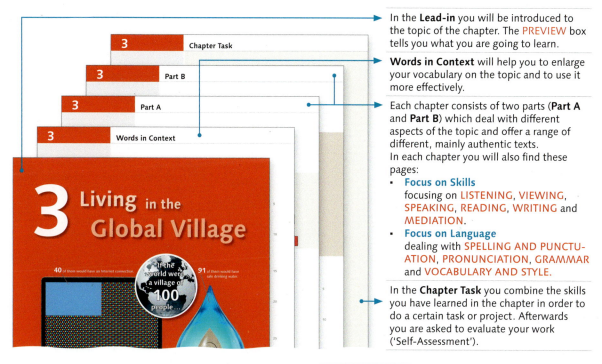

In the **Lead-in** you will be introduced to the topic of the chapter. The PREVIEW box tells you what you are going to learn.

Words in Context will help you to enlarge your vocabulary on the topic and to use it more effectively.

Each chapter consists of two parts (**Part A** and **Part B**) which deal with different aspects of the topic and offer a range of different, mainly authentic texts.
In each chapter you will also find these pages:

- **Focus on Skills**
  focusing on LISTENING, VIEWING, SPEAKING, READING, WRITING and MEDIATION.
- **Focus on Language**
  dealing with SPELLING AND PUNCTUATION, PRONUNCIATION, GRAMMAR and VOCABULARY AND STYLE.

In the **Chapter Task** you combine the skills you have learned in the chapter in order to do a certain task or project. Afterwards you are asked to evaluate your work ('Self-Assessment').

Following the chapters and literature modules, there is a **reference section** which you can turn to for information and extra exercises on specific fields of English:

- The **Skills File** (pp. 120–161): This is a dictionary of the skills (i.e. communicative skills and study skills) that you will need for successful work in English, with exercises that help you to practise them.
- **Preparing for a Speaking Exam** (pp. 162–165): Here you will find tips for doing well in speaking exams.
- **Language Practice** (pp. 166–191): Here you can do extra work in the fields of grammar, style and vocabulary.
- **Communicating across Cultures** (pp. 192–195): Here you will learn how to communicate successfully with people of other cultures.
- **Language Awareness** (pp. 196–199): These pages will explain how language can be used in order to have a certain effect on people, e.g. to convince them, but also to manipulate them.
- **Reading File** (pp. 200–209): Here you can practise reading literary texts.
- **Vocabulary** (pp. 210–217): These pages offer lists of useful vocabulary and phrases for each chapter.
- **Glossary** (pp. 218–221): This is a list with explanations of terms you need for text and literary analysis.
- **Verbs for Tasks** (p. 224): Here you will find explanations of the words ('Operatoren') often used in tasks, especially in exams.

Abbreviations and labels used in *Context Starter*

adj	adjective	**PREVIEW**	refers to the advance organizer (chapter preview) in the margin of the Lead-in of each chapter.
adv	adverb		
AE/BE	American English / British English	**LANGUAGE HELP**	will give you ideas, words and phrases to get started on tasks.
ca. *(Latin)*	circa = about, approximately		
cf.	confer (compare), see	**TROUBLE SPOT**	will point out language difficulties and common mistakes.
derog	derogatory *(abfällig, geringschätzig)*	**CHALLENGE**	marks a more difficult text or task.
e.g. *(Latin)*	exempli gratia = for example	**SUPPORT**	refers you to the Support and Partner Pages (pp. 112–119) where you can find more help to do the assignment.
esp.	especially		
et al. *(Latin)*	et alii = and other people/things		
etc. *(Latin)*	et cetera = and so on	**YOU CHOOSE**	lets you decide which of the two given assignments you would like to do.
ff.	and the following pages/lines		
fml/infml	formal/informal English	*metaphor	indicates that a word or expression (here: *metaphor*) is explained in the Glossary (pp. 218–221).
i.e. *(Latin)*	id est = that is, in other words		
jdm./jdn.	jemandem/jemanden	▶ S21	directs you to the Skills File (here: Skill 21).
l./ll.	line/lines		
n	noun	▶ L7	directs you to the Language Practice section (here: Language task 7).
pt(s)	point(s)		
p./pp.	page/pages	▶ LA1	directs you to the Language Awareness section (here: part 1)
pl	plural		
sb./sth.	somebody/something	CD 04	indicates that the sound file can be found on the accompanying audio CD (here: Track 4).
sing	singular		
sl	slang	DVD 07	indicates that the film or video clip can be found on the accompanying video DVD (here: Track 7).
usu.	usually		
v	verb	Webcode star-07	can be entered at www.cornelsen.de/webcodes to connect you directly to a specific website or download (e.g. a worksheet).
vs. *(Latin)*	versus *(gegen, im Gegensatz zu)*		

About the photograph on the cover of this book

Cloud Gate is a public sculpture by Anish Kapoor in Millennium Park in the American city of Chicago, Illinois. The design won a competition to decide which sculpture would stand in the park. Cloud Gate's construction lasted two years, and it was officially dedicated on May 15, 2006. Nicknamed 'The Bean' due to its shape, the sculpture has been described by *The New York Times* as a 'tourist magnet'. Visiting pedestrians can walk under and around it, and its curved, reflective surface presents a different view from every angle.

Anish Kapoor, an Indian-born British artist, has a reputation for sculptures of extreme size and scale set in urban environments. Born to a Hindu-Jewish family in Mumbai in 1954, he has lived and worked in London since the 1970s. Kapoor's public sculptures can be viewed in major cities all around the world, including Chicago, Jerusalem, Paris, London and New York.

Find more material about Cloud Gate here: **Webcode** star-01

Contents

Chapter 1   The Time of Your Life

Page	Function	Part of chapter/Title	Text type/Media	Communicative and language skills	Text type to be produced
10	Lead-in				
12	Words in Context	Teen years, in-between years	Informative text	Vocabulary skills Language awareness	
	Part A	Hopes, fears and realities			
14		A1 Let's talk about … *Emine Saner*	Newspaper interview	Speaking Mediation G–E	Discussion
16	Focus on Skills	A2 Speaking		Speaking Language awareness	Discussion
17		A3 Teen fears: the top ten	Chart	Speaking	Presentation
18		A4 Teen loses a leg, not his dream *Misti Crane* Check-up: Writing	Newspaper article	Language awareness Writing	Comment
20		A5 Sailor girl Check-up: Listening	Radio report	Listening 🎧 Speaking Language awareness	Discussion
21	Focus on Language	A6 Pronunciation		Speaking	
	Part B	Spread your wings			
22		B1 Make it count Check-up: Speaking	Film clip	Viewing ▶ Speaking	Discussion
22		B2 Greyhound Tragedy *Richard Brautigan* Check-up: Reading	Short story	Speaking Reading Language awareness Writing	One-minute-speech Poster/ Ending of short story
25	Focus on Skills	B3 Writing (1): Planning your writing		Writing	Outline
26		B4 Dare to be daring *Dilbahar Askari* Check-up: Mediation	German essay	Mediation G–E Writing	Email Email
27		B5 Choices *Tess Gallagher*	Poem		
28	Chapter Task	Taking part in a tryout/Assessment		Speaking	Speech
29	Check-up boxes	Figuring out your score/Interpreting your score			

Focus on Literature 1   Narrative Prose – the Novel

Page	Function	Part of chapter/Title	Text type/Media	Communicative and language skills	Text type to be produced
30		Why read?	Quotes	Speaking	
30		A Getting started: Gathering information Notes from the Midnight Driver *Jordan Sonnenblick*	Front cover of a novel Blurb Novel extract	Vocabulary skills	
32		B Developments: How does the plot unfold?			
32		B1 A human service assignment	Novel extract	Writing	Letter/Script
34		B2 Surprises	Novel extract	Writing	Diary entry
35		C Tying up the strings: How could the story end?			

5

Contents

Chapter 2 — Communicating in the Digital Age

Page	Function	Part of chapter / Title	Text type / Media	Communicative and language skills	Text type to be produced
36	Lead-in				
38	Words in Context	Keeping in touch in the 21st century	Informative text	Vocabulary skills Language awareness	
	Part A	**Changing ways of communicating**			
40		A1 The connected generation	Cartoon		
40		A2 The comeback of the written word *Gideon Spanier*	Newspaper article	Mediation E–G Writing	Report Comment
42	Focus on Skills	A3 Writing (2): Structuring a text and connecting ideas		Writing	Comment
43		A4 Conversation – a vanishing skill? *Martha Irvine*	Newspaper article	Writing Language awareness	Summary
45	Focus on Skills	A5 Listening	Podcast	Listening 🎧	
	Part B	**Parents, friends and strangers**			
46		B1 Parental spies *Bella Qvist*	Magazine article	Language awareness Writing	Comment
47		B2 Teenagers and their parents: two sides	Infographic	Speaking	Discussion
48		B3 What you should know	Podcast	Listening 🎧 Speaking	Discussion
49		B4 I C U *Chris Colfer*	Novel extract Movie scene	Language awareness Viewing ▶	
51	Focus on Language	B5 Grammar: The simple form and the progressive form			
52		B6 Nowhere to hide *Yuriko Wahl-Immel*	German magazine article	Mediation G–E Writing	Letter to the editor
53		B7 The cyberbullying virus	Video	Viewing ▶ Speaking	Talk show
54	Chapter Task	Taking part in a competition / Self-Assessment	Audio file with instructions	Listening 🎧 Writing	Audio track Report

Focus on Literature 2 — Narrative Prose – the Short Story

Page	Function	Part of chapter / Title	Text type / Media	Communicative and language skills	Text type to be produced
56		A Getting started: What are we told? Borrowing a Match *Stephen Leacock*	Short story		
58		B The narrator's point of view: Who tells the story?	Short story extracts		
59		C Understanding the construction of plot: How short can a short story be? The Canal Path Murders *Margaret Hodgson* A Story in Six Words *Attributed to Ernest Hemingway*	Microfiction	Writing	Story Microfiction

6

Contents

Chapter 3   Living in the Global Village

Page	Function	Part of chapter/Title	Text type/Media	Communicative and language skills	Text type to be produced
60	Lead-in				
62	Words in Context	Life in a global village	Informative text	Vocabulary skills Language awareness Writing	Essay
	Part A	**Global citizens in a global economy**			
64	Focus on Skills	A1 Mediation: Indien und Amerika brauchen einander *Anette Dowideit et al.*	German article	Mediation G–E	Email
66		A2 Assembled in China	Infographic Statistics		
67		A3 The Fairphone – the world's first fair-trade smartphone	Interview	Listening 🎧 Writing Speaking/Speech	Article
68	Focus on Language	A4 Vocabulary and Style: Using the correct register		Vocabulary skills Language awareness	
69		A5 A vision of the future in China *Cory Doctorow*	Novel extract	Language awareness Writing	Letter/Continuation of story
	Part B	**Looking after the global village: ecological issues**			
72		B1 Pacific plastic	Cartoon		
72		B2 Junk raft completes voyage to Hawaii *Kim Hampton*	Online article Video	Writing Viewing 🎬 Speaking	Summary
74	Focus on Skills	B3 Writing (3): Writing paragraphs	Informative text	Writing	
75		B4 Another use for plastic bottles	Film report	Viewing 🎬	
75		B5 Reducing campus waste	German podcast	Mediation G–E Listening 🎧	
76		B6 Whatever happened to the hole in the ozone layer? *Martyn Chipperfield*	Online article Infobox		
77		B7 How international cooperation reduced CFC consumption	Graph	Writing	Article
78	Chapter Task	Thinking globally – acting locally/Self-Assessment		Mediation G–E	German article

Focus on Literature 3   Poetry

Page	Function	Part of chapter/Title	Text type/Media	Communicative and language skills	Text type to be produced
80		A Getting started: Thinking beyond words *Happiness Roger McGough*	Poem		
81 83		B Enjoying poetry: Finding your style B1 Choosing a favourite B2 A poetry performance	Poems Video	Viewing 🎬	
84 84 85		C You're a poet and don't know it! C1 Completing a poem *The Word Party Richard Edwards* C2 Making up your own poem	Poem Cinquains	Speaking Writing	Performance of poem Cinquain

Contents

Chapter 4   Going Places

Page	Function	Part of chapter/Title	Text type/Media	Communicative and language skills	Text type to be produced
86	Lead-in				
88	Words in Context	The importance of speaking languages	Informative text	Vocabulary skills Language awareness Writing	Article
	Part A	**In a foreign classroom**			
90		A1 What a year at a US high school offers	Word cloud	Writing	Email
91		A2 Going to school in another country Memories from Reutlingen *Emma Brighton*	Extract from exchange student's report	Language awareness Writing	Email
93	Focus on Skills	A3 **Viewing:** Life at an elite boarding school	Documentary film	Viewing 🎬 Language awareness	
94		A4 Life at an elite boarding school	Documentary film	Viewing 🎬	
95		A5 Hosting exchange students *Hillary Clinton*	Speech	Listening 🎧 Writing	Flyer/Written discussion
96	Focus on Skills	A6 **Reading:** The European Day of Languages *Maia Srebernik*	Web article	Reading	
98		A7 Why English is so hard *Anonymous*	Poem	Language awareness Writing	Stanza
	Part B	**Work and life experience**			
99		B1 Summer camps	Film clip	Viewing 🎬	
100		B2 Become a volunteer	Charity's website	Mediation E–G Speaking	One-minute talk
102		B3 Nervous about being a camp counsellor? *Lucy Harper*	Blog entry	Language awareness Writing	Comment
104	Focus on Language	B4 Spelling and punctuation			
105	Focus on Skills	B5 **Writing (4):** Proofreading	Student email	Writing	Email
106	Chapter Task	Applying for a job at a summer camp/Self-Assessment	Mediation G–E		Application video

Focus on Literature 4   Drama

Page	Function	Part of chapter/Title	Text type/Media	Communicative and language skills	Text type to be produced
108		A From page to stage: Performing a script Multiple Choice *Roger Hall*	Drama extract	Speaking	Performance of a scene
110		B Understanding dramatic conflict	Drama extract	Speaking Writing	Performance of a scene

Support and Partner Pages

Page		Part of chapter/Title		Communicative and language skills	
112	Chapter 1	Differentiation and partner work		Language and skills tasks	
113	Chapter 2	Differentiation and partner work		Language and skills tasks	
115	Chapter 3	Differentiation and partner work		Language and skills tasks	
118	Chapter 4	Differentiation and partner work		Language and skills tasks	

Contents

Reference Section

Skills File

120		Listening and viewing skills
120	S1	Listening for information
121	S2	Viewing a film
122		**Reading and text skills**
122	S3	Marking up a text
123	S4	Skimming and scanning
124	S5	Identifying text types
126	S6	Reading and analysing non-fiction
127	S7	Reading and analysing narrative prose
127	S8	Reading, watching and analysing drama
128	S9	Reading and analysing poetry
130		**Speaking skills**
130	S10	Giving a presentation
132	S11	Communicating in everyday situations
133	S12	Having a discussion
135		**Writing skills**
135	S13	The stages of writing
136	S14	Creative writing
136	S15	Writing a formal letter or email
137	S16	Writing an application
139	S17	Argumentative writing
141	S18	Writing a review
143	S19	Writing a report
144	S20	Writing a summary
146		**Mediation skills**
146	S21	Mediation of written and oral texts
148		**Study and language learning skills**
148	S22	Making and taking notes
149	S23	Dealing with unknown words
149	S24	Learning new words
151	S25	Using a dictionary
152	S26	Using a grammar book
153	S27	Working with visuals
154	S28	Working with charts and graphs
156	S29	Working with cartoons
157	S30	Doing project work
158	S31	Using search engines
160	S32	Learning languages with electronic devices
159	S33	Assessing yourself and giving feedback
161	S34	Finding and developing your individual language learning skills

Preparing for a Speaking Exam

162	SE1	Finding out about the exam
163	SE2	Monologues
164	SE3	Dialogues/Interacting

Language Practice

166		**Focus on Grammar**
166	L1	The tenses: verb forms
167	L2	Simple present and present progressive
168	L3	Present perfect simple and present perfect progressive
169	L4	Present perfect and simple past
170	L5	Simple past and past progressive
171	L6	Past perfect and simple past
172	L7	*Will*-future and *going to*-future
173	L8	The passive
175	L9	Conditional sentences
176	L10	Indirect speech
177	L11	Relative clauses
177	L12	The gerund
178	L13	Participle constructions
180		**Focus on Style**
180	L14	Formal and informal English
180	L15	Linking your sentences
183	L16	Emphasis
184		**Focus on Vocabulary**
184	L17	Spelling
184	L18	Using the exact word
184	L19	Common collocations with prepositions
185	L20	One word in German – two in English
186	L21	Verbs of reporting
187	L22	Germanisms
187	L23	Suffixes
188	L24	Prefixes
189	L25	Opposites
189	L26	Using the right expressions for *lassen*
190	L27	Using the right expressions for *wollen*
190	L28	Using the right expressions for *sollen*
191	L29	Comparing and contrasting

Communicating across Cultures

192	CC1	Everyday English
193	CC2	Politeness
193	CC3	Expressing your opinion politely
194	CC4	Dealing with conflicts and misunderstandings
195	CC5	Dealing with cultural differences

Language Awareness

196	LA1	Varieties of English
197	LA2	Communication problems
198	LA3	Similarities and differences of languages
199	LA4	Influencing through language

Reading File

200	RF1	Love in the digital age
204	RF2	You need to love yourself first
205	RF3	Falling in love – then and now
207	RF4	Can life teach you a lesson?

210	**Vocabulary (Chapters 1–4)**
218	**Glossary**
222	Acknowledgements
224	**Verbs for Tasks ('Operatoren')**

1 The Time of Your Life

Download a chronological word list here: **Webcode** star-60

▶ L2: Simple present and present progressive, p. 167
▶ L4: Present perfect and simple past, p. 169

1 Success
2 Creating something new
3 Personal happiness
4 Security
5 Adventure
6 Working in a team
7 Making the world a better place
8 Following your inner voice
9 Challenge

1 Putting yourself in the picture
  a Choose a person from one of the photos above. Put yourself in that person's place and imagine what your life is like, what you enjoy about it, what you had to do to reach this goal. Collect ideas.
  b Work with a partner. Without naming the photo, tell your partner about 'your' life. Your partner will guess which picture you have chosen. Then swap roles.

2 Finding headings
  a On the left, there is a list of headings numbered 1–9. Match the photos with headings that you find suitable.
  b Compare results with your partner. Explain your choices and discuss the cases where you differ.

Lead-in

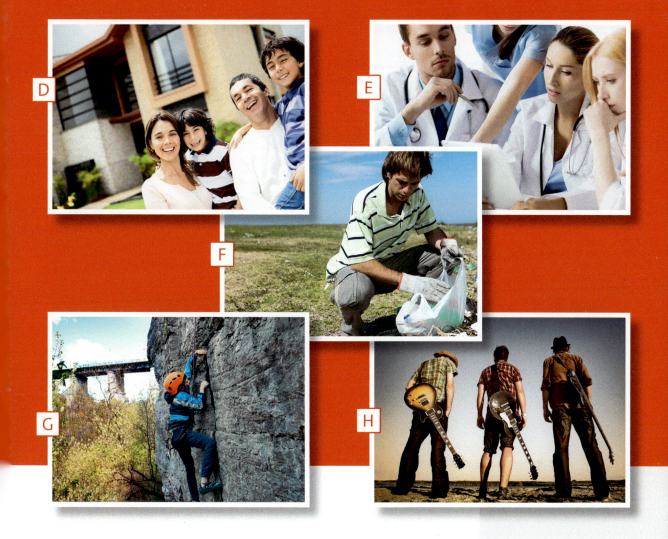

3 **Ranking priorities**
   a **THINK:** Go back to the headings in task **2** and decide what role they play in your own life. Rank them according to their importance to you.
   b **PAIR:** Compare lists with your partner. Together, choose the three priorities that are important to both of you.
   c **SHARE:** Link up with another pair and discuss your choices. Together, choose three priorities that are most important to all of your group.
   d **SPEAKING** Make a list of your top priorities on the board. Discuss the reasons why they are more important to you than the others.

▶ S12: Having a discussion, p. 133
▶ L29: Comparing and contrasting, p. 191

PREVIEW

Main topics
- Young people's dreams, p. 14
- Teen worries, p. 17
- Living your dream, p. 18
- Making choices, p. 22

Skills in focus
- Speaking, p. 16
- Writing: Planning your writing, p. 25

Language in focus
- Pronunciation, p. 21

Chapter Task
- Making a speech, p. 28

In this chapter you will read and hear about the lives of teenagers like you, their hopes, dreams and fears. In a number of places, you will have the chance to practise your speaking skills. Finally you will give a speech for your partner school's debating team. ▶ PREVIEW

The Time of Your Life   Chapter 1

Words in Context

🎧 **CD** 02
Listen to an audio version of the text on the CD or download it here:
 Webcode star-03

▶ L28: Using the right expressions for *sollen*, p. 190

Teen years, in-between years

A time of contradictions
Adolescence – the stage of life between childhood and adulthood – is a period of transition and conflict. Young people are expected to assert themselves, to plan for their future and to play a more active role in the community. In most Western countries, you come of age when you are 18, which means that you have the same rights and responsibilities as an adult. Yet some teenagers do not want to become independent so quickly. They enjoy the positive sides of family life and some even consider their parents to be their friends.
Of course, friends play a considerable role in their lives. It's important for teenagers to gain acceptance and status within their peer group. Sometimes they may also feel forced by peer pressure to wear the right clothes or own the most trendy gadgets. Teens who appear cool and self-confident on the outside may in fact be self-conscious and worry a lot about their looks or their popularity.

Pressure to achieve
Teenagers are exposed to a variety of influences. They often feel under pressure to meet their parents' expectations, by getting good marks at school for example, by finding an internship or gaining admission to the 'right' college or university. They are expected to give serious consideration to their future without knowing for sure what this future will be. While some young people may submit to the pressure to conform, some follow their inner voice instead and strive hard to reach their personal goals. They put a lot of energy into making their dreams happen and are willing to take risks to test their limits. A few achieve early fame and become role models for others in their age group.

The search for identity
In general, adolescence is a time in which young people search for their identity. They tend to experiment, for example with their appearance. Some also rebel against their social environment and do not care if their behaviour seems strange or even provocative to parents or teachers. At the same time they yearn for the security and stability provided by parents, teachers and instructors, or close friends.

▶ L8: The passive, p. 173

■ **TROUBLE SPOT**
(Schul-)Note = **mark**
Not: ~~note~~

▶ Vocabulary, p. 210

Chapter 1 — The Time of Your Life

1 A time of conflicts and contradictions
  a Look at the text closely and list at least three examples of conflicts or contradictions that affect teenagers.
  b Compare lists with your partner. Add any other examples that you can think of. You will need your list for task **4**.

2 Collocations
  a Collocations are combinations of words that are often used together, e.g. *a close friend, reach a goal*. Find some of the collocations used in the text by combining words from the table below (some words can be combined with more than one other word):

give	acceptance
meet	consideration
peer	environment
role	expectations
gain	group
social	model
take	pressure
under	risks

  b Write a short text on the topic 'Advice for teens' using 5–6 of the collocations.

3 Phrases into English
In each of the following sentences, a useful phrase from the text is missing. Copy and complete the sentences. If you aren't sure how to translate the German words, look at the text again.
  1 In Germany, you aren't allowed to start a business until you have (*volljährig werden*).
  2 Social Studies is the subject where young people learn about their (*Rechte und Pflichten*).
  3 For most teenagers, their peer group (*eine erhebliche Rolle spielen*).
  4 Some teens feel (*unter Druck, sich anzupassen*).
  5 While some (*sich dem gesellschaftlichen Druck unterwerfen*), others rebel.
  6 Due to the internet, teenagers are (*mehr Einflüssen ausgesetzt*) than ever before.
  7 Teenagers are often more willing than adults (*an ihre Grenzen zu gehen*).
  8 Some young people (*viel Energie investieren in*) reaching their goals.

4 Writing
Choose one of the examples you collected in task **1**. Explain why this conflict affects your age group and how teenagers can cope with it. Write about 150 words. Use words and phrases from the text where possible.

▶ L19: Common collocations with prepositons, p. 184

■ **TROUBLE SPOT**
ein Ratschlag = **some advice/ a piece of advice**
Not: ~~an advice~~

▶ L27: Using the right expressions for *wollen*, p. 190
▶ L28: Using the right expressions for *sollen*, p. 190

1 Part A

Hopes, fears and realities

A1 Let's talk about ...   *Emine Saner*

In the following texts, three UK teenagers talk about the joys and challenges they face being part of the so-called 'Generation K' – a generation named after Hunger Games *heroine Katniss Everdeen and often characterized as addicted to electronic media and as experiencing life as a permanent struggle and dystopia.*

Isaac Grinnell, 16, Leeds
There is definitely pressure at school. I've got mock exams starting soon, and school piles on the pressure to do well. That makes you feel nervous. Things like university fees worry me a lot because I don't know whether I will be able to afford to go, even though I really want to.

Stuff like alcohol hasn't been a problem for me because my parents have always brought me up thinking it wasn't appropriate for my age. But when I'm walking to school there are lots of people smoking, and I see pictures on Facebook of people drinking alcohol.

Body image affects boys too. There is pressure to look a certain way, and social media heightens it – for men, it's to be really fit and have muscles.

I feel like people my age have grown up with some serious and frightening events going on around us. It's not necessarily that I'm worried that, say, I walk into Leeds and there's going to be a terrorist attack; it's more that I'm worried about how it affects other people. After the Paris attacks, I got worried about people living in Paris, and also about migrants having to flee from their country. It all just adds to the pressure – that you're thinking about them, while also trying to do your exams.

Keiarnya Grant-Blissett, 20, student, Manchester
While I was growing up, my mum had a lot of control over my social media and what TV programmes I watched, so I think I was protected from some of the negative aspects, but now you go on and it's: 'You need to be this if you want to be perfect.' Social media isn't great at showing the diversity of people, and it does make you question yourself. There is so much expectation on how young women should dress, and there is too much sexualisation. But if you wear tight clothes or too much makeup, you get shamed for that as well. I live my life how I want.

I took a step back from social media so I could focus on studying, but I still find there is too much media around. Sometimes when I've spent too long online I think I could have read a book, or gone out exploring.

There was a lot of pressure at school – from the moment you pick your GCSEs, you feel that if you do well you'll get into college, and then you'll get into university and then you'll get a good job. But even if I do this degree, am I going to get a job? That worry is always there.

My mum has always made sure we've had anything we needed, but I've seen her struggle financially – she's a carer – and it's made me want to do well so I can give back to her and make her proud.

---

3 **pile on sth.** make sth. increase quickly
11 **heighten sth.** make sth. bigger
33 **GCSE** (= General Certificate of Secondary Education) *here:* courses for British school certificate usually taken around the age of 16
34 **degree** academic qualification
37 **carer** person who looks after and worries about people very much

Hopes, fears and realities

Willa Duggan, 15, Surrey

There can be a lot of pressure, and I feel like the decisions we make now will have a big impact on our future lives, but generally, picturing what adulthood might be like, I feel like I don't really have a lot of responsibilities right now, and so I don't really feel like it's a miserable time. I do think about things like whether I'll be able to afford a house in the future. I would need my parents' support – it's harder for people to do it on their own.

Climate change really scares me. My mum is really passionate about politics, so I learn a lot from her and I watch the news. I feel like politicians are all quite well off and have a good lifestyle, and don't really know how a lot of people live.

I spend a lot of time on social media – Facebook, Snapchat and Instagram are the main ones. I feel like it's a bit of a competition. People judge you by how many followers you have or the pictures you post. It becomes a bit of an obsession to check up on people to see what they're doing, rather than getting on with your own life. I'm pretty attached to my phone. When I'm on my phone, all my friends are messaging each other and I feel like, if I'm away from it, I'm being left out. It's hard to be the person who doesn't go on it.

From: ' "We've grown up with some frightening events": UK teenagers' hopes and fears', *Guardian*, 19 March 2016

51 **obsession** state of being completely filled with thoughts of a particular thing or person in a way that is not normal

▶ COMPREHENSION ◀

1 A group puzzle
   a You will be assigned a number between 1 and 3. The 1s make notes on Isaac, the 2s on Keiarnya, and the 3s on Willa.
   b Form groups of 3 (all numbers must be represented in each group). Present 'your' person to the other group members.

▶ S22: Making and taking notes, p. 148

▶ ANALYSIS ◀

2 Different attitudes
In your group, compare the three teenagers: What attitudes do they have in common, in what way do they differ?

▶ L29: Comparing and contrasting, p. 191

▶ BEYOND THE TEXT ◀

3 SPEAKING **Comparing teenage values and worries**
   a In your group, discuss your reactions to the teenagers' statements. Compare their hopes and fears with those of German teenagers (if necessary, go back to your findings to tasks **3**, p. 11 and **4**, p. 13). Choose someone to take notes on your discussion.
   b Present your ideas to the rest of the class.

▶ S10: Giving a presentation, p. 130

4 MEDIATION (English → German) **A conversation**
In a conversation with your mum, she states that many young people today are under a lot of pressure. In German, make notes on the text in **A1** so that you can tell her about the ideas of the young people mentioned in the article. Speak for about two minutes.

▶ S21: Mediation of written and oral texts, p. 146

1 Part A

A2 FOCUS ON SKILLS SPEAKING

▶ Preparing for a Speaking Exam, pp. 162–165

Speaking is hardly a new skill for you. However, keeping up your end of a conversation or speaking in a clear and structured way may be difficult and need some practice when you are using a foreign language.

1 Dialogues

In *dialogues speakers usually use typical forms of interaction:
1 opening a conversation
2 asking sb. to explain sth.
3 repeating what has just been said
4 commenting on what has just been said
5 suggesting a new topic
6 agreeing with what has just been said
7 disagreeing with what has just been said
8 closing the conversation

In each form of interaction, typical phrases are used by the speakers.

a The article about the three teenagers on p. 14f. is based on an interview. Below there are some phrases that might have been used in the interview with Isaac. Match them with the categories above.
   A Could you say a bit more about …
   B Hi, Isaac. Thank you for taking part in this interview.
   C It's weird that …
   D Now, let's talk about …
   E Oh, is that so? …
   F Well, I agree with your idea that …
   G Well, thank you for …
   H You said that … What does that mean?

b Together with a partner, add more phrases to all of the categories.
c Compare lists with other pairs. Add useful phrases that aren't on your list.

2 A discussion
a Choose one of the following topics to discuss with your partner:
   - Teenagers today are very keen on status symbols.
   - Being young means rebelling against authority.
b Try to keep the conversation going for at least two minutes (keep track of your time). Use some of the phrases you have collected.

3 LANGUAGE AWARENESS Speaking to different people
Imagine you were talking about the topics from task **2** in a different context:
1 to your host parents on an exchange visit to the UK or USA
2 to your principal at school
3 to a friend your age
4 at an international youth conference on teenage behaviour.
In what way would this discussion be different from the one you held? Name three possible differences.

4 Monologues
In some situations (e.g. oral exams), you are asked to deliver a *monologue, i.e. to give a short presentation.
Partner B: Go to p. 112.
Partner A:
a In a monologue, describe the picture on the left to your partner. Tell him/her what you think it is trying to convey. Try and talk for at least two minutes. ▶ LANGUAGE HELP
b When you are finished, listen to your partner's talk. Keep track of the time (two minutes are required!).

LANGUAGE HELP
- maze
- ladder
- lay sth. across sth. else

LANGUAGE AWARENESS
To be successful in any communicative situation (i.e. be convincing, helpful, friendly, polite etc.) you need to adapt your **style** (i.e. be more or less formal) and **register** (i.e. use or avoid certain words) to the other person and situation.

▶ LA4: Influencing through language, p. 199

Hopes, fears and realities

A3 Teen fears: the top ten

In a survey, 2500 Irish teenagers were asked to name the fears and situations that cause them stress. Here are the ten worries that were named most often:

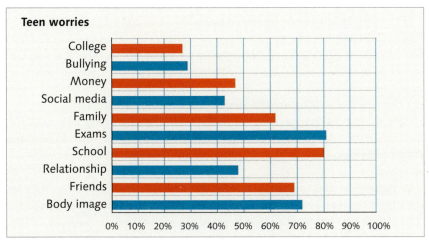

From: „TeenMentalHealth Report Day 2, *The Irish Examiner*, 31 March 2017

▶ L12: The gerund, p. 175

▸ COMPREHENSION ◂

1 Understanding statistics
Present the most important findings of the survey by replacing the numbers in the following text by phrases:
  The students who took part in the survey were asked (1). Four out of five named (2) as something they worry about. Roughly two out of three also expressed fear of (3). A little less than half of the students worry about (4). The problem named least often is (5).

▶ S28: Working with charts and graphs, p. 154

▶ L8: The passive, p. 173

▶ L29: Comparing and contrasting, p. 191

▸ BEYOND THE TEXT ◂

2 Doing a class survey
Do a survey in your class to find out whether your classmates are worried by the same problems as the Irish teenagers.
  a Use the webcode to download a questionnaire and decide how to collect the data as efficiently as possible.
  b Carry out the survey and present the results as percentages.
  c Compare your class's results with those of the Irish teenagers.
  ▶ LANGUAGE HELP

Find a questionnaire here:
Webcode star-61

▶ S10: Giving a presentation, p. 130

3 SPEAKING **Presenting results**
Analyse the results of your class survey. Use words and phrases from task **1** for help.

> **LANGUAGE HELP**
> - The Irish students often worry about …, whereas we …
> - The most common worry in our class is …
> - Surprisingly, only … named …

Part A

A4 CHALLENGE Teen loses a leg, not his dream *Misti Crane*

- What do you expect the text to be about after reading the title?
- Skim ll. 1–44 for one minute to correct your expectations or add details.

If Zach Hanf's plans to become a trauma surgeon work out, he'll be the guy countering the crisis, scrambling to help someone pull through.

In October, Hanf was the patient, mangled by a car crash and near death. The 18-year-old was driving on Rt. 13 in Perry County after a movie and a stop at a fast-food restaurant with his then-girlfriend when he drifted left of center. The Somerset teen crashed head-on into a refrigerated box truck. He has no memory of the wreck, which severed his left foot. He doesn't recall the flight to Ohio State University's Wexner Medical Center or the first several weeks in intensive care.

Hanf, a cross-country standout at Sheridan High School, was left with an above-the-knee amputation, fused vertebrae in his lower back, two plates in his left arm and a plate in his right foot. His brain was injured, his spleen removed. Surgeons operated 13 times.

Dr. Daniel Eiferman, the trauma surgeon who first cared for Hanf and has since become his friend, said he could scarcely believe it when the teen kept hanging on.

'The truth is he lost an ungodly amount of blood. His blood pressure was so low,' Eiferman said. 'He's only alive because of how good of shape he was in.'

Hanf's heart was strong from running, Eiferman said, and kept providing his body with oxygen long after most other hearts would fail to do so.

Hanf didn't leave rehab at Dodd Hall until early December. He got his prosthesis in January. Four days later, encouraged by another amputee at the gym, he walked without help.

'He took my crutches away, and, by golly, I walked,' Hanf said. 'They were cautious, really slow steps, but they worked.'

The only pain that continues to bother him is in his lower back.

Hanf said he has wanted to be a trauma surgeon since he was a child. He recently attended Ohio State University's MD Camp, a three-week program for young people considering medical careers. And he is set to begin his studies at the university's Newark campus in August.

'I've always wanted to be in a life-or-death situation where I could help someone else,' he said. Now, he sees it as a way to give back.

Hanf's mother, Jennifer Soto, said she remembers her son's passion for medicine starting when he was in elementary school, watching *House* and *Trauma: Life in the E.R.* on television. Watching Hanf go through so much has been hard on the family, she said. 'We have a strong faith and belief that everything happens for a reason, so that is what we clung to.'

When Hanf first realized he'd lost his leg, he asked how soon he could stand – and eat, Soto said. Eiferman said he remembers the teen thanking him.

'It wasn't "Poor me,"' Soto said. 'It spoke volumes to us as parents and to the doctors that it wasn't going to bring him down. His story is about courage, determination and will and strength. I'm his biggest fan.'

The wreck perpetuated her son's drive to be a surgeon, she said, and gave him perspective about what it's like to be a patient.

'The only thing that's going to stop him is if he physically cannot do it. He has proven you can do anything you put your mind to.'

▶ S4: Skimming and scanning, p. 123

1 **trauma surgeon** ['trɔːmə 'sɜːdʒən] *Unfallchirurg/in*
  counter sth. (v) deal with sth.
2 **scramble** (infml) hurry
  pull through (infml) survive
6 **refrigerated box truck** lorry that is equipped to keep esp. food cool
7 **sever sth.** ['sevə] cut sth. off
  recall sth. remember sth.
8 **intensive care** *Intensivstation*
9 **cross-country standout** excellent long-distance runner
10 **fused vertebra** ['vɜːtɪbrə] (pl **vertebrae**) *gestauchter Lendenwirbel*
11 **spleen** *Milz*
14 **hang on** (infml) not give up
15 **ungodly** large, unbelievable
17 **provide sb./sth. with sth.** give sth. to sb./sth.
19 **rehab** (infml) = rehabilitation
  prosthesis [prɒsˈθiːsɪs] *Prothese*
20 **amputee** sb. who has had an amputation
22 **crutch** *Krücke*
  by golly (infml, old-fashioned) *Donnerwetter!*
27 **be set to do sth.** plan to definitely do sth.
32 **House, Trauma: Life in the E.R.** names of medical series on US television; **E.R.** = emergency room (in a hospital) *Notaufnahme*
35 **cling to sth.** (clung – clung) hold on to sth.
38 **speak volumes** *Bände sprechen*
39 **determination** will to do sth.
41 **perpetuate sth.** (fml) maintain sth., secure sth.

Hopes, fears and realities

45 Eiferman said the physical demands of surgery are something he and Hanf have discussed. Hanf said he has thought of becoming a prosthetist as a backup plan.

Hanf's injuries could limit him in the operating room, but he's mature and has demonstrated great strength, Eiferman said. 'He's overcome bigger obstacles already.'

And Hanf has something that most doctors don't.

50 'We all have sympathy, but Zach will really have empathy,' Eiferman said.

From: *The Columbus Dispatch*, 10 July 2013

COMPREHENSION

1 Understanding Zach
 a Work together with a partner. One of you makes notes on what Dr. Eiferman says about Zach, the other on what Jennifer Soto, Hanf's mother, says.
 b Tell each other what you have found.

ANALYSIS

2 Examining a person's character
Examine Hanf's reaction to his accident: what do you find heroic or inspiring about it? Write down reasons and examples.

3 CHALLENGE Verbs + infinitive or gerund?
Some English verbs are followed by the gerund (*-ing* form), some by the infinitive with *to*. Look at the text again and choose the correct form in the sentences below. (In one case both forms are possible.)
 1 Zach remembers to take / taking his first steps.
 2 He kept to fight / fighting for a full recovery.
 3 He continues dreaming / to dream of becoming a surgeon or prosthetist.

4 LANGUAGE AWARENESS Using direct speech and quotations
In some parts of the text the author uses direct speech and quotations. Find examples and assess their effect on the reader. Present your findings to the class.

BEYOND THE TEXT

5 WRITING Zach as a role model? SUPPORT p. 112
Use your notes from tasks **1** and **2** to write a comment on the statement 'Zach Hanf is a good role model for other teens' (ca. 200 words).

Check-up WRITING
Choose the answers that best describe you.
1 a I thought about what I wanted to say, but I didn't make any notes.
  b I made an outline of my ideas before I started writing.
  c I wrote down my ideas using keywords before actually writing the text.
2 a My comment has a topic sentence and a conclusion, but I didn't write in paragraphs.
  b My comment is well organized, but it's all one paragraph.
  c My comment has a clear structure, which is reflected in the paragraphs.
3 a I used linking words wherever possible to connect my statements.
  b I used a few linking words in my comment.
  c The only linking words I used were conjunctions like *but* and *so*.
4 a Most of my sentences are simple main clauses.
  b My sentences often contain subordinate clauses.
  c I used subordinate clauses a few times.

Now go to p. 29 to figure out your score and interpret it.

---

45 **physical demands** *körperliche Erfordernisse*
47 **mature** [məˈtʃʊə] *reif*
48 **obstacle** *Hindernis*
50 **empathy** [ˈ---] ability to understand what other people feel

TROUBLE SPOT
reif = (of people) **mature**
    (of fruit) **ripe**

▶ L10: Indirect speech, p. 176
▶ L21: Verbs of reporting, p. 186

▶ L12: The gerund, p. 177

LANGUAGE AWARENESS
When speaking or writing you use words and constructions to convey meaning. By picking specific constructions you can also **influence the readers or listeners**. For example:
quotations → credibility/authority
direct speech → liveliness/authenticity
(rhetorical) questions → involvement of audience

▶ LA4: Influencing through language, p. 199
▶ Focus on Skills: Writing; Structuring a text and connecting ideas, p. 42
▶ S13: The stages of writing, p. 135
▶ S33: Assessing yourself and giving feedback, p. 160

Part A

🎧 **CD** 03
court *Gericht*
authority *Behörde*
issue sb. with a summons *jdn. zu Gericht vorladen*
Gallipoli Turkish peninsula, place of a military operation in World War I

▶ S1: Listening for information, p. 120

▶ L26: Using the right expressions for *lassen*, p. 189

▶ S33: Assessing yourself and giving feedback, p. 160

A5 LISTENING Sailor girl

◀ COMPREHENSION

1 Listening for gist
Listen to a radio report on Laura Dekker. In one sentence, say what it is about.

2 Listening for detail
a Finish the sentences:
 1 Laura was not always able to meet her school deadlines because …
 2 Dutch authorities tried to stop her trip because …
 3 Her trip may be considered easier than Jessica Watson's because …
b Listen again and take notes on the arguments for and against allowing teenagers like Laura and Jessica to undertake dangerous voyages.

Check-up LISTENING
Choose the answers that best describe you.
1 I could understand the spoken text well enough to …
  a … get all the information I needed.
  b … get a general idea of the topic.
  c … get the most important information.
2 The accents of the speakers and the poor tone quality in some parts of the report …
  a … made parts of the text impossible to understand.
  b … made it hard to understand some of the text.
  c … weren't a problem for me.
3 a I ignored the words I didn't understand and concentrated on the rest.
  b I guessed the meaning of unfamiliar words from the context they were used in.
  c I got confused every time someone used a word I didn't know.
4 a I wrote down the arguments in keywords in the order they were named.
  b I read the task carefully and divided my notepad into 'pros' and 'cons'.
  c I just listened, then I wrote down what I could remember.
Now go to p. 29 to figure out your score and interpret it.

▶ S12: Having a discussion, p. 133

🟧 **LANGUAGE AWARENESS**

In order to **adapt your language to a certain situation**, you must quickly analyse the situation:
• Are you and your communication partner(s) at eye level?
• Has the other person more/less knowledge of the issue?
• Are you/they emotionally involved?

▶ LA4: Influencing through language, p. 199

▶ L26: Using the right expressions for *lassen*, p. 189

▶ L28: Using the right expressions for *sollen*, p. 190

◀ BEYOND THE TEXT

3 SPEAKING **A hearing**
A student from your school wants to take a break from his/her education for a year to cycle around the world. Before granting the student permission, the school wants to hold a meeting with
 • the head teacher (1)
 • the student (2)
 • the student's best friend (3)
 • the student's parents (4, 5)
 • the form teacher (6).

a LANGUAGE AWARENESS Form six groups. Each group prepares a role card. Consider whether your role is emotionally involved, holds a certain form of authority or is in a professional and/or private relationship with the others and make your character speak and act accordingly. Choose someone to take part in the hearing.
b Hold the discussion: the head teacher calls on the participants to present their arguments, then makes a decision and explains his/her reasons.

Hopes, fears and realities

A6 FOCUS ON LANGUAGE: Pronunciation

Your class has been invited to hear Laura Dekker speak about her adventures on the high seas (cf. p. 20). After her talk, there's a question-and-answer session.

1 Misunderstandings
Listen to what happens when your classmate Lukas asks a question. What causes the confusion in this situation?

2 German-English trouble spots
Read about some typical trouble spots for German speakers and practise saying the words given below. Then listen to the audios and check your pronunciation:
  a **Voiced and voiceless consonants:** In German, consonants in final position are always voiceless: *Sieg* ends in [-k], not [-g], *Lob* ends in [-p], not [-b]. In English, however, consonants in final position can be voiced or voiceless. Pronounce the following pairs of words: *block – blog, feet – feed, rope – robe, safe – save, batch – badge, since – sins.*
  b **a/e:** Words like *man* and *men*, *mash* and *mesh* sound the same if you don't take care to pronounce the vowels correctly as either [æ] or [e]. Pronounce the following words: *bat – bet, pan – pen, had – head, land – lend.*
  c **The *th*-sound:** Some Germans replace the English *th*-sound with [s] or [z], but this may cause misunderstandings because in English there is a distinction between *s* and *th* (e.g. *think* is not the same as *sink*!). Careful: There are two sounds used for *th*: voiceless as in *think* [θɪŋk], voiced as in *this* [ðɪs]. Pronounce the following words and phrases: *mouse – mouth, tense – tenth, sink – think; three-fourths, the fifth brother, within these thick walls, neither Selma nor her sister Thelma*
  d **Linking *syllables:** In English, vowels at the beginning of a syllable are linked with the final consonant of the preceding syllable, even if it's in a different word, e.g. *an‿open‿ending*. Similarly, the definite article *the* is pronounced [ðɪ] if the next word begins with a vowel sound. Pronounce these phrases: *an‿apple‿a day, a box‿of‿eggs, not‿at‿all, an‿awesome‿experience; the oranges and the apples, the old castle, the aunts and the uncles*

3 Pronunciation practice
Partner B: Go to p. 112.
Partner A:
  a Read the following words aloud (once only!), leaving a short pause after each word:
    grade – logs – trays – dad – faith – things – leave – eyes – sand – worth.
    Your partner will tick the words he/she heard on a worksheet.
  b Then compare your list with your partner's results.
  c Use the webcode to download a list of words. Now your partner will read out some words to you.
  d Mark the words you have heard, then compare lists. Where did your partner have difficulty pronouncing the words?

🎧 **CD** 04
Listen to the audios on the CD or download them here:
 Webcode star-06

🎧 **CD** 05

🎧 **CD** 06

🎧 **CD** 07

🎧 **CD** 08

■ **LANGUAGE AWARENESS**
Only very few people manage to speak a foreign language without being recognized as a non-native speaker. It is totally acceptable to have **traces of your mother tongue** in your English, but make sure to know about typical German–English trouble spots in order to avoid misunderstandings on your behalf. Compare e.g.
I don't want to eat that foot.
I don't want to eat that food.

▶ LA3: Similarities and differences of languages, p. 198

Find the list of words here:
 **Webcode** star-07

1 Part B

Spread your wings

B1 Make it count

In 2012, a major sports company hired American film-maker Casey Neistat to make a movie on the topic 'make it count'. He decided to spend his budget travelling the world with a friend. Watch their video 'Make it count'.

▶ S2: Viewing a film, p. 121
▶ S25: Using a dictionary, p. 151
▶ L18: Using the exact word, p. 182
▶ L20: One word in German – two in English, p. 185

▶ DVD 01

1 Before viewing
  a What do you think the title means? If you need help, look up *count* in a monolingual dictionary and decide which meaning would fit the title.
  b Form small groups and discuss your ideas. Based on your understanding of the title, what do you think the film will be about?

◀ COMPREHENSION

2 VIEWING Connecting title and content
  a After watching the film, compare it with your expectations.
  b Relate the title to the content of the film.

◀ BEYOND THE TEXT

3 Working with quotations from the film
  a Watch the film again, paying special attention to the quotations that are flashed on the screen. Choose one that particularly appeals to you.
  b Get together in groups again. Tell the others which quotation you chose, why you chose it, and what you think it means. Discuss the attitudes to life that are reflected in the quotations.

Check-up SPEAKING (Discussions)   ▶ S33: Assessing yourself and others, p. 160
Choose the answers that best describe you.
1 In classroom discussions,
  a I often play an active role.
  b I seldom play an active role.
  c I sometimes play an active role.
2 When someone addresses me,
  a I have to think about the words I need before I answer.
  b I can reply without hesitating.
  c I don't always know what to say.
3 a I sometimes have to search for the right word.
  b I can express myself clearly and fluently.
  c I can't always express what I want to say.
4 a Mostly I just speak my mind, but sometimes I ask somebody a question.
  b I hardly ever speak directly to other participants.
  c I'm good at getting other people to talk.

Now go to p. 29 to figure out your score and interpret it.

B2 Greyhound Tragedy *Richard Brautigan*

SPEAKING What is worse: to try and fail, or not to try at all? Give a one-minute speech.

Greyhound = Greyhound Lines, the largest North American intercity bus company
2 **weep** cry
corpse [kɔːps] dead body
3 **Oregon** state on the west coast of the USA
5 **Depression** cf. Fact File, p. 23
6 **Penney's** American chain of department stores
compassionate caring
8 **service** religious ceremony

She wanted her life to be a movie magazine tragedy like the death of a young star with long lines of people weeping and a corpse more beautiful than a great painting, but she was never able to leave the small Oregon town that she was born and raised in and go to Hollywood and die.

Though it was the Depression, her life was comfortable and untouched because her father was the manager of the local Penney's and financially compassionate to his family.

Movies were the religion of her life and she attended every service with a bag of popcorn.

22 Chapter 1 The Time of Your Life

Spread your wings

Movie magazines were her Bible that she studied with the zealousness of a doctor of divinity. She probably knew more about movies than the pope.

The years passed like the subscriptions to her magazines: 1931, 1932, 1933, 1934, 1935, 1936, 1937, until September 2, 1938.

Finally it was time to make her move if she were ever going to go to Hollywood. There was a young man who wanted to marry her. Her parents were very enthusiastic about his prospects. They approved of him because he was a Ford salesman. 'It's a company with a fine tradition,' her father said. Things did not look good for her.

She spent months building up the courage to go down to the bus station to find out how much the fare to Hollywood cost. Sometimes she spent whole days thinking about the bus station. A few times she even got dizzy and had to sit down. It never dawned on her that she could have called on the telephone.

She made it a point during those nervous months never to go by the bus station. Thinking about it all the time was one thing but actually seeing it was another. [...]

Time was running out like the popcorn at a Clark Gable picture. Her father had been dropping a lot of 'hints' lately about her being out of high school for three years and perhaps it was time for her to think about doing something with her life.

He was not the local manager of Penney's for nothing. Recently, actually about a year ago, he had become tired of watching his daughter sit around the house all the time reading movie magazines with her eyes wide as saucers. He had begun to think of her as a bump on a log.

Her father's hints happened to coincide with the young Ford salesman's fourth proposal of marriage. She had turned down the other three saying that she needed time to think it over, which really meant that she was trying to build up enough courage to go down to the bus station and find out what the fare to Hollywood cost.

At last the pressure of her own longings and her father's 'hints' made her leave the house early one warm twilight, after getting out of doing the dinner dishes, and walk slowly down to the bus station. From March 10, 1938, until the evening of September 2, 1938, she had been wondering what a bus ticket to Hollywood cost.

The bus station was stark, unromantic, and very distant from the silver screen. Two old people were sitting there on a bench waiting for a bus. The old people were tired. They wanted to be now at wherever they were going. Their suitcase was like a burned-out light bulb.

The man who sold the tickets looked as if he could have sold anything. He could just as well be selling washing machines or lawn furniture as tickets to other places.

She was red-faced and nervous. Her heart felt out of place in the bus station. She tried to act as if she were waiting for somebody to come in on the next bus, an aunt, as she worked desperately to build up enough courage to ask how much it cost to go to Hollywood, but it didn't make any difference to anybody else what games she pretended.

Nobody looked at her, though she could have rented herself out as an earthquake beet. They simply didn't care. It was a stupid night in September and she just didn't have enough nerve to find out how much the fare to Hollywood cost.

She cried all the way home through the warm, gentle Oregon night, wanting to die every time her feet touched the ground. There was no wind and all the shadows were comforting. They were like cousins to her, so she married the young Ford salesman and drove a new car every year except for the Second World War.

She had two children that she named Jean and Rudolph and tried to let her beautiful movie star death go at that, but now, thirty-one years later, she still blushes when she passes the bus station.

From: Richard Brautigan, *Revenge of the Lawn*, 1971

---

10 **zealousness** ['zeləsnəs] enthusiasm
11 **divinity** the study of religion
   pope head of the Roman Catholic Church
12 **subscription** Abonnement
16 **prospects** ['prɒspekts] probable chances of success
   approve of sb./sth. think sb./sth. is good
19 **fare** transportation cost
20 **dizzy** schwindlig
   dawn on sb. jdm. dämmern
22 **make it a point to do sth.** make doing sth. a rule for oneself
24 **Clark Gable picture** movie with Clark Gable (famous actor, 1901–1960)
25 **hint** subtle suggestion
29 **eyes wide as saucers** eyes wide open in amazement
30 **bump on a log** (AE, infml) (here) person you want to get rid of
31 **coincide with sth.** [ˌkəʊɪnˈsaɪd] happen at the same time as sth.
   proposal of marriage Heiratsantrag
36 **twilight** phase between daylight and darkness
39 **stark** bare
   silver screen Kinoleinwand
50 **she could have rented herself out as an earthquake beet** she was shaking and very red in the face
52 **nerve** (AE, infml) courage
57 **Jean and Rudolph = Jean Harlow and Rudolph Valentino** Hollywood stars of the 1920s and 1930s who both died young.
   let her beautiful movie star death go at that gave up her dream of dying as a movie star

FACT FILE

The worst economic crisis in American history, the **Great Depression**, began in October 1929. When stock prices fell sharply, panic broke out on Wall Street. Investors (and ordinary people) frantically tried to get their money back, but many banks were unable to pay, so they were forced to close down. Many businesses failed and millions of Americans lost their jobs. It wasn't until the 1950s that the American economy recovered its former strength.

Part B

*exposition • *rising action
*climax • *falling action
*epilogue

> **LANGUAGE HELP**
> - The conflict is established in the first …
> - The *tension rises when …
> - The *climax is brought about by …
> - In this section, the *tension falls off rapidly as …

▶ S7: Reading and analysing narrative prose, p. 127
▶ Focus on Literature: Short stories, pp. 56–59
▶ RF1, p. 200

▶ S14: Creative writing, p. 136

▶ S33: Assessing yourself and giving feedback, p. 160

— COMPREHENSION ◀

1 The main aspects of the story
Make notes on the following aspects of the story: its time, *setting, main *characters and the sequence of events. Compare with a partner.

— ANALYSIS ◀

2 The text structure
  a Divide the story into sections. Give each section a label from the list on the left.
  b Analyse the function of each section in a few sentences. ▶ LANGUAGE HELP

3 LANGUAGE AWARENESS Using adjectives and adverbial phrases
Collect adjectives and adverbial phrases from ll. 1–9 and 39–49 of the text. Explain how their uses and meanings add to the description of the setting and atmosphere in the text. Make use of these findings for your writing in tasks **4** to **6**.

4 The movie industry
Examine the role of the movie industry (e.g. Hollywood, star cult, movie magazines) in the story. Write about 300 words. ▶ Focus on Skills: Writing, p. 25

5 A short story
Check the Glossary (pp. 218–221) for a definition of *short story*. Analyse to what extent the 'Greyhound Tragedy' is a typical short story.

— BEYOND THE TEXT ◀

6 WRITING Variants of the story YOU CHOOSE

  a Make a poster for a film version of this story. Choose photos of people for the main roles; add captions and slogans to make the film sound interesting.

  b Imagine the girl overcomes her fear, buys a ticket, and boards a Greyhound bus for Hollywood. Write a new ending for the story.

Check-up **READING**
Choose the answers that best describe you.
1 a I understood the text easily with the help of the annotations.
    b I didn't understand some parts of the text.
    c I understood the gist of the text, but not every detail.
2 When I didn't understand a word,
    a I just skipped over it if it wasn't important.
    b I used the context and/or my background knowledge to guess the meaning.
    c I looked it up in the dictionary.
3 While looking for relevant details for task **3**,
    a I re-read the text quickly.
    b I scanned the text.
    c I read the text again, word for word.
4 While working on task **3**,
    a I wrote down a few examples.
    b I wrote down a couple of line numbers.
    c I made notes on the text (examples and line numbers).

Now go to p. 29 to figure out your score and interpret it.

Spread your wings

B3 FOCUS ON SKILLS WRITING (1)
Planning your writing

This is the first of four pages dealing with writing. There is one in each chapter.

▶ Focus on Skills: Writing, p. 42, p. 74, p. 105

1 Examining the task
Before you start thinking about your writing task, make sure you know exactly what you are supposed to do.

▶ S13: The stages of writing, p. 135

You are working on task **4** on p. 24. Which of the following belong to the task?

A	comment on the influence of the movie industry on the lives of ordinary people
B	explain the symbolic meaning of the name 'Hollywood'
C	summarize the plot of the story
D	say what you think of the girl's behaviour
E	point out places in the story where the movie industry plays a role

2 Collecting information
There are different ways of collecting ideas for a task.
*If you are asked to **present your own ideas on a subject**, a good way to begin is by brainstorming and/or by making a mind map.*
*If you are asked to **analyse a given text**, begin by reading the text closely for relevant sections. Make notes, including line numbers and quotations if the language itself is important.*

Go back to text **B2** on pp. 22–23 and identify relevant passages. Make notes on aspects you want to mention.

▶ S22: Making and taking notes, p. 148

3 Outlining
An outline helps you to organize your material in a structured way. It shows the relative importance of points listed and the logical connections between them. If you stick to your outline when writing, it will be easy for your readers to follow your line of argumentation.

Make sure your outline has a convincing structure before starting to write. Making changes here is much easier than later in the writing process!

Copy and complete the outline for task **4** on the right, or create a new outline of your own. Don't forget to add ideas for your introduction and conclusion!

4 Writing
Use your outline from **3** to write the analysis required in task **4** on p. 24.

I Role of movie industry in girl's life
   a examples from story
      1 wish to die as a film star
      2 frequent visits to cinema
      3 …
   b effects on her life
      1 lethargic, no initiative
      2 …
II Influence of movie industry on …
   a …

The Time of Your Life   Chapter 1

Part B

B4 Dare to be daring Dilbahar Askari

The writer, a graduate from the Hebel-Gymnasium in Lörrach, was 20 years old when she wrote this essay.

„Glücklich verheiratet, Mutter, guter Job, großes Haus und viel Geld", so lautet ein Eintrag in einer Abizeitung 2011, Kategorie ‚Ich in zwanzig Jahren'. Die Beiträge variieren kaum: Bilderbuchkarriere, gutes Einkommen, eigenes Haus, Familie, Sicherheit. Willkommen in der **Generation Ratio**. Wir sind jung, zielstrebig und vernünftig. Wir sind furchtbar erwachsen. Und das vor
5 unserer Zeit.

Sicher: Vernunft ist eine Tugend. Ein gewisses Maß an **Vernunft** ist sogar lebenswichtig. Aber wir sind gerade 20 und reden, als hätten wir die Welt gesehen. Als hätten wir die universal geltende Faustregel erfasst: Setze auf Sicherheit und du wirst deine Portion Glück bekommen. Passe dich an die Bedürfnisse der Allgemeinheit an und du wirst dich ganz schnell nach vorne spielen.
10 Unser Übergang von der Schule in die Struktur der Gesellschaft verläuft nahtlos, easy, ohne weitere Komplikationen. Zukunft im Einfamilienhaus plus Gatte plus Hund. [...]

Es ist Unsicherheit, es ist Angst, es ist eine allumfassende **Verunsicherung**, die uns so handeln lässt. Die die Bücherfanatikerin dazu bringt, in ihrer Studienwahl von Literatur auf BWL umzuschwenken, die den Abiturienten, der keinen Plan hat, brav sein Zeugnis zücken und seine
15 Noten mit den Jobprognosen abgleichen lässt. Die uns unsere Kinderträume an den Nagel hängen lässt und dazu bringt, die wenigen **Idealisten** in unseren Reihen mit einem müden, überheblichen Lächeln bedenken lässt. „Ach Kinder, das bringt doch eh nichts." [...]

Es brummt uns der Kopf. Es fällt uns leichter, auf Sturm und Drang zu verzichten, um gleich in ruhige Gewässer zu gelangen. Die pragmatischen Sätze unserer Eltern werden erst zu unseren
20 Mantras und schließlich zu unseren eigenen Worten. Wir sind uns sicher, alles richtig, da vorbildlich, zu machen, dabei merken wir gar nicht, wie falsch wir liegen. Denn wir verpassen damit die Freiheit. Die **Freiheit**, die uns erlaubt, in diesem Moment, in dem nichts entschieden und in festen Bahnen ist, unabhängige Entscheidungen zu treffen.

Eine Freiheit, die uns, da wir jung und ungebunden sind, ermöglicht, **kompromisslos** unseren
25 Träumen zu folgen. In dieser Größenordnung wird sie uns womöglich nie wieder begegnen. [...] Denn Vernunft ist nur gut, solange sie nicht als Vorwand dient. Es ist gefährlich, sein Erwachsenenleben mit Kompromissen zu beginnen. Schon Victor Hugo hat einmal gesagt „Die Zukunft hat viele Namen: Für Schwache ist sie das Unerreichbare, für die Furchtsamen das Unbekannte, für die Mutigen die Chance." Wir sollten die Mutigen sein.

From: www.fudder.de, April 2012

▶ S21: Mediation of written and oral texts, p. 146

LANGUAGE LEARNING SKILLS

Of course, a **German-English dictionary** can be helpful in mediation tasks. But sometimes you will have to get culture-specific words across into the other language for which there is no proper translation, so you would only lose time and effort trying checking it. In those cases it's better to paraphrase a word.

1 MEDIATION (German → English) **Explaining the writer's ideas**
SUPPORT p. 112
Your American friend complains that many of his friends are only interested in having a successful career and asks if it's like that in Germany too. Write an email in which you explain Askari's ideas in your own words (ca. 150 words).

2 WRITING **Reacting to the article** YOU CHOOSE

a Write a reply to your friend's email, describing what German teenagers of your generation think about their future lives (ca. 100 words).

OR

b CHALLENGE Use Askari's criticism of her generation to assess the protagonist's behaviour in the 'Greyhound Tragedy' (Text **B2**, p. 22) (ca. 200 words).

Spread your wings

Check-up **MEDIATION** ▶ S33: Assessing yourself and others, p. 160
Choose the answers that best describe you.

1. **a** I read the text first, then I looked at the task.
   b Before reading the text, I examined the task to see what I was expected to do.
2. **a** I noted down the points from the text that answered the question/task.
   b I noted down important aspects of the text.
3. When I couldn't express a word or phrase in the other language, …
   a I checked it in a dictionary.
   b I tried to paraphrase it.
4. If there was something in the text the person I was mediating for couldn't understand because of cultural differences, …
   a I tried to explain it to him/her.
   b I checked whether I really needed it.
5. While writing my English text, …
   a I chose the text form and style to fit the task.
   b I wrote in the style I always use, then added a couple of phrases to make it look like an email.

Now go to p. 29 to figure out your score and interpret it.

B5 Choices *Tess Gallagher*

I go to the mountain side
of the house to cut saplings,
and clear a view to snow
on the mountain. But when I look up,
5   saw in hand, I see a nest clutched in
the uppermost branches.
I don't cut that one.
I don't cut the others either.
Suddenly, in every tree,
10 an unseen nest
where a mountain
would be.

From: Tess Gallagher, *Midnight Lantern*, 2011
www.poetryfoundation.org/poem/178872

▶ Focus on Literature: Poetry, pp. 80–85
▶ RF2, p. 204
▶ RF3, p. 205

2 **sapling** young tree
3 **clear a view** enable a view
5 **saw** (n) tool used to cut trees
 be clutched into sth. be squeezed into sth.

COMPREHENSION

1. **Understanding the speaker** SUPPORT ▶ p. 113
   Describe the *speaker's actions and the reasons for them.

ANALYSIS

2. **Examining choices**
   a Analyse the meaning of the title by explaining the choices made by the speaker. SUPPORT ▶ p. 113
   b The speaker's choices are closely connected with *symbols. Name them and analyse their meaning in the context of the poem.

3. **Explaining choices**
   'The speaker in the poem "Choices" chooses __ over __.' Complete the sentence with one of the pairs of opposites on the right, then explain why you think it fits the text (ca. 200 words).

*the living • the lifeless
the future • the present
imagination • pragmatism*

BEYOND THE TEXT

4. **Discussing choices**
   a Like the speaker in the poem, young people must make choices that can have far-reaching effects. In a group, discuss the decisions facing you in the coming years and how you feel about making them.
   b The film *Billy Elliot* also deals with a boy who has to make difficult choices. Watch it and examine how and why he makes his decisions.

▶ Vocabulary, p. 210

Chapter Task

Taking part in a tryout

While you are spending a year at an American high school, you decide to try out for the Debating Team to improve your speaking skills. When you arrive at the tryout, you are handed a card with the topic:

> ### Do Teens Need Dreams?
>
> Does our generation have a dream? Does it need a dream?
> Prepare a short *speech on this subject (no more than three minutes).

You have 15 minutes to prepare your speech.

1 Collect ideas: think of the different people and points of view you have been confronted with in this chapter. Which of them could you use as examples to support your own views? Make notes that help you when presenting your opinion.
2 SPEAKING Practise your speech with a partner. Your partner watches the time and makes suggestions about how you can make your speech more effective. Then swap roles.
3 SPEAKING Join up with another pair. Each student should make their speech while the two students who are listening to it for the first time assess them (cf. below).

▶ S33: Assessing yourself and giving feedback, p. 160

Find the assessment sheet here:
Webcode star-08

▶ S33: Assessing yourself and giving feedback, p. 160

Assessment

Give the speaker a mark of 1 to 5 (5 is highest) in each of the following categories:

Criteria	Revision and practice
1 The speaker's position is clear from the beginning. The arguments are presented in an orderly way.	▶ S10: Giving a presentation, Step 9, p. 130 ▶ Workbook, p. 14, ex. 14; p. 69, ex. 16
2 The speaker speaks slowly and clearly. Pronunciation and intonation are correct.	▶ Focus on Language: Pronunciation, p. 21 ▶ Workbook, p. 9, ex. 7
3 The speaker uses relevant, easily understandable vocabulary.	▶ L18: Using the exact word, p. 184 ▶ Workbook, p. 12, ex. 12; p. 13, ex. 13
4 The speaker keeps eye contact with the listeners and gives them the feeling that he/she is talking to them.	▶ S10: Giving a presentation, Step 10, p. 130 ▶ Workbook, p. 14, ex. 14; p. 69, ex. 16

Add up your points (from both judges). If you receive 35 points or more, you have made the team! Congratulations!

If you aren't completely satisfied with your performance, consult the pages listed above under 'Revision and practice'.

Check-up boxes

Figuring out your score

See how many points you get for each answer, then add them up for each skill to interpret your score:

WRITING p.19		LISTENING p.20		SPEAKING p.22		READING p.24		MEDIATION p.27	
Task	Points	Task	Points	Task	Points	Task	Points	Task	Points
1a	1	1a	3	1a	3	1a	3	1a	1
1b	3	1b	1	1b	1	1b	1	1b	2
1c	2	1c	2	1c	2	1c	2	2a	2
2a	1	2a	1	2a	2	2a	2	2b	1
2b	2	2b	2	2b	3	2b	3	3a	1
2c	3	2c	3	2c	1	2c	1	3b	2
3a	3	3a	2	3a	2	3a	2	4a	1
3b	2	3b	3	3b	3	3b	3	4b	2
3c	1	3c	1	3c	1	3c	1	5a	2
4a	1	4a	2	4a	2	4a	2	5b	1
4b	3	4b	3	4b	1	4b	1		
4c	2	4c	1	4c	3	4c	3		

Interpreting your score

WRITING 10–12 points	7–9 points	4–6 points
You feel comfortable with writing tasks. Pay attention to your strengths and develop them further.	You have a good basis, but also weaknesses. Go to the Focus on Writing pages in each chapter for more help and practise the techniques presented there.	You will find help in the Focus on Writing pages (p.25, p.42, p.74, p.105). Consult S13: The stages of writing (p.135) for more help. S14–20 (pp.136–145) can help you with special text forms.

LISTENING 10–12 points	7–9 points	4–6 points
You have little trouble with spoken English. Listen to recorded English whenever you have the chance (audiobooks, DVDs, etc.).	You have a good basis, but also weaknesses. Go to Focus on Skills: Listening (p.45) and S1: Listening for information (p.120) for more help. Concentrate on your listening skills when you do Chapter 2.	You will find help in Focus on Skills: Listening (p.45) as well as in S1: Listening for information (p.120). Listen to English on the internet (podcasts, internet radio) in your free time.

SPEAKING 10–12 points	7–9 points	4–6 points
You are good at expressing yourself fluently.	You have a good basis, but also weaknesses. Go to Focus on Skills: Speaking (p.16) and S10–12 (pp.130–134) for more help.	You will find help in Focus on Skills: Speaking (p.16) and S10–12 (pp.130–134). Learn useful discussion phrases and practise speaking English as often as possible.

READING 10–12 points	7–9 points	4–6 points
You have well-developed reading skills.	You have a good basis, but also weaknesses. Go to Focus on Skills: Reading (p.96) and S4–9 (pp.123–128) for more help.	You will find help in Focus on Skills: Reading (p.96) and S4–9 (pp.123–129). You also need more practice: read English texts in your free time.

MEDIATION 9–10 points	7–8 points	5–6 points
You feel confident with mediation tasks.	You have a good basis, but also weaknesses. Go to Focus on Skills: Mediation (p.64) and S21: Mediation of written and oral texts (p.146) for more help.	You will find help in Focus on Skills: Mediation (p.64) and S21: Mediation of written and oral texts (p.146). S25: Using a dictionary (p.151) could also be helpful.

Focus on Literature 1

| NOVEL pp. 30–35 | SHORT STORY pp. 56–59 | POETRY pp. 80–85 | DRAMA pp. 108–111 |

Find statements and further material on reading here:

Webcode star-09

Why read?

THINK: Make a list of everything you have read in the past six months.
PAIR: Compare lists with a partner, and discuss similarities and differences.
SHARE: In class point out and comment on the different reasons why you read.

Now use the webcode to download statements from others talking about why they read as well as further material on reading. Choose the one you can identify with, and the one you find most surprising, and exchange your comments with your partner.

Narrative Prose – the Novel

'A novel takes you somewhere and asks you to look through the eyes of another person, to live another life.'
Barbara Kingsolver (American novelist, born 1955)

Discuss Barbara Kingsolver's statement about novels, considering novels you have personally read and enjoyed.

A Getting started: Gathering information

Notes from the Midnight Driver Jordan Sonnenblick

The following quote is from the *blurb of Jordan Sonnenblick's *novel.

> Left home alone and frustrated about his parents' failed marriage, Alex Gregory gets totally drunk on vodka, then borrows his Mum's car to drive to his Dad's house. By the next morning he has a pounding headache and a date in court.

Before reading

- In small groups, talk about what you associate with the title, the front cover of *Notes from the Midnight Driver* as well as with the text from the *blurb. Speculate about what the novel may be about.
- State whether the cover makes you curious about the novel and the 'other world' it will take you to. Why does it have this effect on you? Exchange views in your group.

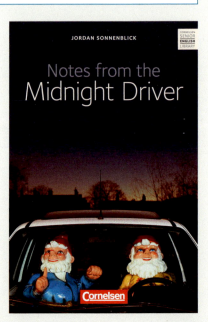

The following extract is the beginning of Jordan Sonnenblick's novel. Read the text and see what you think of Alex Gregory.

▶ A CLOSER LOOK

> **A CLOSER LOOK**
> In order to **enjoy reading a novel** it is important to develop a certain reading speed. The main thing is to **concentrate on *context and sense**. If the text makes sense to you, don't worry about individual words you don't know. Try to use your **word-guessing skills**, and if they don't help, use a **dictionary**.

Focus on Literature

Novel

LIT 1

Last September
GNOME RUN[1]

 CD 09

It seemed like a good idea at the time. Yes, I know everybody says that – but I'm serious. As insane[2] as it looks in retrospect[3], I was fully convinced on that particular Friday evening last September that stealing my mom's car and storming my dad's house was a brilliant plan. And not brilliant, as in, 'That was a brilliant answer you gave in Spanish today.' I mean brilliant, as in, 'Wow, Einstein,
5   when you came up with that relativity thing, and it revolutionized our entire concept of space and time while also leading all of humankind into the nuclear age, that was brilliant!'

The plan had a certain elegant simplicity, too. I would drink one more pint of Dad's old vodka, grab Mom's spare car keys, jump into the Dodge, and fire that sucker up. Then I would speed through the deserted, moonlit streets, straight and true as a homing missile, or at least straight and true as
10 a sober person who actually knew how to drive. When I skidded triumphantly into Dad's driveway, I would leap nimbly from the car, race to the front door, ring the bell with a fury rarely encountered by any bell, anywhere – and catch my father with the no-good home-wrecking wench who was once, in a forgotten life we used to have, my third-grade teacher.

Okay, perhaps these plans would theoretically work better if the planner were not already com-
15 pletely intoxicated. But I'd never gotten drunk before – so how was I supposed to know I'd get so smashed so quickly? And hey, if my mom had really wanted to keep me from driving drunk without a license at age sixteen, would she have gone out on a date and left me home with a car, a liquor cabinet, and some keys?

I rest my case[4].

20 So I downed some more booze straight from the bottle and lunged for the key ring, grabbing it by the wooden number 1 I have made for my 'Number One Mom' in Cub Scouts. I threw on my Yankees jacket, slammed my way out of the house, got into the car, and started it. Then I believe there was some drama with the gear stick and the parking brake, and probably a bit of fun with the gas pedal.

25 The next thing I knew, I was hanging out the passenger door, puking up vodka and Ring Dings. When I got my eyes sort of focused, I could see that the car was up on a lawn. When I got them even more focused, I could see that my last salvo of vomit had completely splattered two shiny black objects – the well-polished shoes of one angry police officer. He yanked me out of the car, largely by the hair, and stood me up. I remember him saying, 'Look at that! Look what you did.' I also remem-
30 ber trying to follow his pointing finger. And when I finally zoomed in on what was lying in front of the car I couldn't believe it. There was a detached head about ten feet in front of the bumper!

The cop sort of puppet-marched me up to the horrific scene and forced my head down close to the carnage. This head was seriously injured, to be sure. It was upside down, smashed up against a tree stump. There was no body in sight. I whirled around so fast that the cop almost lost hold of
35 me, and crouched to look under Mom's car. Sure enough, an arm and a leg were sticking out from underneath the left front wheel.

'Officer, sir, did I – is he – is – ummm …'

I could feel the tears welling up. My eyes burned, and the next wave of acid was coming up my throat in a hurry.

40 'Yes, son. You ruined my brand-new shoes, smashed up your car, and decapitated Mrs. Wilson's French lawn gnome. You're in some serious …'

'Lawn gnome? LAWN GNOME?'

From: Jordan Sonnenblick, *Notes from the Midnight Driver*, 2014 (first published 2006)

---

[1] **gnome run** [nəʊm] *wordplay/pun on 'home run' = score won by a particularly good hit in a baseball game
[2] **insane** [–'–] crazy
[3] **in retrospect** ['retrəspekt] looking back at past events, often with a changed opinion
[4] **I rest my case** said by lawyers when they have finished their speech

LIT 1   Novel

gnome • fire that sucker up homing missile • sober skidded • nimbly encountered • wench intoxicated • smashed booze • lunged • gear stick parking brake • puking Ring Dings • salvo • vomit yanked • detached • bumper puppet-marched • carnage smushed • welling up • acid decapitated

▶ S23: Dealing with unknown words, p. 149

> **A CLOSER LOOK**
>
> The **first-person *narrator** can only talk about things he or she has seen or heard, and about their own thoughts and feelings. They can also leave out things about themselves or only give hints to the reader.

▶ S7: Reading and analysing narrative prose, p. 127

> **TROUBLE SPOT**
>
> **character** ['kærəktə] = Figur
> **figure** ['fɪgə] = Gestalt, Zahl

 CD 10

[1] **frankly** honestly
[2] **verbally abusive** saying rude and disrespectful things
[3] **imbecile** ['imbəsi:l, AE: -sl] idiot
[4] **berate sb.** (fml) jdn. beschimpfen
[5] **Yiddish** the language of Eastern European Jews and their descendants worldwide

1 First impressions
Talk to your partner about your first impression of the beginning of *Notes from the Midnight Driver*. Point out passages that you find interesting / funny / thrilling / hard to understand, including the title.

2 Dealing with unknown words
a From the list of words and expressions on the left, which ones did you think you could ignore and still understand the rest of the sentence, and which ones made you stop and think? Make a table with the headings: *ignored*, *guessed from context*, and *needed dictionary*. Add any other words from the *extract that puzzled you.
b Compare tables with a partner and explain which strategies you used.

3 Understanding what we are told and who is telling us
a Read the *extract again. Analyse what kind of person the *narrator seems to be from the way he tells the reader about himself, his views and the 'midnight incident'. ▶ **A CLOSER LOOK**
b Imagine someone had made a video of the incident. Describe what you would see and hear in the video.
c Discuss with your partner what the *setting as well as the behaviour of the main *character make you anticipate with regard to the story.

B Developments: How does the plot unfold?
B1 A human service assignment

After the incident described at the beginning of the *novel, Alex gets a court sentence of 100 hours of human service time, which he is to do in the nursing home where his mother works.

Before reading
- Jot down 8–10 words or phrases you associate with '100 hours of human service time in a nursing home'.
- Discuss what such a sentence would mean for you, and what it probably means for a sixteen-year-old boy like Alex.

The following *extract is from the first of several letters from Alex to Judge Trent after the court sentence. Find out what Alex's first reactions to his new 'job' are.

    I think it is great that you gave me a chance to right my wrongs and learn from my mistakes, even though my accident did not hurt anybody but myself. However, I have just completed my first visit to the nursing home, where I worked with a very interesting ~~patient~~ resident named Solomon Lewis, and I feel you should change my assignment.
    First of all, while I know the assignment is to serve humans, I am just not qualified to assist   5
Mr. Lewis. Apparently, he has some problems with memory and attention that should be handled by a competent mental-health professional, rather than a teenager. He is also, frankly[1], verbally abusive[2]. Within minutes of meeting me, Mr. Lewis called me an imbecile[3], said I was 'not a rocket scientist' and 'irritating', and suggested that maybe the other ~~pati~~ residents should be mercy-killed. He also berated[4] me repeatedly in some foreign language, which the nurses said   10
must be something called 'Yiddish[5].'

32
Focus on Literature

Secondly, nobody alerted⁶ me to this ahead of time, but Mr. Lewis is afflicted⁷ with a serious health problem called 'emphysema⁸'. He started choking to death right in front of me, and I didn't have the skills to help him. A nurse had to come rushing in with a big mask and give him some
15 kind of emergency breathing treatment. [...]

In closing, I feel that I have grounds for concern here. I am glad to do human service so that I can learn a valuable life lesson about responsibility and trust. However, I am just not qualified to meet Mr. Lewis's needs. The home should replace me with a psychiatrist/linguist/paramedic/saint, and the court should find me a new assignment that will be less traumatic for my sensi-
20 tive⁹ adolescent¹⁰ mind.

From: Jordan Sonnenblick, *Notes from the Midnight Driver*, 2014 (first published 2006)

⁶ **alert sb. to sth.** point sth. out to sb.
⁷ **be afflicted with sth.** *(fml)* suffer from sth. *(usu. an illness)*
⁸ **emphysema** [ˌemfɪˈsiːmə] lung disease
⁹ **sensitive** easy to upset
¹⁰ **adolescent** [ˌædəˈlesnt] between 13 and 18 years old

1 Understanding a *character
a In pairs, exchange your first impressions about Alex's feelings towards his human service assignment. Discuss whether you would have reacted similarly if you had been in Alex's shoes.
b Decide which three of the adjectives on the right fit your view of Alex best, and discuss your choices with your partner. Give reasons.
c Using the adjectives on the right, choose three to characterize Mr Lewis from Alex's *point of view, and compare your choices with your partner's.

2 Analysing ways of *characterization ▶ A CLOSER LOOK
a Examine how the *narrator, Alex, characterizes Mr Lewis in his letter.
b Analyse Alex's choice of words and their *connotations when writing about Mr Lewis and his behaviour.
c Explain to what extent Alex's report serves to characterize him as much as the person he is describing.

3 Analysing a character's *diction
a Analyse the *style and *tone of Alex's letter, and make a chart in which you list comical and formal elements.
b Evaluate the effect created by the *juxtaposition of these elements.

4 WRITING Changing perspectives YOU CHOOSE
a **CHALLENGE** Write a formal letter from Judge Trent in response to Alex's letter in which she explains to him that he must stay with this particular resident despite the problems he has mentioned.
OR
b Judge Trent talks to Alex on the phone to tell him that he must do his assigned job. Write down the script of their conversation and act it out with a partner.

---

arrogant • charitable • clever concerned • conscientious demanding • easy-going helpful • helpless hypocritical • intelligent naïve • reasonable rebellious • respectful disrespectful • selfish serious • sympathetic troublesome • understanding

■ **TROUBLE SPOT**
sympathetic [ˌsɪmpəˈθetɪk] = *mitfühlend*
likeable [ˈlaɪkəbl] = *sympathisch*

■ **A CLOSER LOOK**
A *narrator characterizes someone either **directly**, i.e. by making statements about them, or **indirectly** by their behaviour and speech. A first-person narrator also gives clues about himself by the way he characterizes others.

▶ S15: Writing a formal letter or email, p. 136

LIT 1   Novel

B2 Surprises

The following *extract is from a chapter just after halfway through the *novel, called 'A Night for Surprises'. Alex has organized a charity concert in the nursing home, in which he himself plays the guitar and Annette and Steven, a duo from his school that he calls the cha-KINGS, play piano and drums.

Read the extract to discover what kind of changes have occurred since Alex's first experiences with Solomon (Sol) Lewis (extract **B1**), and briefly exchange views with a partner afterwards.

🎧 CD 11

[sidebar glossary:]
[1] **chafe sb.** make sb.'s skin sore by rubbing it
[2] **schmegege** (Yiddish) person who upsets you
[3] **eerie** scary
[4] **creeped out** (infml) scared
[5] **remotely** (here) slightly
[6] **eyewear** eye-glasses
[7] **no dice** (AE, infml, old-fashioned) no luck
[8] **inevitable** [ɪnˈevɪtəbl] not to be avoided
[9] **billow** be blown up with air, thus looking bigger (usu. of clothes)
[10] **mound of sth.** (here) large amount of sth. in a pile
[11] **horrific** terrible
[12] **tongue depressor** [tʌŋ] (AE) long flat wooden instrument that doctors use to press down your tongue when looking at your throat
[13] **undies** (infml) underwear
[14] **latch** metal device used to hold a lid or door shut
[15] **gullible** [ˈɡʌləbl] too willing to believe what other people tell you
[16] **launch yourself somewhere** go somewhere with a lot of energy
[17] **stairwell** place where stairs lead from one storey to another
[18] **slaughter** [ˈslɔːtə] (here) violent act of murder
[19] **Tito Puente** (1923–2000) Latin jazz and salsa musician

But I was feeling pretty good when we walked offstage for intermission after my witty announcement of 'We're going to … uh … take a break now and then … um …. play some more if you're still here." Laurie told me how great she thought it was, the manager gave me a thumbs-up, and my parents smiled and started to walk over to me. But Sol grabbed my arm first. 'Alex, I need you to do something for me.'   5

'I'm kind of busy right now, Sol. And I have to play again in a few minutes. Are you having a good time?'

'Sure, sure. You're magnificent, Alex. But can you run up to my room and get my other eye-glasses?'

'What's wrong with the ones you're wearing?'   10

'They chafe[1] me and I can't see right. If the night nurse hadn't been such a schmegege[2] and moved everything around in my room last night, this wouldn't have happened. Look, would you just go?' By now, I felt like everyone in America was staring at me, the mean kid who wouldn't get an old man a pair of glasses.

'Fine. Where should I look for them?'   15

'If I knew where to find them, I would have worn them in the first place. I don't know, they're the only pair of glasses in my room. How hard can it be for a talented young guy like yourself?'

I looked around for Steven and Annette to tell them where I was going, and that I'd be right back, but they must have run out to the bathroom or something. Laurie saw, and said, 'Don't worry, Alex. I'll tell the Cha-KINGS where you went.'   20

[…]

Sol's floor was eerily[3] deserted, because everybody was downstairs. It kind of felt like I was in one of those dreams where you show up at your school, and there's nobody in the halls. So it gets darker and darker, and you try to run out, screaming. But it's too late, because a hand reaches out and …   25

Well, anyway, I started to get a little creeped out[4]. In the room, I didn't see anything in the open that looked remotely[5] similar to eyewear[6]. I quickly opened each drawer of Sol's dresser, but no dice[7] there either. By this point, I kept waiting for the inevitable[8] masked killer to grab me, which added to the intensity of my search. I got down to the bottom drawer, which contained nothing but billowing[9] mounds of[10] Sol's underwear – boxers, by the way. I knew the glasses might be beneath the piles in there, but actually moving the boxers was a horrific[11] thought on its own. So I found an unused, wrapped tongue depressor[12] on top of the dresser, popped it open, and sort of stirred the undies[13] around. I hit something solid, and forced myself to reach in. A case! I pulled it out and pushed the little latch[14] device that opened the lid.   30

But there were no glasses inside, just a big old key. Hmm. Where were the glasses? Were there any glasses? Was this a … a … a trick? Oh, my God! I thought. Sol's up to something. How could I be so gullible[15]? I launched myself[16] out the door and down the fire stairs, still holding the case. When I came out of the stairwell[17], my fears became a reality. Okay, not the slaughter[18] ones, but the trickery ones. I could hear Steven's drums start up on a fast Latin tune. When Annette jumped in, I recognized it as a Tito Puente[19] chart called 'Para Los Rumberos' that I knew Steven loved.   35

What on earth were they doing?   40

34   Focus on Literature

Novel LIT 1

Then I heard my beloved Tele[20] jumping into action. But I had never played it like this. The notes were rippling[21] forth in a torrent[22], faster than I would have been on my best day, and with the kind of timing I would have killed for. I came screeching[23] around a corner into the rec
45 room[24], and saw a tableau[25] I'll never forget. The nurses were up on their feet, swaying[26]. The orderlies[27] were getting down. Even many of the residents were standing and shimmying[28] like people with actual, biological hip joints[29]. And in front of this frenzied[30] hotbed of[31] party power, a man was wailing[32] on MY guitar.

A man whose glasses were chafing him.

50 Sol looked all the way to the back of the room at me, and mouthed[33] the word that I absolutely knew was coming: 'Gotcha!'[34]

What was I going to do? I walked up to the front, and stood between my mom and Laurie, in Sol's seat. Laurie had a huge grin going, and whispered to me, 'This is amazing. He's incredible!'

I didn't say a word. I could feel the redness of my face, but Laurie didn't notice. My mom put
55 her arm around my shoulder and said, 'Oh, Alex. What a wonderful surprise! I don't know how you did it, but it's like you've brought Mr. Lewis back to life!'

From: Jordan Sonnenblick, *Notes from the Midnight Driver*, 2014 (first published 2006)

[20] **Tele** type of guitar
[21] **ripple** move in small waves
[22] **torrent** large amount of sth. moving very fast (*usu. water*)
[23] **screech** make a loud, unpleasant sound as you move
[24] **rec room** room in an official building where people can play games, relax, etc.
[25] **tableau** [tæˈbləʊ, ˈtæbləʊ] (*here*) scene
[26] **sway** move slowly from side to side
[27] **orderly** assistant nurse
[28] **shimmy** (*v*) move your hips and shoulders as you dance
[29] **hip joint** *Hüftgelenk*
[30] **frenzied** fast and hectic
[31] **hotbed of sth.** place where sth. is happening a lot
[32] **wail** make a long sound
[33] **mouth sth.** [maʊð] move your lips as if you are saying sth.
[34] **gotcha** = I got you said to sb. you have successfully tricked ('*Reingefallen!*')

1 Understanding the action
Outline the *action narrated here. It will be useful to form a mental image of the *setting, the *characters and their behaviour.

2 Analysing character development and *style
a Read the *extract again closely, and explain what you learn about Sol from his behaviour as described by Alex.
b Examine whether the *narrator, Alex, has changed since you first encountered him and explain why you think so.
c Study the style of Alex's narration of the incident, especially the situation in Sol's room, and state how this contributes to your view of him as a person.
d Focus on Laurie's behaviour, and decide if the turn of events is a surprise for her as much as for her friend Alex. Identify the clues in the text.

3 WRITING A diary entry
Write a diary entry as close to Alex's *style as a *narrator as possible (cf. **B1**, task **2c**, **3a**), in which he describes his feelings after the concert, including his friend's and his mother's reactions to the development.

▶ S14: Creative writing, p. 136
▶ L5: Simple past and past progressive, p. 170

C Tying up the strings: How could the story end?

1 Making intelligent guesses ▶ A CLOSER LOOK
In pairs, speculate and make notes on how you expect the *novel to go on and eventually end. Consider what you know from the *extracts and make some intelligent guesses.

2 Looking at the storytelling
Explain why or why not you would like to see more of life through Alex's eyes by reading the complete *novel *Notes from the Midnight Driver*. Consider what you found funny, surprising, or exciting – or even boring – in the three extracts.

A CLOSER LOOK

It is possible to make intelligent guesses about a *novel ending by looking at how the *plot develops, how the *characters behave in certain situations, and also by knowing a bit about **patterns of storytelling** as well as about the real world. However, the *author of a novel may add a **surprising twist** at the end. So stay on your toes and **keep guessing** – and finally decide whether the ending fulfills the reader's expectations or not, and why.

2 Communicating in the Digital Age

A

B

Download a chronological word list here: **Webcode** star-62

- S27: Working with visuals, p. 153
- L2: Simple present tense and present progressive, p. 167
- L3: Present perfect and present perfect progressive, p. 168

LANGUAGE HELP
- One / The main advantage is that …
- A weak point of … is …
- The disadvantage of … is…
- The biggest drawback of … is …
- With … you can/cannot …
- Both/Neither of them …

Find a tool to make your poster:
Webcode star-11

1 Talking about pictures
  a THINK: Choose one of the photos A–D. Imagine the 'story' behind the pictures: speculate on the *setting, the situation, the people and their relationship. (Give the people names if necessary.)
  b PAIR: Find a partner who has chosen a different photo. Tell each other about your photos and the stories you invented.
  c SHARE: Link up with another pair and tell each other your stories. Discuss the role that communication plays in each of them.

2 Thinking about communication
  a BRAINSTORMING: Collect all the ways you can think of that people use to communicate (face-to-face conversation, phone call, email, …).
  b Form small groups. Each group chooses one form of communication and compiles a list of the advantages and disadvantages. ▶
  c On the basis of your findings, say in what situations and/or with whom your form of communication would be appropriate or not. Create a poster with dos and don'ts.
  d GALLERY WALK: Present and discuss your posters. If possible, refer back to your stories from task **1**.

Lead-in

In this chapter you will discuss how digital media affect our lives, especially the way we communicate with each other. At the end you will work on a project in which you will take part in a (fictitious) competition. The more you know about the topic, the more you can contribute to your task. ▶ PREVIEW

PREVIEW

Main topics
- Ways of communicating today, p. 40
- Monitoring your child's online behaviour, p. 46
- The problem of cyber-bullying, p. 48

Skills in focus
- Writing: structuring a text and connecting ideas, p. 42
- Listening, p. 45

Language in focus
- Grammar: The simple form and the progressive form, p. 51

Chapter Task
- Taking part in a competition, p. 54

Words in Context

🎧 CD 12
Listen to an audio version of the text on the CD or download it here:
Webcode star-12

▶ Vocabulary, p. 212

Keeping in touch in the 21st century

The online world
Computers and the internet have had a great impact on our everyday lives. We use search engines to surf the web; we retrieve information, do shopping and banking; we download material, share photos and news with friends and we even apply for jobs or university places – all via the internet. Online encyclo- 5
paedias, video-sharing or microblogging websites allow ordinary people to upload content to the net and thus to gain access to a global audience (at least in theory). This interactive aspect of the internet, sometimes referred to as Web 2.0, has turned formerly passive consumers into active contributors.

The internet in your pocket
Thanks to the invention of hand-held devices like tablet PCs and smartphones, the internet has gone portable, with far-reaching consequences for society. Information available online – train times, ticket prices, maps – can be accessed when and where it is needed: on the go, at work or at home, wherever there is a wireless connection. Apps (short for applications) and QR (quick response) 15
codes enhance the usefulness of portable devices in a variety of situations.

The rise of social networking
The number of channels now available for communication influences the way we deal with each other. As the amount of digital text-based communication steadily increases from year to year, traditional forms of linking up (phone 20
calls, face-to-face conversation) appear to be losing popularity.
At the centre of the new digital culture are social networking sites (SNS) that allow their users to share pictures, instant messages, activities and interests. Since their first appearance around the turn of the century, they have mushroomed to become global meeting points that link hundreds of millions of 25
people worldwide. Originally they appealed mainly to a young audience that used them to make new contacts and post photos and messages, but today more and more older people are discovering their usefulness as well.
By representing themselves as a 'community' of 'friends', SNS can create a false sense of security that leads some teenagers to post personal information 30
or private photos that can be copied and passed on by anyone. The anonymity of cyberspace also makes it easier for cyberbullies to torment their victims without fear of legal consequences.

1 Organizing information
Copy the table below, then use the information from the text above to complete it.

topic	its uses	its effects
the internet		
portable internet device		
social networking site		

Keeping in touch in the 21st century

2 Doubly useful words

Many English words can be used both as nouns and as verbs (e.g. 'Can I borrow your *phone*?' – 'Will you *phone* me?').

a In each of the sentence pairs below, replace the tilde ('~') by a word from the text that can be used in both sentences, either as a noun or as a verb:
1. a The internet has become a communications channel that ~s millions of people around the world.
   b To open the application form, just follow the ~ in the email.
2. a The ~ of digital media on our lives cannot be overestimated.
   b Undeniably, the internet ~s the way we work and communicate.
3. a Can you ~ your Facebook profile on your mobile?
   b For this map you need internet ~.
4. a Facebook makes it easy to ~ old friends.
   b We stayed in ~ via email while I was in New Zealand.

b Write four more sentence pairs like those in **a** using the following words: *fear, appeal, increase, form*. Use your dictionary if necessary.

3 Collocations

Collocations are combinations of words that often 'go together' (e.g. *gain experience, a serious problem*).

▶ L19: Common collocations with prepositions, p. 184

a Form six collocations using the words in the two boxes below. Look at the text again if you need help:

upload	audience
legal	consequences
surf	content
personal	device
portable	the web
global	information

■ **TROUBLE SPOT**

viele Informationen (pl) = **a lot of information** (sing)
eine Information = **a piece of information** (sing)
Not: *an information*

b Choose four collocations and use each one in a sentence.

4 Activate your passive vocabulary

Translate the following sentences. The text will help you with the underlined parts:
1. <u>Dank des Smartphones</u> können wir überall <u>auf Informationen aus dem Internet zugreifen</u>.
2. <u>Immer mehr Menschen entdecken die Nützlichkeit</u> des mobilen Internetzugangs.
3. <u>Seit Erscheinen</u> des Smartphones ist die Zahl der <u>verfügbaren</u> Apps <u>ständig gestiegen</u>.
4. <u>Textbasierte Anwendungen steigern</u> die Bedeutung des geschriebenen Wortes.
5. Soziale Netzwerke machen es möglich, mit alten Freunden <u>in Kontakt zu bleiben</u> und <u>neue Kontakte zu knüpfen</u>.

5 Writing

Write a text of about 150 words describing how you use the internet in your everyday life. Use words and phrases from the text where possible.

2 Part A

Changing ways of communicating

▶ S29: Working with cartoons, p. 156

A1 The connected generation

— COMPREHENSION ◀

1 **Talking about the *cartoon**
   a Describe the situation presented in the two panels.
   b Who or what is the cartoonist making fun of?
   c Link up with another student and compare your understanding of the cartoon.

— ANALYSIS ◀

2 **Interpreting image and meaning** SUPPORT ▷ p. 113
   Analyse how facial expression and body language contribute to the *cartoon's message.

— BEYOND THE TEXT ◀

3 **Evaluating the cartoon**
   Discuss how successfully the *cartoon expresses its critique of modern forms of communication.

■ **LANGUAGE AWARENESS**

You have learned that a proper sentence contains at least a subject and a verb. However, in many situations and in many text types it is common to use **incomplete sentences**. For example, the cartoon above omits the subject and/or verb to imitate spoken language (first frame) and a Twitter message (second frame).

▶ LA3: Similarities and differences of languages, p. 198

■ **TROUBLE SPOT**

text (n) = **1.** piece of written language; **2.** text message
text sb. = send sb. a text message

3 **double the number** twice as much as
4 **confound sb.** [–'–] *(fml)* confuse sb.
6 **addict** ['– –] person who cannot stop doing sth. *(usu. taking drugs)*
11 **slide** *(here)* go down by
12 **findings** *(pl)* results
   media regulator ['regjʊleɪtə] government agency that watches and checks the media
13 **authoritative** [–'– – – –] zuverlässig
18 **pithy** short and full of meaning
19 **hence** for this reason
   digital (n) digital media
24 **broadcast sth.** etwas veröffentlichen

A2 The comeback of the written word *Gideon Spanier*

Some people say that the advent of the text message has changed our ways of communicating for the worse. Say why this might be so.

Texting, emails, tweets and other forms of text-based communications on a mobile device are now more popular than making phone calls or talking face-to-face.

The average Briton sends 50 mobile text messages a week, double the number four years ago, which will confound those who thought the SMS was a dying technology. Social media and email are also taking up more of our time – an average of 90 minutes a week (although that might seem impossibly low to some smartphone addicts). Among the 16- to 24-year-olds, 96 % use some form of text-based communication each day to keep in touch with friends and family, 90% send texts and 73% use social media but only 67 % make voice calls. Indeed, the overall amount of time that Britons spent making voice calls on both mobile and landlines fell for the first time last year, sliding 1 %.

These are just some of the surprising findings from media regulator Ofcom's Communications Market Report, an authoritative annual guide that was published today. Watching video and playing games were meant to have taken over our life in the digital age but it turns out that words still matter. If anything, the power of text has increased, which should give hope to anyone who cares about reading – or believes in the future of journalism.

New technology lets us communicate in a pithy and highly effective way in real time, hence the popularity of the text message, the tweet and the live blog. At the same time, digital now allows us easy access to the biggest [collections] of documents and books, which can be searched or sorted at the click of a button. In contrast, it's still frustratingly difficult to search video and images – except by using words.

The rise of mobile devices is important because it gives us more opportunity to consume (and broadcast) content – wherever we are. That is why we have more time to text, write emails, post messages on social media, read e-books and look at apps and websites. [...]

Changing ways of communicating

The Ofcom survey also confirmed another interesting trend: those who own tablets tend to use them most inside the home – 90% of the time – rather than on the go. This suggests that the real attraction of a mobile device – as opposed to a laptop or personal computer – is not so much that it can get a mobile signal from our phone network but that it gives us mobility, from room to room as well as out of the home. The mobile handset has ceased to be just a phone. Now the smartphone and the tablet are more like mobile computers – an internet-connected device on which we can consume content, rather than simply make telephone calls. [...]

It might appear as if our media habits aren't changing that much. We still watch a lot of TV – four hours a day, says Ofcom, the same as a year earlier — but now many of us might also have a mobile device on our lap. This phenomenon has been dubbed the 'second screen'. However, the mobile is so personal that it is arguably becoming the first screen, especially for teenagers, who will often flop down on the sofa in the living room, ignore the main TV set, and immerse themselves in their smartphone.

From: 'The joy of text – it's words that matter in mobile age', *London Evening Standard*, 18 July 2012

FACT FILE
Ofcom stands for 'The Office of Communications'. It is a government-approved authority which regulates the broadcasting industries in the United Kingdom. Ofcom represents the interests of citizens by promoting competition and by banning material that might be considered harmful or offensive.

32 **cease to be sth.** [siːs] stop being sth.
37 **lap** *Schoß*
  dub sth. sth. else name sth. sth. else
38 **arguably** [ˈɑːgjuəbli] quite possibly
40 **immerse yourself in sth.** [ɪˈmɜːs] concentrate totally on sth.

► COMPREHENSION

1 Looking at the text
  a Write eight true/false statements about the trends named in the text. Give them to your partner.
  b Check your partner's sentences and correct the false ones.
  c Check each other's solutions.

2 Summarizing the main points
  a List examples from the text that illustrate how the written word continues to be important in digital media.
  b Outline the reasons the author gives as to why text-based communication hasn't died out.

▶ S20: Writing a summary, p. 144
▶ L7: *Will*-future and *going to*-future, p. 172

3 MEDIATION (English → German) Writing a report
You are working on an *article for your school magazine on the importance of writing in today's world. In German, write a report on the basis of this article (ca. 200 words).

▶ S21: Mediation of written and oral texts, p. 146
▶ L14: Formal and informal English, p. 180

4 LANGUAGE AWARENESS Examining the use of numbers
  a The author uses a lot of numbers and percentages in his text. Find examples and examine their effect on the reader.
  b Together with a partner, discuss how you could benefit from your findings in task **5**.

▶ S21: LA4: Influencing through language, p. 199

► BEYOND THE TEXT

5 WRITING Reacting to the text
Write a comment of 200–300 words on one of these topics. **YOU CHOOSE**

  a 'Forms of text-based communications on a mobile device are now more popular than making phone calls or talking face-to-face' (ll. 1–2). Comment on this development.

  OR

  b Present and discuss trends that have appeared since Spanier wrote his article.

▶ S17: Argumentative writing, p. 139
▶ L18: Using the exact word, p. 184

Part A

▶ Focus on Skills: Writing, p. 25, p. 74, p. 105

A3 FOCUS ON SKILLS WRITING (2)
Structuring a text and connecting ideas

When writing a text, you have to make sure that your line of thought is easy to follow for your readers. For that purpose you should give it a clear structure by using paragraphs (▶ p. 74) and connecting your ideas with linking words.

1 Understanding a badly written text
In the following text, a student comments on the Ofcom survey on how people use their mobile phones (cf. Part **A2**, pp. 40–41).
a Read the text and try to sum up in your own words what the student wants to say here.

> I talk to my friends face-to-face when I meet them in school. When they are not around I prefer to text them. I don't want to disturb them. Texting is much faster than talking. You can leave out the small talk. You can do something else at the same time. You don't hear the sound of
> 5 your friends' voices. You don't know how they feel and what else is going on in their lives. It is difficult to build up a close relationship. Everybody can write things that are not true. You can't look into their eyes, you can't tell if they are lying. I like the fact that communication, e. g. asking for homework or arranging when to meet, has become so
> 10 effective and much less time-consuming. I think this comes at a high price. There is less personal closeness and honesty. A report presents the new developments in our media usage. People communicate more by sending text messages than by talking to each other because of the development of mobile devices. With them you can send and receive
> 15 text messages wherever you are and whenever you want.

b Try to say why it is so difficult to understand the text. Give examples.

2 Writing a well-structured text
a Extract ideas from the text and use them to make an outline for a well-structured text. Divide it into three parts: **introduction, body** (advantages of texting, disadvantages of texting), **conclusion**. Add your own ideas.
b On the basis of your **outline**, write a well-structured text, bearing in mind the following tips and tasks:
  • Follow your outline to give the text a convincing structure.
  • Take a look at the linking words on the left and make sure you know what they mean (you can use the webcode to download example sentences). Use the linking words to connect your ideas in your text.
  • Give the text a meaningful heading.

▶ S13: The stages of writing, p. 135

▶ L15: Linking your sentences, p. 180

all in all • although another point is • because besides • but • however in addition (to) • in conclusion in spite of • moreover • since to sum up

Download example sentences here:
👆 **Webcode** star-13

A4 CHALLENGE Conversation – a vanishing skill?
Martha Irvine

While many people find texting appropriate in most situations, others argue that without face-to-face communication something important is lost.

Anna Schiferl hadn't even rolled out of bed when she reached for her cell phone and typed a text to her mom, one recent Saturday. Mom was right downstairs in the kitchen. The text? Anna wanted cinnamon rolls for breakfast. Soon after, the 13-year-old could hear mom's voice echoing through the house. 'Anna,' Joanna Schiferl called, 'if
5 you want to talk to me, you come downstairs and see me!' Anna laughs about it now. 'I was kind of being lazy,' the teen from suburban Chicago concedes. 'I know that sounds horrible.' Well, maybe not horrible, but certainly increasingly typical.

Statistics from the Pew Internet & American Life Project show that, these days, many people with cell phones prefer texting over a phone call. It's not always young
10 people, though the data indicate that the younger you are, the more likely you are to prefer texting. And that's creating a communication divide, of sorts – the talkers vs. the texters.

Some would argue that it's no big deal. What difference should it make how we communicate, as long as we do so? But many experts say the most successful communi-
15 cators will, of course, have the ability to do both, talk or text, and know the most appropriate times to use those skills. And they fear that more of us are losing our ability to have – or at least are avoiding – the traditional face-to-face conversations that are vital in the workplace and personal relationships. 'It is an art that's becoming as valuable as good writing,' says Janet Sternberg, a professor of communication
20 and media studies at Fordham University in New York who is also a linguist. In the most extreme cases, she's noticed that more students don't look her in the eye and have trouble with the basics of direct conversation – habits that, she says, will not serve them well as they enter a world where many of their elders still expect an in-person conversation, or at the very least a phone call.

25 On today's college campuses, the dynamic is often different. Forget about things like 'office hours,' for instance. Many professors say they rarely see students outside of class. 'I sit in my office hours lonely now because if students have a question, they email, often late at night,' says Renee Houston, an associate professor of communication studies at the University of Puget Sound in Washington state. 'And they never call,
30 ever.' [...]

Mary Ann Allison, an assistant professor of media studies at Hofstra University, has her students keep a log of their own communication habits. 'By paying attention to it, they say, "Wow, it's a really different conversation when you're talking with someone and listening to them,"' Allison says. They key in on body language, facial expressions
35 and tone of voice – all cues that you lose when you can't see or hear someone, or when you're distracted, even in person, by a gadget.

Sternberg, at Fordham, asks her students to give up one form of electronic communication to see what kind of difference it makes in their lives. She also has them practice simple tasks such as standing up in a room full of people and introducing them-
40 selves. Many of them hate the drill, she says, but later tell her how useful it was, especially in the workplace.

TROUBLE SPOT
Handy (German) = **mobile phone** (BE), **cell phone** (AE)
handy (English) = *praktisch, nützlich, handlich*

FACT FILE
The Pew Research Center is a US nonprofit organization that conducts studies by using opinion polls or analysing media content in order to find out what issues, trends and attitudes influence America and the world. The Pew Internet & American Life Project explores the impact of the internet on families, communities, work and home, daily life, education, health care, and civic and political life.

'I'm so glad you agreed to meet in person. There are some things that just can't be said in 140 characters.'

▶ S29: Working with cartoons, p. 156

vanish disappear, no longer exist
6 **concede sth.** admit that sth. is true
11 **divide** (n) barrier, border
 of sorts (infml) (here) in a way
16 **appropriate** [əˈprəʊpriət] fitting, suitable
17 **avoid sth.** keep away from sth.
18 **vital** [ˈvaɪtl] very important
20 **linguist** researcher in the study of language
23 **your elders** people older than you
25 **dynamic** (n) situation
34 **key in on sth.** (v) pay close attention to sth.
35 **cue** signal
36 **distract sb.** [–ˈ–] *jdn. ablenken*
 gadget tool or device that does sth. useful
40 **drill** simple and repetitive exercise

Part A

44 **rush sth.** do sth. too quickly
47 **range** spectrum
48 **adapt** [–'–] change your behaviour to deal with a new situation
49 **gap** Kluft

Interestingly, Anna's mom, Joanna Schiferl, is more worried about the effect that texting is having on her daughter's writing skills than her social skills. Anna tends to rush her writing and pays less attention to grammar, or uses abbreviations she'd use in a text. It is a common observation among parents.

So the key, experts say, is to recognize your weak point and work on developing a wide range of communication skills. 'People with a more flexible style, whether they're communicators in person or through technology, will have an easier time adapting,' Houston says – and will help bridge the communication gap, generational or otherwise.

From: 'Text messaging: is texting ruining the art of conversation?', *The Huffington Post*, 3 June 2012

Find a mind mapping tool here:
Webcode star-14

▶ S20: Writing a summary, p. 144

▶ LA3: Similarities and differences of languages, p. 198

▶ S10: Giving a presentation, p. 130

— COMPREHENSION ◀

1 Looking for the main ideas SUPPORT ▶ p. 114
   a Present the main topics of the text in a mind map.
   b Compare mind maps with a partner. Add any missing points to your own mind map.

2 WRITING **Summarizing the text**
With the help of your mind map, write a summary of the text (ca. 100 words).

3 Examining text features YOU CHOOSE
   a LANGUAGE AWARENESS In the text you can find various forms of questions. Identify them and examine the effect this has on you as a reader.

   OR

   b The author often uses other experiences and opinions. Examine the function this has.

— ANALYSIS ◀

4 Examining the text type
Check the Skills File for different types of non-fictional texts. Decide which category this text belongs to and give reasons.

— BEYOND THE TEXT ◀

5 Presenting an idea
The experts suggest three practical measures that can help students improve their media awareness and social skills. Choose one of them and present it to your class, explaining why you think it would or would not be helpful.

6 WRITING **Discussing an issue**
Work in groups of 4–5. Hold a writing conference on the topic 'Do teens have difficulty with face-to-face conversation?'.

Changing ways of communicating

A5 FOCUS ON SKILLS LISTENING

Listening to spoken English can be a challenge, both in real life and at school. Listening in the context of school is often different from listening in real life, because at school you are usually given some time to prepare and then you listen to the text twice.
Think of situations in which you have listened to someone speaking English: what made it difficult for you to understand the speaker? What strategies helped you?

1 Before listening
Before listening you should try to anticipate as much as you can about the audio, e.g. from its topic or its heading.

You are now going to hear an extract from a podcast called '23 days unplugged'. Speculate what the podcast might be about.

2 Dealing with unknown words
Listen to an excerpt from the podcast. Watch out for the word *capabilities* and the expression *on the fly*. Using the contexts, try to find out what they mean.

🎧 CD 13

3 Listening for gist
When listening to the whole text for the first time, try to relax. Don't panic if you don't understand every word. If you hear an unfamiliar word, try to guess its meaning from the context.

Listen to the entire extract, then choose the right answer: The podcast deals with …
1 … ways to get by without a mobile phone.
2 … how people reacted to living without their mobile phones for a time.
3 … the reasons why it's necessary today to have a mobile phone.

🎧 CD 14

4 Listening for detail
When you listen for the second time, you often listen for specific information. Take notes if you are allowed to. Prepare your notepad so that you can write down the information you need quickly while still paying attention to what is being said. Use keywords, abbreviations and symbols.

▶ S22: Making and taking notes, p. 148

Listen to the podcast once again.
a Take notes to describe how the speaker's life changed after she lost her phone.
b Complete your notes as soon as the recording is over. Then compare notes with your partner.

5 After listening: more practice
Three other people are interviewed in the podcast. Listen again and take notes on each of them: what happened to them, and how do they feel about their experiences?

Communicating in the Digital Age   Chapter 2

Part B

Parents, friends and strangers

B1 Parental spies Bella Qvist

Imagine your parents could see your online activities. How would you feel?

Can giving parents detailed activity reports of their child's online search terms be harmful to young people looking for information on sensitive topics such as religion, sexuality, gender or domestic abuse? [...]

Most security software companies today sell 'family' products, many including reports, notifications and video supervision. But is it right to spy on your child?

The UN convention on the rights of the child stipulates that children have a right to privacy and a right to information. They also have a right to protection from all types of violence and exploitation – and there lies the rub.

With a young generation more internet-savvy than their parents, ensuring online safety for minors surfing an ever-expanding web becomes a hard task. Today's parents don't have an older generation to turn to for tech advice, so many turn to parental control software instead. [...]

Raj Samani, chief technology officer at Intel Security, previously McAfee, applies a family protection pack with informed consent and says his children approve of his monitoring because he is transparent about the reasons for it.

'My daughter tried to communicate with somebody and I got the notification. And actually what she was doing was unsafe so I ended up having a conversation with her, explaining the concept of anonymity.' [...]

Samani says parents and children do need to have a discussion about when monitoring should stop: 'To me I think it comes down to a point where you have got that level of understanding and maturity.'

Cyber security consultant Dr Jessica Barker questions whether parental monitoring is fair on children, and says it can intrude into their privacy. Referencing research by Professor Sonia Livingstone on internet governance and children's rights, she goes so far as to say it can be harmful.

'If [children] feel they are being monitored that undermines any kind of relationship of trust. They might be using the internet in a healthy way to get information and support, and feel that they are not able to do that because they are being monitored.'

She brings up the issue of teenagers wanting to explore their gender or sexuality in private. If parents have a problem with that, or even use filters blocking LGBT sites, that could cut off access to something hugely helpful, a service previous generations didn't have.

From: 'Parents, is it ok to spy on your child's online history?', *Guardian*, 5 November 2015

Vocabulary (margin notes):

6 **stipulate sth.** determine sth. firmly
8 **rub** *(fml)* problem, difficulty
9 **internet-savvy** *(infml)* clever at using the internet
10 **minor** underaged person not considered an adult
14 **informed consent** *Einverständniserklärung*
15 **monitor sb./sth.** watch sb./sth. closely over a period of time
27 **reference sth.** refer to sth.
28 **governance** act of controlling sth.
30 **undermine sth.** make sth. weaker
35 **LGBT** = lesbian, gay, bisexual and transgendered

Parents, friends and strangers

COMPREHENSION

1 Looking for the main idea
Which of the following best describes the topic of the text? Give reasons.
- Security software for families that helps monitor online behaviour
- Chances and challenges of parental online monitoring
- The dangers of parents monitoring their children's online activities

2 Making notes on the text
Make notes on Mr Samani and Ms Baker's attitudes toward parental online monitoring. You will need these notes when working on task **5**.

▶ S22: Making and taking notes, p. 148

3 LANGUAGE AWARENESS **Using participles**
The writer often uses participle constructions instead of relative clauses.
a Identify the participles in ll. 2, 4, 9, 10, 19, 27, 34 and if possible rewrite the sentences using relative clauses.
b Say why the writer may have preferred the participle construction over the relative clause.

▶ L13: Participle constructions, p. 178

ANALYSIS

4 Analysing the text structure
a Divide the text into parts and think of a title for each part.
b Explain the argumentative structure of the text based on the order of its parts.

LANGUAGE AWARENESS

Using a participle construction instead of a relative clause or an adverbial clause merely seems to be a question of grammar. In fact, it is also very much a matter of style: some sentence patterns are considered more formal than others. They are therefore used in writing rather than in speaking and in formal rather than in informal contexts. In order to add some formality to a text, it might therefore be advisable to include such constructions.

BEYOND THE TEXT

5 WRITING **A comment** SUPPORT ▶ p. 114
Write a comment on the Samanis' solution for protecting their children in the online world. Use your notes from task **2** to back up your statements.

B2 Teenagers and their parents: two sides

COMPREHENSION

1 Working with infographics
Partner B: Go to p. 114.
Partner A: Look at the table below. It represents the results of a survey published in 2017 about the online experiences of 805 15- to 16-year-olds living in Germany. Work on task **a**.
a Match the percentages A–E to the statements 1–5.

A	74%	1	have had their computer infected by a virus or malware
B	44%	2	have shared too much personal information online
C	39%	3	have been exposed to too much advertising
D	37%	4	have been victims of cyberbullying
E	25%	5	have seen distressing or frightening content

b Tell your partner what you think is true. Ask him/her for the right figures.

Go on to task **c** on the next page.

▶ LA1: Varieties of English, p. 196
▶ LA3: Similarities and differences of languages, p. 198
▶ S17: Argumentative writing, p. 139
▶ L29: Comparing and contrasting, p. 191
▶ S28: Working with charts and graphs, p. 154

Part B

c Listen to what your partner tells you about how parents check their teenage children's online behaviour. Then tell him/her what is true using the information from the infographic below.

Parental controls

- **61%** checked which websites their teen visited
- **60%** checked their teen's social media profile
- **48%** looked through teen's phone calls / messages
- **39%** used parental controls for teen's online activites
- **16%** used monitoring tools to track teen's location with his/her mobile phone

From: *pewinternet.org*, January 2017

▶ LANGUAGE HELP
- I can't believe that …
- I think it's really surprising/shocking that …
- I wouldn't have expected that …
- I was amazed to learn that …

▶ BEYOND THE TEXT

2 SPEAKING Discussing an issue
Form a group with another pair. Discuss the facts that surprised you.
▶ LANGUAGE HELP

B3 LISTENING What you should know

Bullying is a problem at many schools. Describe different forms of bullying. What do you think cyberbullying is? You are going to hear two experts talking about it in a podcast.

▶ TROUBLE SPOT
Mobbing (German) = **bullying** (English)

 CD 15

at-risk behaviour behaviour that can lead to serious problems
preliminary [prɪˈlɪmɪnəri] not final
absenteeism [ˌæbsənˈtiːɪzəm] fact of being frequently away from school without good reasons
be attuned to sth. [əˈtjuːnd] pay close attention to sth.
target sb. (v) choose sb. as a victim
suspect sth. think that sth. (bad) is true
investigation *Ermittlung*
violation breaking of a rule
adolescent [ˌædəˈlesnt] teenager
victim person who suffers as the result of a crime, accident, etc.
perpetrator [ˈpɜːpətreɪtə] person who does something cruel, illegal, etc.
bystander person who sees an event but isn't involved

▶ COMPREHENSION

1 Listening for gist
Listen to the podcast, then complete the following sentence: 'The experts have advice for three groups of people: parents of …, parents of …, and …'.

2 Listening for detail
a You will be assigned a number between 1 and 3. The 1s take the first topic from task 1, the 2s the second, and the 3s the third. Take notes on what the experts say about your topic.
b Form small groups with others who have the same number as you. Compare your information, making additions or corrections if needed.

▶ BEYOND THE TEXT

3 SPEAKING Discussing an issue
a Form groups of three or four, making sure that members from all three groups (1, 2 and 3) are represented. Tell your group about your topic, listen to the others and take notes.
b Discuss which advice you find helpful and which you would reject.

Parents, friends and strangers

B4 I C U *Chris Colfer*

The narrator Carson Phillips, a senior at Clover High School, wants to study journalism. To make his college application stronger, he decides to set up a literature magazine at his school. As the unpopular Carson and a classmate are the only staff members, he decides to recruit new members by blackmailing other students into joining. Remy, the editor of the class yearbook, is his first victim.

A few weeks ago, I stumbled upon a funny user name on the Clover High School website: YearbookGirl69. I didn't think much of it, a freshman slut under Remy's rule perhaps. However, whoever it was left uptight opinionated comments on almost every page.

5 'Why do the lunch ladies need to be at back-to-school night? Can't they just stay in the kitchen?' was one of the many obnoxious posts. 'I hate lunch ladies more than I hate war!'

Could Remy be pulling a Voltaire? Over the weekend, while I was thinking of ways to blackmail Remy, I messaged YearbookGirl69 privately to test out this theory under
10 the user name BadBoy2012.

'Hey, sexy,' I messaged. 'Love reading your thoughts on the CHS site. We think alike.'
A few minutes later, she responded. 'OMG thanks. I'm so glad some 1 noticed LOL.'
I waited a couple of minutes more, playing hard-to-get, seeing if she'd write more.
'Who is this LOL?' YearbookGirl69 asked.

15 'I like to keep my identity a secret; I'm like Batman,' I replied. 'But with better abs.'
'Hott! Me 2! I like the mystery LOL,' she sent. I don't know what the hell was so funny. Was she seriously laughing out loud every time? 'Can I get a pic of those abs?' she asked.

I copied and pasted a picture of Taylor Lautner's torso from the Internet (I pray no
20 one ever finds that Google image search in my web history).

'©Q#$TWERYJ#$%&!ll' is what I got next. 'Are U even real?'
'Very' I said, and left it at that.

Now, today, while I was in English and the class had their laptops out, I decided to see if I was right about Remy. I was sitting a few seats behind her and had a clear view
25 of her computer.

BadBoy2012 messaged YearbookGirl69. A window popped up on Remy's computer screen. *Bingo!*

'What are you wearing?' BadBoy2012 asked.
I saw Remy's neck blush.

30 'Practically nothing,' Remy responded as YearbookGirl69.
'Send me a pic!' BadBoy2012 said.
Remy looked around the classroom to see if anyone was watching her. I ducked behind my laptop when she glanced my way. I looked back and saw her retrieving a photo from her documents and attach it to the instant-message conversation.

35 A photo of Remy half-naked with a 'sexy face' popped up on my computer screen. It was enough to turn a nun into an atheist. I shut my laptop, ran out of the classroom, and vomited into the nearest trash can. I'm being dramatic – I didn't vomit but I did dry-heave.

'Mr. Phillips, are you all right?' my English teacher asked when I returned to class.
40 'I'm afraid I'm changed for life,' I said, and went back to my seat. Remy rolled her eyes at me as I passed her. *She had no idea what she had just done to herself!*

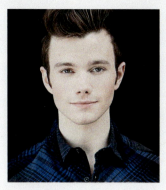

American actor and writer Chris Colfer

senior [ˈsiːnɪə] student in their final year
blackmail sb. *jdn. erpressen*
1 **stumble upon sth.** find sth. by chance
2 **freshman** student in the ninth grade at school
slut *(sl) Luder*
rule *Herrschaft*
3 **uptight** [ˌ-ˈ-] *(sl)* (here) angry
opinionated *(derog)* [əˈpɪnjəneɪtɪd] expressing strong opinions
6 **obnoxious** [əbˈnɒkʃəs] *widerlich*
8 **pull a Voltaire** write using a false name (Voltaire = pen-name of François Marie Arouet (1694–1798), French writer and philosopher)
15 **abs** *(sl)* = abdominal muscles *Bauchmuskeln*
19 **Taylor Lautner** American actor famous for his role in *The Twilight Saga* films
29 **blush** *(v)* go red (usually in the face)
33 **retrieve sth.** *etwas herausholen*
36 **nun** *Nonne*
atheist [ˈeɪθiːɪst] person who does not believe in God
37 **vomit** *sich übergeben*
38 **dry-heave** *würgen*

Part B

44 **rude** very unfriendly
45 **sly** showing you know a secret
manila type of brown paper
48 **petrified** ['petrɪfaɪd] extremely frightened
50 **whimper** winseln
54 **cordially** (fml) herzlich
55 **mandatory** ['mændətəri] verpflichtend
57 **subtle** ['sʌtl] subtil, nicht zu offensichtlich
turn sb. in (infml) jdn. verpetzen
58 **indication** sign

> ### LANGUAGE HELP
> - I think his behaviour is unacceptable because …
> - It isn't fair to pretend …
> - It's all for a good cause …
> - It's Remy's own fault because …
> - Carson doesn't really mean to …
> - His behaviour is defensible because …

▶ S20: Writing a summary, p. 144

LANGUAGE AWARENESS

Abbreviations and short forms are used in different contexts and with different functions. For example, they can save time and increase clarity (in scientific contexts), or create humour or a feeling of belonging (when using a special register or slang).
Explain the following abbreviations and decide in which situation they would be acceptable or expected: H_2O, TMI, ≤, ain't, ©, ∑, TGIF

▶ LA4: Influencing through language, p. 199

▶ S14: Creative writing, p. 136

DVD 02
▶ S2: Viewing a film, p. 121

After school I found Remy sitting on a bench alone. I sat down next to her. I couldn't make eye contact. I'm not sure I ever will again.

'Can I help you, Carson?' she asked rudely.

I slyly handed her a large manila envelope. Inside she found printed copies of the conversations between BadBoy2012 and YearbookGirl69.

She went silent for a good minute and a half. Out of the corner of my eye I saw the papers start to shake in her tight, petrified grip. She looked at me as if I had told her that her father had had a successful sex change while she was at school.

'You're BadBoy2012?' she whimpered.

'I can't even look at you anymore,' I said. 'Not that it was easy before.'

I took a bright yellow flyer out of my back pocket and handed it to her. I left before she could open it. The flyer said:

> YOU ARE CORDIALLY INVITED TO ATTEND A
> MANDATORY MEETING IN THE JOURNALISM
> CLASSROOM FRIDAY AFTER SCHOOL.

I had to make sure it was subtle in case any of my victims tried turning me in, but if Remy's horror was any indication, *that* wouldn't be a problem.

From: Chris Colfer, *Struck by Lightning*, 2012

COMPREHENSION

1 Summarizing the plot
Summarize how Carson tricks Remy into joining his new club.

ANALYSIS

2 Examining a character's behaviour YOU CHOOSE

a Describe the relationship between Carson and Remy. **OR** b Compare Remy's behaviour online and offline. What impression of her character does the text give?

3 LANGUAGE AWARENESS Explaining abbreviations
The author often uses abbreviations in this excerpt.
a Find them and explain what they stand for.
b Explain why they are used in that context.

BEYOND THE TEXT

4 Evaluating a *character
Comment on Carson's behaviour. ▶ LANGUAGE HELP

5 Changing perspectives
Retell the episode from Remy's *point of view.

6 VIEWING Watching a scene from the movie *Struck by Lightning*
Watch the excerpt from the film. It contains the scene you have read.
a Describe how Carson blackmails his fellow students.
b Describe the atmosphere created in this excerpt and analyse how it is achieved.

B5 FOCUS ON LANGUAGE: Grammar
The simple form and the progressive form

*Unlike German, English has two different forms of each tense: a **simple form** and a **progressive form**.*

1 Compare the following examples (three of them are from text **B4**, cf. p. 49):

	simple form	progressive form
present	What do you wear to a job interview?	What are you wearing [today]? (l. 28)
past	I sat down next to her. (l. 42)	I was sitting a few seats behind her. (l. 24)

2 Translate the sentences into German. How can you convey the meanings of the two forms of *wear* and *sit*?

▶ L1–6: Tenses, pp. 164–169

*Verbs that refer to **activities** or events can be used in both forms: in the **progressive form** (if the activity they describe is happening right now or was happening at a certain time in the past) or in the **simple form**. The simple form must be used for momentary actions (she hit him on the head) and actions in a series (I ran to the phone and called the police).*

3 Look at text **B4**, ll. 1–41. Find simple past forms that describe activities.

4 *The **simple past** and the **past progressive** are often used together in the same sentence.*
   CHALLENGE Compare the following sentences from text **B4**:
   1 While I was thinking of ways to blackmail Remy, I messaged YearbookGirl69. (ll. 8–9)
   2 I ducked behind my laptop when she glanced my way. (ll. 32–33)
   Describe the order of events for each sentence. Point out when the simple past and the past progressive are used.

■ **LANGUAGE AWARENESS**
The **progressive form** is very specific to the English language, and this makes it difficult for non-native speakers to use it appropriately. They often overuse it, use it in the wrong contexts or ignore it altogether. For example: What is the correct answer to somebody shouting, "Dinner is ready!" – "I come", "I'm coming" or "I'll come"?
Identify your individual problem areas concerning the progressive form and try to avoid them.

▶ LA3: Similarities and differences of languages, p. 198

*Verbs that describe a **state** cannot normally be used in the progressive form:*
I hate lunch ladies … (l. 6) – Not: I'm hating lunch ladies.

State verbs are mainly verbs of thinking and feeling (think, believe, feel, love, hate, like, etc.) and verbs like be, become, appear, seem, look (aussehen), need, sound, want, etc.
Some verbs have different meanings. They can describe a state or an activity:

state	activity
[…] I didn't think much of it. (l. 2)	[…] I was thinking of ways to blackmail Remy. (ll. 8–9)
That hat looks great on you.	She looked at me. (l. 48)
I […] had a clear view of her computer. (ll. 24–25)	We were just having a quick meal when my mobile rang.

5 Translate the sentences into German. What does the verb mean in each case?

6 Complete the sentences with the correct verb forms – simple or progressive.
   1 Carson (want) to start a school magazine, but he (need) more staff members.
   2 Remy (not realize) that Carson (hide) behind a false identity.
   3 Before she (send) BadBoy2012 a photo, Remy (look) around the room to see if anyone (watch) her.
   4 Carson (think) that Remy (look) really awful in the photo.
   5 He (not be able to) imagine what Remy (think) of when she (take) that photo.

▶ L2: Simple present and present progressive, p. 167

B6 Nowhere to hide *Yuriko Wahl-Immel*

A friend in Canada is taking part in a project on cyberbullying. She asks you about the situation in Germany: who is involved in cyberbullying and what help can be offered? You find this information about a study in Germany.

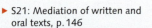

Cybermobbing gehört zum Alltag vieler Kinder und Jugendlicher in Deutschland. „Mädchen werden gerne in die Schmuddelecke gestellt, als Schlampe diffamiert", sagt Soziologin und Psychologin Catarina Katzer, Mitautorin einer am Donnerstag präsentierten umfassenden Studie zum Thema Mobbing im Netz. „Jungen werden oft als ‚Homosau' fertiggemacht. Man versucht, ihnen Pornos mit Männern anzuhängen", schildert die Forscherin eines Kölner Instituts für Cyberpsychologie.

Katzer, die auch Mitbegründerin des Bündnisses gegen Cybermobbing ist, betont: „Das Cybermobbing kann viel schlimmer und dramatischer sein als Mobbing auf dem Schulhof im kleinen Kreis. Früher fühlten sich die Opfer zuhause sicher. Aber heute gibt es keinen Schutzraum mehr. Die Cybermobber kommen ins Kinderzimmer." Der Terror laufe oft über einen langen Zeitraum. [...]

Jeder sechste Schüler hat in der repräsentativen Erhebung angegeben, schon einmal Opfer gewesen zu sein. 19 Prozent bekennen, dass sie bereits Täter waren. Das Phänomen Cybermobbing ist alles andere als ein Randthema, es betrifft viele, kommt in allen Schulformen und schon ab dem Grundschulalter vor. Andere Studien waren zuvor zu dem Ergebnis gekommen, dass ein Viertel oder sogar ein Drittel aller Schüler in Deutschland schon mal Cybermobbing erlebt haben.

„Das Schamgefühl, das Verletztsein ist so schlimm wegen der großen Öffentlichkeit", weiß Katzer. Sogar vermeintlich gelöschte, bloßstellende Fotos von Partys tauchen irgendwo anders plötzlich wieder auf – manchmal Jahre später. „Das macht die Opfer so hilflos und schutzlos. Sie fühlen sich blamiert, verlieren das Vertrauen, wollen die Schule wechseln, auch ihr Freundschaftsbegriff ändert sich mitunter." Die Sensibilität für das Problem ist jedenfalls gewachsen, stellt auch Psychologin Stephanie Pieschl von der Uni Münster fest. „Immer mehr Jugendliche, Eltern, Lehrer und Pädagogen kennen den Begriff." Aber: „Cybermobbing ist noch ein relativ junges Forschungsfeld." Die Schulen sollten beherzt ran an das Problem: „Die Schule ist der ideale Ort, besonders präventiv gegen Cybermobbing vorzugehen." [...]

In der Praxis zeige sich, dass Freunde und Eltern wichtige Stützen für die Opfer sein können. „Ein erfolgreicher Ansatz sind die jugendlichen Mobbingberater, also ältere Schüler, die Jüngeren zum Beispiel erklären, was passieren kann, wenn man ein Bikini-Foto postet." Zu tun gibt es noch viel, betont die Expertin: „Das Thema wird uns alle noch richtig lange beschäftigen und fordern."

From: www.stern.de, 17 May 2013

---

1 MEDIATION (German → English) **Information about a study**
    a The text contains some expressions that you will probably not know how to translate into English: *jdn. in die Schmuddelecke stellen* (l. 2), *Schutzraum* (l. 10), *Mobbingberater* (l. 29). To help you find an English equivalent, describe what they mean in German first. Then paraphrase it in English.
    b Summarize the text in English for your friend (ca. 150 words).

2 WRITING **Reacting to an article**
    Write a letter to the editor in which you react to this article. Comment on how accurate you find the description of the situation in Germany.

▶ S21: Mediation of written and oral texts, p. 146
▶ L21: Verbs of reporting, p. 186
▶ L10: Indirect speech, p. 176
▶ L22: Germanisms, p. 187

▶ S15: Writing a formal letter or email, p. 136

Parents, friends and strangers

B7 The cyberbullying virus

1 Before viewing
The words on the right are all medical terms. Look up their meaning in your dictionary.

infiltrate ['ɪnfɪltreɪt]
pandemic [pæn'demɪk]
susceptibility [sə,septə'bɪləti]
virus contraction
infect/infection
host/carrier [həʊst]
be exposed to sth.
highly contagious [kən'teɪdʒəs]
immune
side effect
strain (of a disease)

— COMPREHENSION ◀

2 VIEWING **Understanding cyberbullying**
a Copy the following table. After watching the film the first time, fill in the table by describing the meanings of the words on the right with respect to illnesses and then with respect to cyberbullying. One example has already been done for you. Compare results with your partner.

word	meaning with respect to illnesses	meaning with respect to cyberbullying
contract a virus	be infected by a virus, become ill	be influenced by cyberbullying and start bullying people, too
infect sb.		
be exposed to sth.		
be a host to sth.		
be contagious		
be immune to sth.		

▶ DVD 03

▶ S2: Viewing a film, p. 121

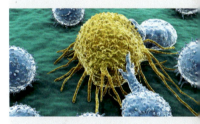

b Write a short text (ca. 100 words) in which you explain the way(s) in which cyberbullying can be compared with an illness.

— ANALYSIS ◀

3 Comparing two parts of the film
There is a break at 2:55. Analyse how the presenter's voice, the background music or the sounds differ in the first and second part of the film and describe their effects.

▶ L29: Comparing and contrasting, p. 191

4 CHALLENGE **Interpreting names**
Except for the victim, all the girls in the film have names with a meaning (Bravery, Compassion, Courage, Envy, Hate, Insecurity and Peer pressure). Choose four of them (two positive and two negative ones) and explain their connections with cyberbullying.

— BEYOND THE TEXT ◀

5 Evaluating the effectiveness of the film
Assess the effectiveness of the film: would it help teenagers deal with cyberbullying? Consider the different groups. ▶ LANGUAGE HELP

■ LANGUAGE HELP
- (to) help teenagers to …
- (to) succeed in doing sth. …
- (to) show examples of … such as …
- (to) make sb. realize how serious … is
- (to) show sb. the effects of their actions such as …

6 SPEAKING **A talk show: 'Does the internet make us ruthless?'**
a Form groups: the victims, students who support the victims, the bullies, students who support the bullies, and the moderators. Give your character a name, prepare their role and decide who will take part in the show.
b Hold the talk show, then assess the performances of the participants.

▶ S12: Having a discussion, p. 133
▶ Vocabulary, p. 212

Chapter Task

Taking part in a competition

To find out about your Chapter Task, listen to the audio file.

1 **LISTENING** **Understanding the task**
  a After listening, copy the sentences and finish them:
   1 The topic of the project is …
   2 The audio track should be … long.
   3 The audio track can take four different forms, namely …
   4 Your group has to consist of … people.
   5 The jury chooses the winner according to four criteria: …
  b Get together with a partner and compare your results so that you know what to do.

2 **Working on the project**
Get into a group and work on the project according to the guidelines in the audio file. Organize your work, make an outline, write your script, practise and record it. If necessary, consult the relevant pages in the Skills File.

3 **Working with the results**
  a Present your audio file to the class. While listening to your classmates' audio files, take notes on their content and their strengths and weaknesses (cf. the criteria in task **1a**). Give feedback.
  b **WRITING** Imagine you write for your school magazine. Write a report about the presentation of the audio files. Focus on 3–4 presentations, summarize their content, say what you enjoyed most and what could have been improved.

CD 16

Download the audio file here:
Webcode star-15

Find a recording tool here:
Webcode star-16

Chapter Task

Self-Assessment

Look at the tables below. Evaluate your own work on the Chapter Task and the chapter itself by giving yourself a grade of **A** (very good), **B** (good), **C** (satisfactory) or **D** (poor). If you aren't completely satisfied with your performance, consult the pages listed under 'Revision and practice' below.

Download a self-assessment sheet here: **Webcode** star-17

▶ S33: Assessing yourself and giving feedback, p. 160

Understanding the task LISTENING

Evaluate how you did when listening to the instructions for the Chapter Task.

Criteria	Revision and practice
1 I understood what I was asked to do in the Chapter Task.	▶ S1: Listening for information, p. 120 ▶ Workbook, p. 23, ex. 8; pp. 56–57, ex. 1–2
2 I understood unknown words by paying attention to their context.	▶ S23: Dealing with unknown words, p. 149 ▶ Workbook, pp. 84–85, ex. 31
3 I noted down many keywords about the content of my classmates' audio files.	▶ S22: Making and taking notes, p. 148 ▶ Workbook, p. 23, ex. 8; p. 84, ex. 30

Working on the Chapter Task

Evaluate how you did when working on your project.

Criteria	Revision and practice
1 I contributed to the organization of our work.	▶ S30: Doing project work, p. 150
2 I gave important input to the outline and the final script of the audio track.	▶ S13: The stages of writing, p. 135
3 I gave important tips on how to improve our audio track before recording it.	▶ S33: Assessing yourself and giving feedback, p. 160 ▶ Workbook, p. 22, ex. 7
4 I contributed my share to the recording of the track.	▶ S10: Giving a presentation, p. 130

Working on the report WRITING

Evaluate your report for the school newspaper on the presentation of the audio files.

Criteria	Revision and practice
1 I knew enough words to write about the topic precisely.	▶ Vocabulary, p. 212 ▶ Texts, pp. 38, 40 ▶ Workbook, p. 17, ex. 1–2; pp. 18–19, Words in Context; p. 20, ex. 3–5
2 My text has an introduction, a body and a conclusion. Its ideas are well structured and connected with linking words.	▶ Focus on Writing, p. 42 ▶ Workbook, p. 22, ex. 7; pp. 72–73, ex. 19
3 I used the correct verb form in my report.	▶ L2: Simple present and present progressive, p. 167 ▶ Workbook, p. 26, ex. 13–14; p. 27, ex. 15

Working on the topics of this chapter

Evaluate your expertise on the topics of this chapter.

Criteria	Revision and practice
1 I knew enough about the forms of digital communication to suggest various ideas for the audio file.	▶ Texts, pp. 38, 40 ▶ Workbook, p. 17, ex. 1–2; pp. 18–19, Words in Context; p. 20, ex. 3–5
2 I understood the positive and negative sides of digital communication and was able to discuss them.	▶ Text, p. 43 ▶ Workbook, p. 24, ex. 10; p. 27, ex. 16

Focus on Literature 2

| NOVEL pp. 30–35 | **SHORT STORY** pp. 56–59 | POETRY pp. 80–85 | DRAMA pp. 108–111 |

Narrative Prose – the Short Story

A Getting started: What are we told?

*The following *short story deals with a chance encounter between former friends. Read the beginning of the story.*

Kenny Paul M. Whiting

I wish I had been in a hurry, on my way to a conference, an interview, one of those game-changing[1] events that can make all the difference[2] in the world. But I wasn't – it was just another Friday evening, hot and stifling[3], and I was on my way home after a ten-hour day at Moore and Breckenridge. That's when I saw Kenny coming up the escalator[4] from the outbound platform[5].

1 While reading
  a Discuss your first impression(s) with a partner. Write down questions you have about the given situation, e.g. about the *narrator (= character/voice telling the story), the *setting (= time and place) and the *plot (= *action).
  b Finish reading the story and make notes relevant to your questions.

It must have been at least five years since we last met. Probably longer. For an instant I hoped he hadn't seen me, or didn't recognize me, but then I knew it was too late.

'Hey, Morris!' He came hurrying over, grinning from one ear to the other. I hoped he didn't notice my embarrassment.

'Hey, man, good to see you,' I said, wrapping my arm round his shoulder. Kenny had always been shorter than me, but somehow he seemed to have become even smaller than I remembered him, as if the passage of time was slowly forcing him to his knees.

'You back in town again?' he asked.

'Yes and no,' I replied. 'I work for a consulting firm, so I'm staying here at a hotel for a while. Normally I work from my office in New York.'

Kenny was looking intently[6] into my eyes, as if searching for something he knew had to be there. I remembered how long ago, when we were friends, Kenny's way of looking at things had reminded me of a dog – dutiful[7] and single-minded.

'I guess you made it big[8], huh? Always knew you were the smart one.' He gave a little laugh.

'What about you? What have you been up to all these years?' From far below, I heard a train grind[9] to a stop at the platform.

'Me?' Kenny grinned as if I had said something funny. 'I'm busy enough just staying out of trouble.'

We both laughed, even though it wasn't funny. I heard the doors of the train hiss shut and the gentle rumble[10] as it started off into the darkness.

I thought of the kind of place Kenny came from, a tacky[11], faceless jumble[12] of budget[13] malls and decaying one-family houses. The sound of ventilators and mosquitos on a hot summer night. When Kenny came home from MIT[14] for the holidays, the TV ran without interruption. No one bothered to ask him how college was. None of them was interested. College was a waste of money, even on a full scholarship[15]. Kenny fought against their indifference for 18 months. Then he gave up. I think that was when we lost contact. Maybe he was embarrassed to show me his weakness. Maybe he just stopped caring.

---

[1] **game-changing** having a major impact
[2] **all the difference in the world** a huge difference
[3] **stifling** ['staɪflɪŋ] stickig
[4] **escalator** (AE) moving stairs
[5] **outbound platform** platform for trains going away from the city
[6] **intently** eindringlich
[7] **dutiful** obedient
[8] **make it big** (infml) be successful
[9] **grind to a stop** stop noisily
[10] **rumble** (n) low sound
[11] **tacky** (infml) showing bad taste
[12] **jumble** (n) disorderly collection
[13] **budget** (adj) cheap
[14] **MIT** = Massachusetts Institute of Technology, a private university in Cambridge, Massachusetts
[15] **scholarship** amount of money given to sb. by an organization to help pay for their education

Short Story — LIT 2

'No, just kidding, man. I've been doing all kinds of stuff. Mostly repair work. My brother-in-law has got a little business going. Making good money. Nothing like you, of course.'

Kenny looked down at his shoes, as if he had said something improper. I thought of the time when
35 I had brought Kenny home to meet my parents. How out of place he had looked on the dark leather sofa. My mom had gone out of her way[16] to be nice to him, asking him about his favorite courses and how many brothers and sisters he had, that kind of stuff. I could feel the whole time how Kenny was suffering, like a mongrel[17] at a pedigree[18] dog show. I never took him there again.

I wanted to get away, back into the safety of my shell, but I also wanted to give Kenny something.
40 Lacking a better idea, I reached into my pocket and produced a business card. 'Listen, Kenny, I've got to run, but here's my number … give me a call when you've got some time on your hands[19] and we can get together someplace.'

Kenny looked at the card in confusion, as if he didn't understand its purpose. Then he drew a stub[20] of a pencil out of his shirt pocket and scrawled[21] something on the back of the card, handing
45 it back to me.

'Why don't you phone me? Seeing as you're a lot busier than I am.'

'I will,' I promised and gave him a quick hug before I turned and hurried down the stairs. But we both knew I was lying.

Unpublished manuscript, 2018

[16] **go out of your way to do sth** make a special effort to do sth.
[17] **mongrel** dog of mixed breed
[18] **pedigree dog** *Rassehund*
[19] **time on your hands** free time
[20] **stub** very short piece
[21] **scrawl sth.** write sth. carelessly

2 Understanding the story
a State spontaneously whether you like the story or not.
b Discuss with a partner the questions raised by the story, and to what extent they are answered. Make sure you have understood the plot and the setting.
c Decide which of the following summaries (1–3) you think fits best.
  1 A young man is going home from work when he runs into an old friend by chance. They talk briefly about their lives, then they make plans to meet again some other time.
  2 A successful young man meets a former friend of his who dropped out of college. He is embarrassed to be seen together with this person and ends the conversation abruptly.
  3 Meeting a former friend by chance, a young man thinks about the past and how their lives have taken different directions. He doesn't know how to deal with the situation.
d Use elements from 1–3 above to create your own summary.

3 Interpreting the ending
a The ending of the story (ll. 46–48) could have various meanings. From the following statements choose the one that you agree with most.
  1 Kenny realizes that his former friend wants to have nothing to do with him.
  2 The narrator wants to end the conversation quickly.
  3 The narrator feels guilty that he can't do anything to help Kenny.
b Discuss your choices in class, referring to details from the story as evidence and adding further interpretation of your own beyond the given sentences.

4 Identifying typical features of a *short story ▶ A CLOSER LOOK
a Note down everything you have found out so far about what is typical of a short story. Use the webcode for more useful material.
b Using your notes from **4a** as well as the definition from the box above, explain what makes 'Kenny' a typical short story.

▶ S7: Reading and analysing narrative prose, p. 127

A CLOSER LOOK
A *short story …
- can usually be read in one sitting,
- deals with one **decisive moment** in a *character's life, or else shows a so-called 'snapshot' of life, i.e. one moment you can think about,
- does not rely on explicit descriptions of *setting, character development or complex *plots like a *novel, but **concentrates** on the one decisive incident for one character.

▶ RF1, p. 200

Find more material on short stories here: **Webcode** star-18

▶ S22: Making and taking notes, p. 148

Focus on Literature

LIT 2 Short Story

B The narrator's point of view: Who tells the story?

Study the following snippets from two different short stories with regard to the question: Who is telling me this?

A

I wish I had been in a hurry, on my way to a conference, an interview, one of those game-changing[1] events that can make all the difference in the world.

From: Paul M. Whiting, 'Kenny', unpublished manuscript, 2018

B

[Her father] was not the local manager of Penney's for nothing. Recently, actually about a year ago, he had become tired of watching his daughter sit around the house all the time reading movie magazines with her eyes wide as saucers[2]. He had begun to think of her as a bump on a log[3].

From: Richard Brautigan, 'Greyhound Tragedy', *Revenge of the Lawn,* 1971

■ A CLOSER LOOK

A story can be told from different *points of view.
A first-person *narrator is a *character in the story who tells us what happened to him or her and how he or she felt about it.
A third-person narrator can have either a **limited view** from only one character, or switch from one character's point of view to another's, or even comment on everything. The third-person narrator with an **unlimited point of view** is also known as **an omniscient narrator**.

[1] **game-changing** having a major impact
[2] **saucer** ['sɔːsə] a small round dish that a cup stands on
[3] **be a bump on a log** (here) person you want to get rid of

1 Understanding perspectives ▶ A CLOSER LOOK
State from whose *point of view each of the quoted passages is told, and identify the important signal words for this particular perspective.

2 Changing perspectives
a Get together in groups of four with two of you choosing passage **A**, and the other two passage **B** to work with:
   A 'Debbie's Call'   **B** 'Greyhound Tragedy'
   1 **Partner A1:** Rewrite the passage, using a third-person *narrator limited to the American caller.
   2 **Partner A2:** Rewrite the passage, using a third-person narrator who switches perspectives.
   3 **Partner B1:** Rewrite the passage from the first-person *point of view of the daughter.
   4 **Partner B2:** Rewrite the passage from the first-person point of view of the father.
b Compare your texts and discuss what different effects you have achieved by the change in point of view.

■ LANGUAGE HELP

- A … *narrator invites / asks the reader to …
- A … narrator can show / illustrate / put himself or herself into …
  The reader can identify with … / walk around in a *character's shoes / may find it easier to understand a character's *action / to follow the *plot when there is a … narrator.
- A narrator with an unlimited *point of view helps the reader to …

3 Drawing conclusions
Using your results from **2b**, discuss and sum up in class what the advantages and possible disadvantages of each type of *narrator might be.
▶ LANGUAGE HELP

■ TROUBLE SPOT

*author = Schriftsteller/in, Autor/in
*narrator = Erzählinstanz/ Erzählstimme

C Understanding the construction of plot: How short can a short story be?

Extremely short stories, called *microfiction or flash fiction, are becoming increasingly popular.

Read the following examples and see if you can make sense of them immediately.

The Canal Path Murders Margaret Hodgson
She could hear the sounds of heavy footsteps as she hurried down the lonely canal path after dark.
A man's hand grabbed roughly at her sleeve and she spun round, her legs weak with fear. He was holding a gun and stared stupidly at her. 'You dropped this', he said.
From: *Best Practice*, 2012

A Story in Six Words
For sale: baby shoes. Never worn.
Attributed to Ernest Hemingway (1899-1961)

1 **Looking at the texts** ▶ A CLOSER LOOK
A good story needs a good *plot. Determine to what extent the examples given above fulfil the requirements of a plot.

2 **Analysing the plot** ▶ A CLOSER LOOK
Explain how a reader manages to 'get' the *plot despite the shortness of the text.

3 WRITING **Clarifying the plot**
Choose one of the *microfictions ('The Canal Path Murders' or 'A Story in Six Words') to rewrite as a fuller story to make the *plot explicit. Share your stories in class and evaluate them with regard to clarity, logic and concentration on the main elements. Discuss which version appeals to you more: the extremely short one or the extended one.

4 WRITING CHALLENGE **Writing microfiction**
Write your own *microfiction and read the results aloud in class. You can have a vote on the best stories and perhaps publish them in your school magazine.
Practical suggestion: Start out writing a long story, then take out bit by bit until you are left with an end product that is at the same time extremely short and exciting.
Use the webcode to download tips on writing microfiction.

▪ A CLOSER LOOK
The writer E.M. Forster explained the difference between *plot and **story** like this:
'The King died and then the Queen died' is a story.
'The King died and then the Queen died of grief' is a plot.
In a story the events are connected by '**and then**,' in a plot the events are connected by '**because**'.

Find more examples of microfiction here:
 Webcode star-19

▶ S14: Creative writing, p. 136

Find more tips here:
Webcode star-20

3 Living in the Global Village

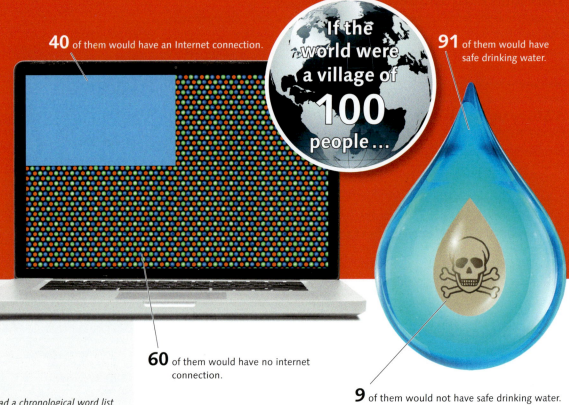

40 of them would have an Internet connection.

If the world were a village of **100** people…

91 of them would have safe drinking water.

60 of them would have no internet connection.

9 of them would not have safe drinking water.

Download a chronological word list here: **Webcode** star-63

■ **FACT FILE**

At present, the total number of people on the Earth amounts to roughly 7.5 billion (7,500,000,000).

▶ L9: Conditional sentences, p. 173

Find a tool to make your poster here: **Webcode** star-22

1 Thinking about what we have

a Carry out a quick survey in your class. How many of you have an internet connection in their household? How many have their own computer?

b Use the data above to estimate the total number of people in the world without internet access and without clean water.

c If your class were the whole world, how many of you would have an internet connection? Explain why your result is different to the result of your survey from **a**.

d Using data available online, choose alternative statistics and design your own poster to show the world as a village.

Lead-in

A
- Applying to work for six months in Australia
- Buying cheap products made in other countries
- Wearing clothes with brand names

B
- Watching the live TV broadcast of the football World Cup
- Subscribing to satellite TV
- Dancing in a club in Cologne to music mixed in London

C
- Following Theresa May on Twitter
- Listening to speeches on the radio from the United Nations
- Helping Greenpeace by writing a letter to an oil company

D
- Flying to Vietnam on holiday
- Taking part in a web discussion on women's rights
- Visiting Asia on a school exchange

2 Looking at different aspects of globalization

a The boxes above contain examples of four different aspects of globalization (A, B, C and D). They are:
- political globalization
- social globalization
- cultural globalization
- economic globalization

Decide which is which, and explain your choices.

b After reading the examples in the boxes, brainstorm different ways in which globalization affects you.

c Create a mind map entitled 'Globalization and me'. You may use the webcode to find a mind mapping tool. Use the mind map to record your results from task **2b**. You should add to your mind map as you work through Chapter 3.

Find a mind mapping tool here:
Webcode star-23

In this chapter you will learn about how globalization affects your life and the lives of people around the world. You will also look at ways people are dealing with some of the environmental problems of globalization. ▶ PREVIEW

PREVIEW

Main topics
- Globalization and what it means, p. 62
- How and why countries need each other, p. 66
- Environmental damage, p. 72
- Ideas for sustainable living, p. 75

Skills in focus
- Mediation, p. 64
- Writing: writing paragraphs, p. 74

Language in focus
- Vocabulary and style, p. 68

Chapter Task
- Creating a poster that encourages people to get involved locally, p. 78

Living in the Global Village · Chapter 3

3 Words in Context

CD 17
Listen to an audio version of the text on the CD or download it here:
Webcode star-24

TROUBLE SPOT

technology = *Technik*
technique [tek'ni:k] = method, way of doing sth.

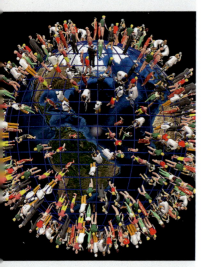

Life in a global village

Global village
'Global village' is a *metaphor used to show that geographical distances and time differences in the world can be overcome through modern technology. People in a village live close to each other, know each other personally and rely on each other. Email and social networks allow us to connect virtually with people everywhere as if they were living next door. News is spread instantaneously and simultaneously. English as a world language is taught and spoken around the globe. Likewise, companies are now producing and selling their products worldwide. Thus, the world has become more interconnected and it is becoming increasingly interdependent on social, economic, cultural and political levels. Ideas from one part of the world can now spread quickly to others. However, this does not necessarily mean that those ideas will be embraced in other parts.

Global business
Large multinational corporations have provided jobs for people all over the world. These large global players often outsource the production of goods from developed to developing countries, which produce goods cheaply, because wages are much lower there. Some people are critical of outsourcing, but most western consumers are still happy to buy these imported goods cheaply.
In recent years there has been a growing divide between the rich and the poor, as wages have been cut for workers while profits have increased for the shareholders of companies.

Environmental impact
Another aspect of the idea of the global village is that some problems concern not only individual states but the whole world. The increase in industrialization and agriculture has a deep impact on the planet. This can be seen in deforestation, water pollution, depletion of the ozone layer and, most importantly, in global warming and climate change. Environmental damage does not stop at national borders, which means that pollution and the destruction of the natural world affect us all. Pollution of an ocean by one or two large industrial countries, for example, affects all the countries around it that rely on it for fish.

Political globalization – solving problems together
When one country cannot solve environmental problems alone, global teamwork can help. New ideas are needed to help people live in more sustainable ways, but natural resources can only be protected through international cooperation. Fortunately, international organizations such as the United Nations and non-governmental organizations (NGOs) provide a place where countries can work together to share solutions and agree on rules to deal with common problems.

▶ Vocabulary, p. 214

Life in a global village 3

1 Changes and challenges
  a **Partner A:** Read the text closely. Make notes on ways society is influenced by globalization.
  Partner B: Read the text closely. Make notes on problems the world is facing.
  b When you have finished making notes, explain them to your partner.
  c Get together with another pair and compare results.
  d Add any useful information, vocabulary or examples to your mind map from the Lead-in.

▶ S22: Making and taking notes, p. 148

Find a mind mapping tool here:
Webcode star-25

2 Definitions
  a Find the highlighted words in the text which mean:
   1 nations where the standard of living is still lower than the world average
   2 moving the production of goods to a new place to save labour costs
   3 companies with operations in many different countries
   4 the cutting down of trees in a large area
   5 different countries working together
  b DEFINITIONS GAME: Choose two highlighted words from the text and in two minutes write down a definition for the class without using the word itself. Then, one student shares his or her definition with the class. The person who correctly guesses the word chooses the next player, who then defines a new word.

▶ S25: Opposites, p. 189

3 Phrases into English
In each of the following sentences, a useful phrase from the text is missing. Copy and complete the sentences. If you aren't sure how to translate the German words, look at the text again.
  1 In a globalized world, *(werden Nachrichten schnell verbreitet)*.
  2 The globalized economy has helped *(Arbeitsplätze zu schaffen)* in regions where employment used to be rare.
  3 Globalization has also created problems that *(die Entwicklungsländer betreffen)*.
  4 Hopefully, nations will cooperate *(um diese Probleme gemeinsam zu lösen)*.

▶ L8: The passive, p. 172

4 Collocations
Combine words from the boxes on the right to make collocations. For help look at the text on p. 62.

environmental	change
multinational	village
social	resources
ozone	countries
imported	layer
climate	damage
developing	pollution
global	corporations
water	goods
natural	networks

▶ S19: Common collocations with prepositions, p. 184

5 WRITING An essay
Use five of the collocations from task **4** to describe in a short essay how globalization affects your life.

▶ S13: The stages of writing, p. 135

3 Part A

Global citizens in a global economy

A1 FOCUS ON SKILLS MEDIATION

▶ S21: Mediation of written and oral texts, p. 146

Mediating is a technique used to make communication possible between persons who do not share a common language. More specifically, it means summarizing (either orally or in writing) a spoken or written text in another language.

1 Summarizing content
Imagine an American friend comes across the following article and sends you an email asking, 'Why do they mention the USA in the article?' Read the text and try to answer your friend's question in one sentence.

Indien und Amerika brauchen einander
Anette Dowideit et al.

Menschen sind heute auf eine Weise verbunden, die noch vor zehn Jahren niemand für denkbar gehalten hätte. Zum Beispiel Yasmeen Malik und Dixie. Die zehnjährige Yasmeen aus Richmond im amerikanischen Bundesstaat Virginia braucht wie viele Kinder Hilfe bei den Hausaufgaben, besonders in Mathe. Die bekommt sie von Dixie. „Sie ist meine Lieblingsnachhilfelehrerin", sagt Yasmeen. Das Besondere: Die beiden haben sich noch nie gesehen. Dixie sitzt nicht mit Yasmeen am Schreibtisch, sondern am anderen Ende einer Internetleitung, die durch Ozeane zur indischen Stadt Bangalore führt. 5

Dixie heißt auch gar nicht wirklich Dixie, sie hat vielmehr einen komplizierten indischen Namen, den sich Yasmeen nicht merken kann. An Yasmeens Computer ist ein Mikrofon angebracht und eine spezielle Software der Internetfirma TutorVista installiert. Ihre Eltern zahlen jeden Monat 100 Dollar an die Firma. Dafür darf Yasmeen sich nachmittags in das Netzwerk der Firma einwählen und bekommt Nachhilfestunden, meistens von Dixie. 10

Früher hatte die Schülerin einen Nachhilfelehrer, der tatsächlich mit ihr am Tisch saß. Doch der Unterricht bei Dixie ist genauso gut, nur eben viel günstiger. Das kommt daher, weil in Indien Miete, Essen und alles andere weniger kosten als in Amerika. Wie so oft erzeugt die Globalisierung Gewinner und, zumindest kurzfristig, Verlierer. Der alte Nachhilfelehrer daheim in Virginia verliert – falls er nicht einen neuen Job findet. Familie Malik dagegen profitiert: Yasmeen kann sich aussuchen, wann und wie viel Nachhilfe sie braucht, und ihre Eltern zahlen weniger Geld für den Unterricht als früher. Und auch Dixie gehört zu den Gewinnern: Sie hat einen für indische Verhältnisse gut bezahlten Job. 15 20

Damit aber hängt Dixies Schicksal nicht mehr davon ab, wie gut die Wirtschaft in Indien läuft, sondern davon, wie es um sie in den USA bestellt ist. Denn wenn Yasmeens Mutter oder Vater auf einmal durch die Krise ihren Job verlören und zu Hause blieben, dann müssten sie das Geld für die Nachhilfe ihrer Tochter vielleicht sparen. 25

Globalisierung ist allerdings viel mehr als Geld und Jobs, vor allem für Menschen, die weit weg von uns sind. Für den 31-jährigen Aniruddha Shanbhag lässt sich die Globalisierung in drei Buchstaben zusammenfassen: MTV. Anfang der 90er-Jahre bekam er in seiner Heimat, in Indien, erstmals den amerikanischen Musiksender zu sehen. Und die Videos amerikanischer und europäischer Bands haben das südasiatische 30

Global citizens in a global economy 3

Land ebenso verändert wie viele andere Regionen der Welt: Statt für die traditionelle Musik ihres Landes interessierten sich Jugendliche wie Aniruddha plötzlich für Bands wie Metallica und Nirvana. Und statt eines klassischen indischen Wickelrocks für Männer trugen junge Leute lieber absichtlich aufgeschlitzte Jeans. Kurz nach MTV kam auch Coca-Cola nach Indien, und in den vergangenen Jahren folgte die Burgerkette McDonald's.

Unter dem Eindruck von MTV ist Aniruddha Toningenieur geworden, dann hat er für einen Internetshop Musik-CDs aus anderen Ländern eingekauft. Inzwischen verkauft er Versicherungen für eine Tochterfirma des deutschen Allianz-Konzerns. Sieben Sprachen hat sich Aniruddha nebenher angeeignet. Auf Deutsch bringt er nur ein paar Worte über die Lippen, aber er weiß, dass Bayern München Rekordmeister ist.

Es sind Menschen wie Aniruddha, die die Globalisierung unumkehrbar machen. „Wenn ich mich nur mit Indien befassen könnte", sagt er, „wäre mir die Welt wahrscheinlich zu eng geworden."

From: Die Welt, 24 January 2009

2 Looking for details

Your American friend then writes: 'I am doing a project on how lives in India are shaped by globalization. What does the article say about globalization? Can you help?' Now that you have given her the basic idea of the text, you can help her with the details. It is important to remember what information your friend needs and in what form she needs it.

Step 1: **Find the important information in the text.** Always check with your task! (Here, you should concentrate on how people's lives in India are shaped by globalization). Then, in English, make notes about the passages. You might have to paraphrase or explain terms or phrases you do not know in English. Do not try to translate word for word because your friend does not need (or expect) you to.

Step 2: **Structure your information by making an outline.** You can change the order that is given in the text.

Step 3: `LANGUAGE AWARENESS` **Explain phrases and aspects** you can't transfer into the other language easily.

Step 4: **Now write the required text**, keeping in mind the format and the person you are mediating for (here it's an email to your friend). Adapt your *style and *register to suit both. Don't forget to start your email with information about the source of the text, so your guest can find it again if she needs to. (ca. 100 words)

▶ LA3: Similarities and differences of languages, p. 198
▶ S22: Germanisms, p. 187

3 Communicating information `YOU CHOOSE`

a Meanwhile, another friend in London is compiling information on the history and global influences of MTV for a school project. Send him an email in which you point out the information from the article that may be relevant for his project.

OR

b Your former host family in Australia is looking for a private tutor for their 14-year-old daughter. Write them an email in which you outline the information from the article that will help them.

3 Part A

List of countries
Australia • Canada • China • Finland
Germany • Guyana • India
Indonesia • Japan • Malaysia
Poland • Romania • South Africa
South Korea • Taiwan • Thailand
United Kingdom • USA

A2 Assembled in China

1 Thinking about what you own
  a State where you think your phone was made.
  b Look at the infographic below and say where parts of popular phones come from. Use the list of countries on the left to help you.

Where phones come from …

  c If you named a single country in your answer to task **1a**, how should you now change your answer?
  d Work in a small group. Brainstorm a list of the advantages and disadvantages of so many different countries contributing to the production of mobile phones. Compare your answers in class, and add more ideas to your list.

2 Globalization in figures

🇩🇪	US $ 28.86	average hourly wage in Germany (2016)
🇨🇳	US $ 4.11	average hourly wage in China (2013)

🇩🇪	43	weekly working hours of young adults in Germany (2015)
🇨🇳	48	weekly working hours of young adults in China (2015)

🇨🇳	ca. 2.381 billion	mobile phones assembled in China (2017)
🇩🇪	ca. 24.1 million	mobile phones sold in Germany (2017)
🌍	1.5 billion	mobile phones sold worldwide (2016)

From: conference-board.org, 2017; statista.com

▶ S28: Working with charts and graphs, p. 154

  a Examine the statistics above and explain why no mobile phones are produced in Germany.
  b Speculate on how these statistics show that Germany and China need each other. State your answer in a short text.
  c Add new ideas and examples to your mind map from the Lead-in (p. 61, task **2c**).
  d **CHALLENGE** Find out about the journey made by some of your clothes before you bought them. Present your results.

▶ S31: Using search engines, p. 158

66   Chapter 3   Living in the Global Village

Global citizens in a global economy 3

A3 LISTENING The Fairphone – the world's first fair-trade smartphone

1 Before listening

You are going to listen to a radio report on Bas van Abel, who has developed the Fairphone.

a Study the Fact File below. Then read statements 1–3 below and choose the best of the underlined words to complete the statements.

> ■ **FACT FILE**
>
> **Fair trade**
> The idea behind fair trade is to pay producers a guaranteed higher price so that they can improve their standards of living and plan for the future. Most fair-trade products are basic farmed goods like sugar, chocolate, bananas, tea and coffee. A large proportion of fair-trade food is grown organically.
>
> Starting in the late 1960s with hand-made clothes and ornaments, fair trade now accounts for €1.2 billion sales in Germany (2017).
> Western consumers choose fair-trade products if they want to share wealth more equally. They accept higher prices and trust that the extra money they pay goes to the small farmer. (see also p. 154, Practice)

Bas van Abel

1 Important fair-trade goods are e.g. <u>food and drink / art / electrical products</u>.
2 Fair trade helps <u>producers / consumers</u> in developing countries.
3 Fair-trade products are <u>usually / never / seldom</u> more expensive to buy.

b Having read the Fact File, explain what you would expect from a Fairphone.

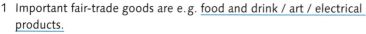
— COMPREHENSION ◀

2 Listening for gist

Listen to the radio report and say what a Fairphone is in one sentence.

🎧 CD 18

▶ S1: Listening for information, p. 120

3 Listening for detail

a Say whether the following statements are true or false.
  1 Bas van Abel wanted to offer consumers an alternative to the mobile phones on the market.
  2 Bas van Abel's Fairphone project only works with one or two partners.
  3 The Fairphone project is trying to get people to think differently about mobile telephones.

b Take notes on the different ways the Fairphone project is trying to improve the current situation. SUPPORT ▶ p. 115

▶ S22: Making and taking notes, p. 148

— BEYOND THE TEXT ◀

4 WRITING An article for your school magazine

Write an article for your school magazine in which you describe the Fairphone project and assess how effective it is in helping change the situation in developing countries. Do some research if necessary.

▶ S13: The stages of writing, p. 135

▶ S19: Writing a report, p. 143

5 SPEAKING Giving a one-minute speech

Do you buy fair-trade products? Why (not)? Give a one-minute speech.

3 Part A

▶ Focus on Vocabulary, pp. 184–191
▶ L14: Formal and informal English, p. 180

A4 FOCUS ON LANGUAGE: Vocabulary and style
Using the correct register

You can express yourself more precisely and thus make your texts more interesting to read by paying careful attention to the vocabulary and style you use in your writing. This includes:
- *using a wide range of vocabulary;*
- *avoiding commonly overused words;*
- *choosing the correct *register.*

1 Using precise words and the correct register
In your article for the school magazine on the Fairphone your English teacher has found the following sentences. The words and phrases underlined in red are not precise or are overused.

> Bas van Abel had an interesting idea: he wanted all the people involved in the making of mobile phones to have good lives. He tried to do this by giving them nicer working conditions and more money.

▶ S25: Using a dictionary, p. 151
▶ L18: Using the exact word, p. 184

a Work with a partner. Using the words in the right column in the table below, rewrite the sentences from above to convey precisely what you mean. Consult your dictionary for additional options.

	Replace with
had	came up with / invented / developed
interesting	impressive / thought-provoking / fascinating
idea	concept / plan
people	workers / employees
making	production / manufacture / construction
good lives	a better standard of living / improved living conditions
do	achieve / accomplish
give	offer / provide / present
nicer	improved / better
more money	improved pay / higher wages / a better salary

■ **LANGUAGE AWARENESS**

Register describes the level of language that is used in different contexts or situations or to address different target groups, e.g. peers, family or bosses. The four most common registers are:
formal English (e.g. 'offspring'): used for academic purposes or in contact with people of higher authority
neutral English (e.g. 'child'): used for most written texts
informal English (e.g. 'kid'): mostly used in spoken English
slang (e.g. 'kiddo'): typically used by particular social groups or in particular social contexts

▶ LA1: Varieties of English, p. 196
▶ LA4: Influencing through language, p. 199

b ■ **LANGUAGE AWARENESS** Together with a partner, write out two alternative versions of the given sentences, one in order to advertise the Fairphone in a scientific magazine, the other to tell friends about this idea. Use the appropriate register.

2 Nations and languages
a Look at the flags in **A2** 'Assembled in China' (p. 66) again. Then continue the table below with the other countries.

Flag	Country: He is from …	Nationality: He is a/an …	Language: She speaks …	Adjective: She has … friends.
	Germany	*German*	*German*	*German*

Download the table here:
 Webcode star-26

b Looking at the adjectives and nationalities, see if you can find some simple rules or ideas about how nationality words are used in English.

▶ L23: Suffixes, p. 185

Global citizens in a global economy

A5 A vision of the future in China
Cory Doctorow

Describe the photo and the situation it depicts. Explain the effect it has on you.

The following extract from the novel For the Win *is set in an imaginary future where western consumers have stopped buying products made in China.*

Lu had worked as a security guard in a factory in Shilong New Town, a city that made appliances for sale in Britain. [...] The entire city, four million people, did nothing but make appliances for sale in Britain, a country with eighty million people.

Then, one day, the factories on either side of Lu's had closed. They had all made goods for a few different companies, employing armies of young women to run the machines and assemble the pieces that came out of them. Young women always got the best jobs. Bosses liked them because they worked hard and didn't argue so much – at least, that's what everyone said.

When Lu left his village in Sichuan province to come to south China, he'd talked to one of the girls who had come home from the factories for the Mid-Autumn Festival, a girl who'd left a few years before and found wealth in Dongguan, who'd bought her parents a fine new two-storey house with her money, who came home every year for the Festival in fine clothes with a new mobile phone in a designer bag, looking like an alien or a model stepped fresh out of a magazine ad. 'If you go to a factory and it's not full of young girls, don't take a job there,' was her advice. 'Any place that can't attract a lot of young girls, there's something wrong with it.' But the factory that Lu worked at – all the factories in Shilong New Town – were filled with young girls. The only jobs for men were as drivers, security guards, cleaners and cooks.

The factories boomed, each one a small city itself, with its own kitchens, its own dormitories, its own infirmary and its own customs checkpoint where every vehicle and visitor going in or out of the wall got checked and inspected. And these indomitable cities had crumbled. The Highest Quality Dishwasher Company factory closed on Monday. The Boundless Energy Enterprises hot-water heater plant went on Wednesday. Every day, Lu saw the bosses come in and out in their cars, waving them through after they'd flicked their IDs at him. One day, he steeled his nerve and leaned in the window, his face only inches from that of the man who paid his wages every month.

'We're doing better than the neighbors, eh, Boss?' He tried for a jovial smile, the best he could muster, but he knew it wasn't very good.

'We do fine,' the boss had barked. He had very smooth skin and a smart sport-coat, but his shoulders were dusted with dandruff. 'And no one says otherwise!'

'Just as you say, boss,' Lu said, and leaned out of the window, trying to keep his smile in place. But he'd seen it in the boss's face – the factory would close. The next day, no bus came to the bus-stop. Normally, there would have been fifty or sixty people waiting for the bus, mostly young men, the women mostly lived in the dorms. Security guards and janitors didn't rate dorm rooms. That morning, there were eight people waiting when he arrived at the bus-stop. Ten minutes went by and a few more trickled to the stop, and still no bus came. Thirty minutes passed – Lu was now officially late for work – and still no bus came.

---

3 **appliance** [əˈplaɪəns] machine usually used in the household
21 **infirmary** [ɪnˈfɜːməri] facility serving as a hospital
22 **indomitable** [ɪnˈdɒmɪtəbl] unconquerable
26 **flick** make a light sharp movement
steel your nerve prepare yourself mentally or emotionally for sth. unpleasant
29 **jovial** [ˈdʒəʊviəl] cheerful and friendly
30 **muster sth.** gather sth. together
37 **janitor** [ˈdʒænɪtə] a person employed to look after a building
38 **trickle** move forward slowly

Part A

41 canvass sb. ['kænvəs] ask sb. about his or her opinion
45 scorching very hot
47 bare sth. uncover or reveal sth.
cake up *(here)* cover up
48 condenser dryer dryer for clothes
screeching screaming in a high voice
49 smock loose, lightweight overgarment worn to protect clothing while working
padlocked fastened with a portable or detachable lock
51 duffel-bag large bag for carrying personal belongings
66 abandon sth. [ə'bændən] give sth. up
67 flail move as if to hit sth.

He canvassed his fellow waiters to see if anyone was going near his factory and might want to share a taxi – an otherwise unthinkable luxury, but losing his job was even more unthinkable. One other guy, with a Shaanxi accent, was willing, and that's when they noticed that there didn't seem to be any taxis cruising on the road either. So Lu, being Lu, walked to work, fifteen kilometers in the scorching, melting, dripping heat, his security guard's shirt and coat over his arm, his undershirt rolled up to bare his belly, the dust caking up on his shoes. And when he arrived at the Miracle Spirit condenser dryer factory and found himself in a mob of thousands of screeching young women in factory-issue smocks, crowded around the fence and the double-padlocked gate, rattling it and shouting at the factory's darkened doors. Many of the girls had small backpacks or duffel-bags, overstuffed and leaking underwear and make-up on the ground.

'What's going on?' he shouted at one, pulling her out of the mob.

'The bastards shut the factory and put us out. They did it at shift-change. Pulled the fire-alarm and screamed "Fire" and "Smoke" and when we were all out here, they ran out and padlocked the gate!'

'Who?' He'd always thought that if the factory were going to shut down, they'd use the security guards to do it. He'd always thought that he, at least, would get one last paycheck out of the company.

'The bosses, six of them. Mr Dai and five of his supervisors. They locked the front gate and then they drove off through the back gate, locking it behind them. We're all locked out. All my things are in there! My phone, my money, my clothes –' Her last paycheck. It was only three days to payday, and, of course, the company had kept their first eight weeks' wages when they all started working. You had to ask your boss's permission if you wanted to change jobs and keep the money – otherwise you'd have to abandon two months' pay.

Around Lu, the screams rose in pitch and small, feminine fists flailed at the air. Who were they shouting at? The factory was empty. If they climbed the fence, cutting the barbed wire at the top, and then broke the locks on the factory doors, they'd have the run of the place. They couldn't carry out a condenser dryer – not easily, anyway – but there were plenty of small things: tools, chairs, things from the kitchen, the personal belongings of the girls who hadn't thought to bring with them when the fire alarm sounded. Lu knew about all the things that could be smuggled out of the factory. He was a security guard. Or had been.

From: *For the Win*, Tor Teen, New York, 2010. The text has been abridged by the publisher.

COMPREHENSION

1 Working out the events in a story
Put the following events in the order in which they happen.
1 Lu walks 15 kilometres in the heat to work.
2 The factory is closed, the gates are padlocked, and the workers are locked out.
3 The factory boss tells Lu that all is well with the factory.
4 The bus does not turn up to take Lu to work.
5 The factories near Lu's factory close down.

Global citizens in a global economy

2 LANGUAGE AWARENESS Understanding the past perfect
a Read the first sentence of the text. Explain why the narrator writes 'Lu had worked', rather than the usual narrative simple past 'Lu worked'.
b Decide whether the verbs in brackets should be simple past or past perfect.
1 Lu couldn't pay for a taxi, as his employers (not pay) him yet.
2 Lu knew Beijing very well, as he (be) there many times.
3 Lu: '(you ever visit) China before your trip in 2017?'
  His friend: 'Yes, I (travel) to China once before.'
4 Before he (move) to Shilong last year, Lu (work) in Shanghai for two years.

▶ L6: Past perfect and simple past, p. 171

─── ANALYSIS ◂

3 Examining the narration
Decide which of the following statements about this text is correct.
1 The story is told from the perspective of a third-person *narrator with a *point of view limited to a factory girl.
2 There is no narrator in the text as most of it consists of quotations.
3 Lu is the narrator of the story.
4 The story is told from the perspective of a third-person narrator with a point of view limited to Lu.
5 The story is told from the perspective of an omniscient narrator.

▶ Focus on Literature: The narrator's point of view, p. 58
▶ S7: Reading and analysing narrative prose, p. 127

4 Finding examples to support your views
a Find two sentences from the text which prove your answer to task 3 is correct and write them down.
b Work with a partner. Look at the sentences you have selected and discuss the effect they have on you. Share your results with the class.
▶ LANGUAGE HELP

LANGUAGE HELP
- create a distance between …
- affect the reader's connection to a character
- create suspense
- adopt the perspective of …
- create empathy for …
- identify with …

5 CHALLENGE Thinking about globalization
At present, much of the world's manufacturing is done in China. Imagine what the background to this story is and describe a scenario which has resulted in Chinese factories shutting down. Two ideas you can consider are how globalization works and how consumers spend their money.

─── BEYOND THE TEXT ◂

6 WRITING Thinking about the workers YOU CHOOSE

a Imagine you are one of the young factory workers who has lost her personal possessions in the factory lock-out. Write a short letter home describing what has happened and what you are going to do about it.

OR

b How do you think the workers at the factory gates will react to the situation they are in? Continue the story. SUPPORT p. 116

▶ S14: Creative writing, p. 136

Part B

▶ S29: Working with cartoons, p. 156

Looking after the global village: ecological issues

B1 Pacific plastic

Cups, shopping bags, food packets ... have you ever wondered where it all ends up? The Great Pacific Garbage Patch is an area of the ocean in which there is a high concentration of floating plastic particles. The circular ocean current causes garbage to collect in a large area in the middle of the ocean.

————————————————————————— COMPREHENSION ◀

1 **Talking about a *cartoon**
  Describe the situation in the cartoon.

————————————————————————— ANALYSIS ◀

2 **Analysing a cartoon**
  Discuss how effectively the cartoon expresses its criticism.

————————————————————————— BEYOND THE TEXT ◀

3 **Giving your opinion**
  Evaluate the cartoon. Give reasons for your response.

B2 CHALLENGE Junk raft completes voyage to Hawaii
Kim Hampton

The following text shows a spectacular way of drawing people's attention to the Pacific Garbage Patch.

▶ L13: Participle constructions, p. 178

With the hundreds of thousands of tons of plastic debris floating around in the Pacific, it would have been difficult to spot the one collection of garbage moving with a purpose. A bunch of plastic bottles, strapped together with old aluminum spars and topped with an airplane cockpit and a mast, would have barely stood out from the mass of plastic garbage in the Pacific […], yet this questionable craft has carried two brave men across the Eastern Pacific, and into the history books. An elated Marcus Eriksen spoke with YachtPals just moments ago: 'It's awesome! It's just starting to dawn on me what a big deal this really is!' 5

Nearly three months ago, Dr. Marcus Eriksen and Joel Paschal sailed out from Long Beach, California, on a boat made of 15,000 plastic bottles and a[n] old Cessna 310 fuselage, which they appropriately named 'Junk'. Eriksen and Paschal took this little 2,600 mile cruise in order to bring awareness to the issue of ocean pollution. Just a short while ago, the team made land at the Ala Wai Harbor Fuel Dock on the Hawaiian island of Oahu – meeting their goal, and then some. 10

With a top speed of 3.2 knots, it wasn't a fast ride, and there were some serious issues, but a steady pace over the last several weeks has brought vessel and crew in to port safely. Thanks to modern communications equipment, Marcus and Joel have been sending in photos and video from sea to bring special attention to the Pacific Ocean pollution and the North Pacific Gyre – a clockwise rotating mass of water roughly twice the size of the U.S., described by the team as a toilet bowl that never flushes. 15

20

3 **spar** type of pole or stick used for the sails of a ship
6 **elated** very excited
7 **it dawned on me** I realized
10 **Cessna 310** ['sesnə] small plane
   fuselage ['fjuːzəlɑːʒ] main body of a plane
14 **and then some** doing more than expected
15 **knot** *Knoten*
19 **gyre** ['dʒaɪə] thing that moves round and round

Chapter 3   Living in the Global Village

Looking after the global village: ecological issues 3

On their final day at sea, Marcus reflected on the epic journey: '2,600 miles of open ocean crossed in 87 days. From our first week of sinking hopes on a sinking raft, through four hurricanes that swept under us, to the unbelievable chance meeting with
25 Roz Savage in the middle of nowhere, we have had quite an adventure. We've collected 10 ocean surface samples using our marine debris trawl, managed to snatch a few large pieces of plastic debris that floated under us, and caught fish with stomachs filled with particles of plastic. Plastic is forever, and it's everywhere.'

Eriksen wrote of his arrival, 'We return [...] to the world of alarm clocks, calendars,
30 cars and shoes. Three months is enough time to forget the world you left and accept a new reality. But not everything is forgotten. I long for my friends, family and fiancée. I crave fresh veggies and exercise. In three months I wonder how I will reflect on this summer? Will there be days when I will find myself wishing to be back on JUNK, even if only for a minute? I don't know what this experience will bring, but it is my inten-
35 tion to use it as a starting point for hundreds of conversations about solutions to the plastic plague. We have, in half a century, transformed two thirds of the ocean surface into a plastic soup. Knowing what I know, it would be immoral to do nothing.'
From: the website of Yacht Pals, 28 August 2008

25 **Roz Savage** (born 1967) English sportswoman who has rowed solo across the Indian, Atlantic and Pacific Oceans
26 **trawl** net thrown behind a boat to catch things
27 **debris** ['debriː] rubbish
31 **long for sth.** desire sth.
32 **crave sth.** want sth. a lot
veggies ['vedʒiz] vegetables
36 **plague** [pleɪg] Pest

COMPREHENSION

1 **WRITING** A summary **SUPPORT** p. 116
Summarize the journey of Eriksen and Paschal.

▶ S20: Writing a summary, p. 144

ANALYSIS

2 **Examining quotes**
a Almost half of the text consists of quotes by Marcus Eriksen. Read the quotes again and make notes on the effect they have on you.
b Write a short statement on the function of the quotes in the article.
SUPPORT p. 116

▶ S22: Making and taking notes, p. 148

BEYOND THE TEXT

3 **VIEWING** 'The Majestic Plastic Bag'
a Watch the video. Describe in one sentence what the film is about.
b Analyse the devices the film-maker uses to make his film effective, e.g.
- the content of the voice-over and the language used
- the speaker's voice
- the music.

🎬 **DVD** 04

▶ S2: Viewing a film, p. 121

4 **SPEAKING** Your contribution
Give a presentation showing what you could do to reduce waste.

▶ S10: Giving a presentation, p. 130

Part B

- Focus on Skills: Writing, p. 25, p. 42, p. 105
- S13: The stages of writing, p. 135

B3 FOCUS ON SKILLS WRITING (3)
Writing paragraphs

A paragraph consists of several sentences that share the same idea. It is used to structure your thoughts and to make it easier for the reader to follow them. The following rules should help:
1. Start with a short topic sentence, in which you describe the main idea of what the paragraph is going to be about.
2. The supporting sentences make up the body of a paragraph. These can also consist of explanations or examples.
3. The concluding sentence summarizes the body of a paragraph and provides a link to the next one.

1 Writing topic sentences

a In the following paragraph the topic sentence is missing ([…]). Three possible topic sentences are listed on the left. Read the paragraph and choose the topic sentence which best describes what the paragraph is about.

Topic sentences:
1. Floods can cause massive damage to buildings and roads.
2. The Earth's climate is getting warmer, and the signs are everywhere.
3. Farmers are afraid that the summer heat is going to damage their wheat before harvest time.

> […] In Europe the summer this year began with lots of rain, which caused terrible flooding. This long rain period was followed by a long period of heat, which caused crops to dry up and die. As global temperatures continue to rise, we'll see more changes in our climate and our environment. These increased temperatures will have severe impacts on people, animals and ecosystems.

b Read the paragraph again and focus on the last sentence. Predict what you expect the next paragraph could be about.

c Here is the second paragraph, without its topic sentence. Read the paragraph to find out what it is about and then write its topic sentence.

> […] Firstly there is a direct impact on people's health. In many countries the rates of diseases such as malaria are increasing as the temperature rises. Secondly, global warming affects people through extreme weather events such as storms and floods. Finally, food supply and clean water supply are threatened. These problems also put pressure on fragile ecosystems.

2 Supporting and concluding sentences

- rising temperatures > animals move north > cooler
- warmer / drier weather > plants dying

a Read the topic sentence of the third paragraph below. Then use the notes on the left to write the supporting sentences. Refer to rule 2 above for help.

The effect of global warming on ecosystems could be very damaging.

- Many animals / plants > become extinct

b Now write the concluding sentence to the third paragraph. Use the note on the left and refer to rule 3 above for help.

3 Writing

Using the techniques here and your mind map, write four paragraphs about how globalization connects people around the world.

Looking after the global village: ecological issues 3

B4 VIEWING Another use for plastic bottles

📹 DVD 05

You will watch a report on a new way of providing light to slums in the developing world.

◀ COMPREHENSION

1 **Examining the use of old bottles**
   a In one sentence summarize how old plastic bottles are used in Manila.
   b For whom and why is this so significant, according to the video?

◀ BEYOND THE TEXT

2 **Brainstorming ideas**
   In a group, brainstorm other ways of reusing plastic bottles. Consider these ideas for local action in your Chapter Task (p. 78).

▶ S2: Viewing a film, p. 121

LANGUAGE AWARENESS
Whenever you address somebody or speak in front of an audience, it is important **to adapt your text** to the people listening to or reading it. This is especially important in (written or oral) mediation as you have to mediate across cultural borders. You have to adjust your language (style, register), the content (e.g. for additional explanations), the way you address people (*Ladies and Gentlemen* vs. *Hey guys, Mr/Mrs X* vs. first names ...) as well as the form of your text to the needs of your audience.

▶ LA4: Influencing through language, p. 199

B5 Reducing campus waste

During your exchange year in the USA, you have joined a committee consisting of students who want to make their high school a more environmentally friendly place. Every student has to contribute suggestions from their home country. You find the following German audio and decide to present it to the group in the form of a report.

1 LISTENING **Listening for gist**
   Listen to the audio and, in English, write down what it is about in one sentence.

2 LISTENING **Listening for detail**
   Listen to the audio for a second time and take notes in German on what German universities have done to conserve the environment.

3 MEDIATION (German → English) **A report**
   Use your notes to write the report for the committee (in English), directly addressing its members, so you can easily present it to them. Use the language help box for some vocabulary you might need. ▶ LANGUAGE HELP
   Remember to focus on what information the committee needs and what format they need it in.

🎧 CD 19

▶ S22: Making and taking notes, p. 148

▶ S21: Mediation of written and oral texts, p. 146

LANGUAGE HELP
- paper cup
- hand dryers
- traffic light
- solar panels
- CO_2 display
- paper towels
- cafeteria
- organic food

Part B

B6 Whatever happened to the hole in the ozone layer? *Martyn Chipperfield*

Work with a partner and use the box below to find out what the ozone layer is.

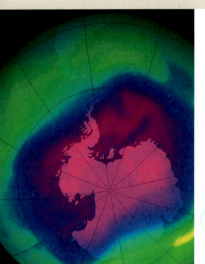

Work in pairs. **Partner B:** Turn to page 117.
Partner A: Read the text below about ozone.

The hole in the ozone layer

Ozone is a naturally occurring form of oxygen with the chemical symbol O_3. It forms a thin layer in the stratosphere between 20 km and 30 km above the Earth's surface. It provides very important protection against the ultra-violet (UV) rays of the sun, absorbing up to 99 percent of harmful radiation. Ozone is measured in Dobson units (DU), a score of 100 DU is equal to a layer of gas one millimetre thick.

1 Answer your partner's questions about ozone.
2 Now ask your partner for information about CFCs:
 - what they are
 - how they affect ozone
 - why they were used
 - where the problems started

Read the text below to find out about the ozone hole.

The 1987 treaty that stopped the pollution causing a hole in the ozone layer is rightly seen as a major success story. It's arguably the most successful international environmental agreement ever. It's true that, 30 years on from the signing of the Montreal Protocol, the Antarctic ozone hole still reappears every year. Yet the protocol really is working and its continued development means that it is doing more good than ever, including helping the fight against climate change.

In 1985, scientists made the unexpected discovery that the Earth's ozone shield, located in the stratosphere about 20 km–30 km above the surface and essential for life, contained a huge hole over Antarctica. The cause was quickly established to be chemicals, notably chlorofluorocarbons (CFCs) used as aerosol propellants and refrigerants, which are stable at low altitudes but release ozone-destroying chlorine and bromine when they break down in the upper atmosphere.

It took just two years for intensive research, building on work on ozone depletion from the 1970s, to provide enough evidence for politicians representing every country in the UN to take action. They agreed to limit production of CFCs and other related gases. Signed on September 16, 1987, the Montreal Protocol put the brakes on increasing ozone depletion. This prevented the catastrophic scenarios of large, global-scale ozone depletion that would have severely damaged animal and plant life at the surface through large increases in ultraviolet (UV) radiation. For example, skin cancer rates in humans would have increased greatly.

Despite the success of the protocol, a large Antarctic ozone hole continues to appear every spring in the southern hemisphere. In fact, the hole continued to grow for almost 20 years after the Montreal Protocol was put in place, with the largest hole recorded in 2006. This is because the process by which the atmosphere can cleanse itself of the stable CFC molecules takes many decades.

Even though the emission of these chemicals has now largely stopped, the CFCs already in the atmosphere will carry on releasing their chlorine and bromine for decades to come, as they are slowly broken down by sunlight in the upper atmosphere.

---

7 **shield** protection against sth.
10 **aerosol** metal container for liquids to be released as spray
 propellant gas that is kept under pressure in a bottle in order to force out its contents (e.g. in spray cans)
11 **refrigerant** substance used e.g. in fridges, freezers or in air conditioning
 chlorine ['klɔːriːn] halogen element that is often used in order to keep water clean
12 **bromine** ['brəʊmiːn] poisonous chemical element (a nonmetallic, halogen liquid)
13 **depletion** (fml) considerable reduction of sth. so that there is not enough left

Looking after the global village: ecological issues

30 As such, the ozone hole will take about three times longer to disappear than it did to appear, eventually closing sometime in the second half of the century.

From: www.theconversation.com

— COMPREHENSION ◀

3 Finding key points
Make notes on the key points of the text. Then outline the article's answer to the question posed in the title.

— ANALYSIS ◀

4 Explaining a sentence
Explain why the author refers to the Montreal Protocol as 'the most successful international environmental agreement ever' (ll. 2–3).

ODS = ozone depleting substance ['əʊzəʊn dɪˌpliːtɪŋ 'sʌbstəns]
CFC = chlorofluorocarbons [ˌklɔːrəʊˈflʊərəʊkɑːbənz]
ODP = ozone depleting potential (a measure of the effect on the ozone layer)

B7 How international cooperation reduced CFC consumption

The graph below shows how the consumption of CFCs has developed since 1986.

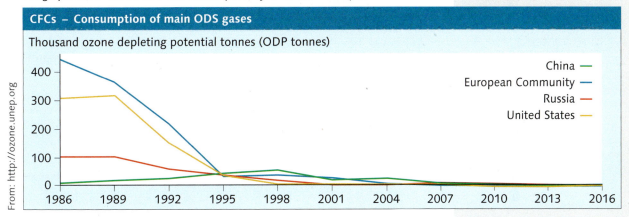

From: http://ozone.unep.org

— COMPREHENSION ◀

1 Dealing with graphs
a Examine the line graph above. Note down key numbers and key dates.
b Now work in pairs. ▶ LANGUAGE HELP
   Partner A: State what information it contains about the consumption of CFC gases in the United States and China.
   Partner B: State what information the graph contains about the consumption of CFC gases in Russia and the European Community to Partner A.

— ANALYSIS ◀

2 Comparing findings
Compare your findings in the line graph to the situation described in Chipperfield's article (text B6, p. 76). SUPPORT ▶ p. 117

— BEYOND THE TEXT ◀

3 WRITING **An article**
a For a project day on environmental protection, write a school magazine article called 'The dwindling ozone hole – a positive example of global teamwork'.
b CHALLENGE ▶ Some ozone-depleting gases are also greenhouse gases that add to global warming. Find examples of international initiatives that aim to reduce greenhouse gases and write an article about them for your school magazine.

| LANGUAGE HELP |
- The graph is about …
- It shows the development of …
- It covers the time period from … to …
- In 1986 … produced … tonnes of CFCs.
- CFC production started/continued to rise/fall in …
- After … production fell rapidly in …
- … production started to fall gradually in …

▶ S28: Working with charts and graphs, p. 154

Find more information for your research here:
 **Webcode** star-27

▶ S13: The stages of writing, p. 135
▶ Vocabulary, p. 214

Chapter Task

Thinking globally – acting locally

In this Chapter Task you will look at different ways of acting locally in order to encourage people to make changes in their lives.

1 How to make a difference
Work in groups of three or four. Look for ideas on your mind maps from the Lead-in (p. 61, task **2b**) about ways people in your area could help create a fairer planet or help protect the environment. (See the ideas box below for extra help.)

> **Ideas box: Thinking globally and acting locally**
> - Reducing the amount of plastic used
> - Stopping coming to school by car
> - Buying only fair trade food, clothes and other goods
> - Drinking tap water instead of mineral water

2 Your plan for encouraging people to act locally
As a group, agree on one idea that people in your area could try out. Decide how you will present this idea in your next lesson on an easily understandable and persuasive poster.

3 Research time
  a Find a German article about how people in your area are changing the way they work, live, eat, shop or spend their free time in order to make the best of globalization.
  b **MEDIATION** (German → English): Write an outline of your article in English. Your aim is to provide information for your group that could be used for your group poster.

4 Share information in class
Back in your groups, present your mediation texts to each other. Together, decide on the most important pieces of information to be included on your poster.

5 Design your poster
- Use your mind maps and the results of your mediation task for ideas.
- Describe the local action people should take: WHAT they should do.
- Describe the problem you are trying to solve: WHY they should do it.
- Make sure your poster grabs people's attention.
- Keep your layout simple:
    – Do not use too many colours or confusing fonts (i.e. the size and style of letters).
    – Use pictures rather than texts to make your point.
Use the webcode to find a webtool that will help you create your poster.

6 Comparing your posters
Share your posters with the rest of the class. Decide whose idea for 'acting locally' was the most convincing and why. Say whose poster you found the most persuasive and why.

▶ L27: Using the right expression for *wollen*, p. 190
▶ L28: Using the right expression for *sollen*, p. 190

Find a webtool for your poster here:
Webcode star-28

Presentation:

A Project ~~xxxxx~~

wich should encourage people.

Social, Nature

Chapter Task 3

Self-Assessment

Look at the tables below. Evaluate how you did when working on the chapter and the Chapter Task by giving yourself a grade from **A** *(very good),* **B** *(good),* **C** *(satisfactory) or* **D** *(poor). If you are not completely satisfied with your performance, consult the pages listed under 'Revision and practice' below.*

Download a self-assessment sheet here: **Webcode** star-29

▶ S33: Assessing yourself and giving feedback, p. 160

Working on mediation tasks MEDIATION
Evaluate how you did when mediating 'Indien und Amerika brauchen einander' (pp. 64–65) and the audio text 'Reducing campus waste' (p. 75).

Criteria	Revision and practice
1 I made notes on the main topic.	▶ S22: Making and taking notes, p. 148 ▶ Workbook, p. 34, ex. 5; pp. 82–84, ex. 28–29
2 I outlined all the essential aspects regarding the main topic.	▶ S20: Writing a summary, p. 144 ▶ Workbook, p. 34, ex. 5; pp. 82–84, ex. 28–29
3 I wrote the email/report from my notes.	▶ S13: The stages of writing, p. 135 ▶ Workbook, p. 34, ex. 5; pp. 82–84, ex. 28–29

Writing paragraphs WRITING
Evaluate how you did when writing paragraphs (see p. 74).

Criteria	Revision and practice
1 I identified the most suitable topic sentence.	▶ S13: The stages of writing, Drafting stage, p. 135 ▶ Workbook, p. 40, ex. 15
2 I wrote the supporting and concluding sentences.	▶ S13: The stages of writing, p. 135 ▶ L15: Linking your sentences, p. 180 ▶ L16: Emphasis, p. 183 ▶ Workbook, p. 40, ex. 15
3 I wrote the paragraphs according to the given rules.	▶ S13: The stages of writing, p. 135 ▶ Workbook, p. 40, ex. 15

Working on the Chapter Task
Evaluate how you did when working on your project for this chapter.

Criteria	Revision and practice
1 I contributed to the decision process concerning our main idea and gave reasons for it.	▶ S30: Doing project work, p. 150 ▶ S12: Having a discussion, p. 133
2 I found a suitable German article and mediated the information for the other members of my group in English.	▶ S21: Mediation of written and oral texts, p. 146 ▶ L21: Verbs of reporting, p. 186 ▶ Workbook, p. 34, ex. 5; pp. 82–84, ex. 28
3 I contributed to creating the poster by arranging the information in an effective and persuasive way.	▶ S10: Giving a presentation, p. 130 ▶ S13: The stages of writing, p. 135

Working on the topics of this chapter
Evaluate your expertise on the topics of this chapter.

Criteria	Revision and practice
1 I dealt with the different aspects of globalization and arranged them in a logical order in a mind map.	▶ Texts, pp. 62, 64, 66 ▶ Workbook, p. 33, ex. 3–4; p. 38, ex. 11
2 I understood the positive and negative aspects of globalization and discussed them.	▶ Texts, pp. 62, 64, 66 ▶ Workbook, p. 34, ex. 5; p. 35, ex. 6

Focus on Literature 3

| NOVEL pp. 30–35 | SHORT STORY pp. 56–59 | **POETRY pp. 80–85** | DRAMA pp. 108–111 |

Poetry

A Getting started: Thinking beyond words

What makes us happy?

- Complete the sentence 'Happiness is …' As in the picture, imagine a specific situation or event that makes you happy.
- Exchange your images with a partner, and put together a series of 'Happiness is …' sentences which are e.g. related to the same topic (school, love, family, …) or use the same verbs, etc.

1 Visualizing the scene
 a Read the text and imagine the 'happy scene' it presents. Compare your ideas with a partner, describing how you imagine the *speaker, the *setting, the people involved, etc.
 b Explain to your partner why you can or cannot identify with the idea of happiness that Roger McGough has put into words.

2 Reading between the lines
▶ A CLOSER LOOK
 a *Poems are 'pictures made out of words' (Karen Finneyfrock, American poet). List the *images used in the *poem 'happiness' to create a 'picture made out of words'.
 b With a partner, brainstorm possible *connotations of the *images. Together with another pair, interpret the images and their connotations, i.e. point out which ideas are being expressed.

Example:

Image	Connotation	Interpretation
'lying in bed ofa weekday morning'	free time, not having to work	leisure, personal liberty to do as you please
…	…	…

3 CHALLENGE Analysing the mood
Examine the use of informal language in the *poem and the effect this has on the mood.

---

happiness
Roger McGough

Lying in bed ofa weekday morning
Autumn
and the trees
none the worse for it.
5 Youve just got up
to make tea toast and a bottle
leaving pastures¹ warm
for me to stretch into

in his cot²
10 the littlefella
outsings the birds

Plenty of honey in the cupboard.
Nice.

From: Roger McGough, *Collected Poems*, 2004

---

¹ **pasture** ['pɑːstʃə] grassland for feeding cows; the circumstances of your life, work, etc.
² **cot** a small bed for a baby

> **TROUBLE SPOT**
> **look unhappy** (adj) = unglücklich/unzufrieden aussehen
> **smile unhappily** (adv) = unglücklich lächeln

> **A CLOSER LOOK**
> Poets (especially modern poets) often use e.g. unusual orthography and grammar. This is called **artistic** or **poetic** licence (= 'dichterische Freiheit') and can also be used as a stylistic device to add poetic meaning.
> Poetic meaning is also created by *connotations. A connotation describes the feelings or ideas that a word or image suggests, in contrasts to its literal or primary meaning (= *denotation).

▶ RF2, p. 204
▶ RF3, p. 205

▶ S9: Reading and analysing poetry, p. 128

Poetry

LIT 3

B Enjoying poetry: Finding your style
B1 Choosing a favourite

Have a look at the six *poems (on this and the following page) and decide which one appeals to you most.
▶ A CLOSER LOOK

Leisure
William Henry Davies

What is this life if, full of care,
We have no time to stand and stare.

No time to stand beneath the boughs³
And stare as long as sheep or cows.

5　No time to see, when woods we pass,
Where squirrels hide their nuts in grass.

No time to see, in broad daylight,
Streams⁴ full of stars, like skies at night.

No time to turn at Beauty's glance,
10　And watch her feet, how they can dance.

No time to wait till her mouth can
Enrich that smile her eyes began.

A poor life this is if, full of care,
We have no time to stand and stare.

From: www.poemhunter.com

im rlly gd @ txting
Kenn Nesbitt

im rlly gd @ txting.
i do it all day lng.
im spedy on the keybrd
n my thms r supr strng.

5　i txt wth all my fmly.
i txt wth all my frnz.
n i rply 2 evry txt
tht nebdy senz.

id rthr keep on txting
10　thn go outsd n play.
i thnk i prbly snd abot
a thsnd txts a day.

im gld 2 no tht u cn
undrstnd me rlly wel.
15　4 if u cldnt rd my txts
id haf to lrn to spel.

From: www.poetry4kids.com

The Kiss
Sarah Teasdale

I hoped that he would love me,
And he has kissed my mouth,
But I am like a stricken⁵ bird
That cannot reach the south.

5　For though I know he loves me,
To-night my heart is sad;
His kiss was not so wonderful
As all the dreams I had.

From: http://en.wikisource.org/

Fog
Carl Sandburg

THE fog comes
on little cat feet.

It sits looking
over harbor and city
5　on silent haunches⁶
and then moves on.

From: www.poetryfoundation.org

A CLOSER LOOK
*Poems often rely on devices such as *rhyme, *alliteration and *assonance as well as *rhythm. They should be read aloud in order to demonstrate the full effect of these qualities.

▶ RF2, p. 204
▶ RF3, p. 205

³ **bough** [baʊ] branch of a tree
⁴ **stream** small narrow river

Find more poetry recitals here:
Webcode star-30

⁵ **stricken** wounded, in trouble
⁶ **sit on one's haunches** in der Hocke sitzen

Focus on Literature

LIT 3   Poetry

Actor
Tanmay Tiwari

He arrived in style, to the delight of the press,
The paparazzi, as usual, were complimenting his dress
The crowd exclaimed, 'He's so fair!'
And then they added, 'We love your hair'.

5   The man blew kisses out of passion,
To the people who adored[1] his fashion.
He stood tall amongst all like a player,
And everybody there, admired his hair.

A woman jumped from the crowd,
10   She wanted to marry him, she screamed aloud.
She also said they'd make a great pair,
And yes, she loved his hair.

Finally, when the actor reached his home,
He wept like a child when he was alone.
15   He touched his head, remembering the crowd's jig[2]
And lastly he removed his wig.[3]

From: www.boloji.com/index

[1] **adore** love sb. very much
[2] **jig** *Freudentanz*
[3] **wig** artificial hair
[4] **pluck** pick
[5] **chalice** [ˈtʃælɪs] (v) *hier: wie einen Kelch in der Hand halten*
[6] **reverent** [ˈrevərənt] showing great respect
[7] **palm** [pɑːm] *Handfläche*
[8] **carve sth.** *etwas schnitzen*
[9] **mould** [məʊld] (v) form

Jealousy
Ruth Ellison

I put out my hand and plucked[4] a rose,
A red satin rose with a velvet scent,
And chaliced[5] its loveliness in reverent[6] palms[7],
Knowing that it was perfect.

5   Then, because I could not make the rose,
And because I could not paint the rose,
Nor carve[8] it, nor mould[9] it,
Nor even draw its beauty in my words,

I slowly closed my fingers over it
10   And crushed it.

From: *Every Man Will Shout*, 1964

▶ S9: Reading and analysing poetry, p. 128

1 Talking about first impressions
Share your chosen *poem with a partner and tell each other what you particularly like about it.

2 Taking a closer look
a With others who have chosen the same poem as you, take a closer look at your poem and analyse
- who the *speaker is, and who is addressed,
- what the topic is,
- how *imagery, rhyme, alliteration, assonance as well as *rhythm contribute to the topic, the atmosphere created, etc.

Discuss how these aspects affect your appreciation of the poem.
b Present your findings to the class.

Poetry

LIT 3

B2 A poetry performance

1 **Before viewing**
   a Brainstorm what it means 'to own a dog'.
   b Look at the title of the *poem you are about to listen to ('How Falling in Love is Like Owning a Dog'), and speculate on possible similarities between falling in love and owning a dog.

2 **VIEWING** First impressions of the performance
   Watch and listen to Taylor Mali perform his poem 'How Falling in Love is Like Owning a Dog' and note down your first impressions. Together with a partner agree on the three most striking features. ▶ LANGUAGE HELP

3 **Focusing on the poem**
   Watch and listen again and jot down the aspects you remember hearing concerning 'love', and connect them to the title.

▶ DVD 06

▶ S2: Viewing a film, p. 121

LANGUAGE HELP
- The *speaker raises/lowers his voice when …
- The speaker repeats/emphasizes/whispers certain words such as …
- He interacts with … / addresses the crowd directly by … / when …
- He pauses / slows down / speeds up whenever …
- His body language / gestures / facial expressions underline/stress/express …

How Falling in Love is Like Owning a Dog
Taylor Mali

First of all, it's a big responsibility,
especially in a city like New York.
So think long and hard before deciding on love.
On the other hand, love gives you a sense of security:
5 when you're walking down the street late at night
and you have a leash[10] on love
ain't no one going to mess with you. […]

Love doesn't like being left alone for long.
But come home and love is always happy to see you.
10 It may break a few things accidentally in its passion for life,
but you can never be mad at love for long.

Is love good all the time? No! No!
Love can be bad. Bad, love, bad! Very bad love. […]

Sometimes love just wants to go for a nice long walk. 15
Because love loves exercise. It will run you around the block
and leave you panting, breathless. It pulls you in several different directions
at once, or winds itself around and around you 20
until you're all wound up and you cannot move.

But love makes you meet people wherever you go.
People who have nothing in common but love
stop and talk to each other on the street.

Throw things away and love will bring them back, 25
again, and again, and again.
But most of all, love needs love, lots of it.
And in return, love loves you and never stops.

From: http://www.taylormali.com

[10] **leash** [liːʃ] *(Hunde-)Leine*

LIT 3 Poetry

4 Analysing the poem
  a After reading the *poem, list the positive and the negative aspects of owning a dog / being in love as mentioned in the poem. Discuss whether this is a fitting *analogy.
  b Try out different ways of reading the poem out loud. Record your version.
  c Form groups of four and play your versions to each other. Discuss which recitals you liked best. Analyse which *stylistic devices were emphasized in the different versions (e.g. *alliteration, *repetition, etc.).

5 Looking into slam *poetry
'Poetry slam blends poetry, performance, and competition in front of an electrified audience. It's a festival, a carnival act, an interactive class, a town meeting, a con game, and a poetic boxing match, all rolled into one.'
Mark Kelly Smith, *The Complete Idiot's Guide to Slam Poetry*.
Watch some more slam poetry on video-sharing channels on the internet, work out the rules and discuss which of the labels above fits this *genre of poetry best.

Find a recording tool here:
Webcode star-31

C You're a poet and don't know it!
C1 Completing a poem

Use the webcode to download a copy of the *poem with gaps, and fill in the green gaps by choosing one of the words on the left.
Similarly, fill in the yellow gaps by choosing one of the phrases on the right.
There are more words and phrases than you need.
Note: Read the word or phrase you want to use out loud to make sure both *rhythm and *rhyme fit.

Find the poem here:
Webcode star-32

The Word Party Richard Edwards

Left words	Poem	Right phrases
careless	Loving words clutch¹ crimson roses,	build bridges
complicated	rude words sniff and pick their noses,	hold hands
favourite	sly words come dressed up as foxes,	make or break a friend
foreign	short words stand on cardboard boxes,	show off, bending metal
favourite	common words tell jokes and gabble,	only want to mumble
hard	_____ words play Scrabble,	yawn and suck their thumbs
impolite	_____ words stamp around and shout,	give out farewell posies
long	_____ words stare each other out,	thank you for your trouble
loud	_____ words look lost and shrug,	
playful	_____ words trip on the rug,	
simple	_____ words slouch with stooping shoulders,	
swear	Code words carry secret folders	
technical	Silly words flick rubber bands,	
unfamiliar	Hyphenated words _____,	
	Strong words _____,	
	Sweet words call each other 'petal'	
	Small words _____,	
	Till at last the morning comes.	
	Kind words _____,	
	Snap! The dictionary closes.	

¹ **clutch** (v) hold tightly

From: www.cfcl.com

Poetry — **LIT 3**

1 **Reading for gist**
Read the completed *poem once or twice, then choose from the sentences below the one that summarizes best what you think the poem is about:
1 Language consists of a big variety of words like a big crowd at a party.
2 Like the people that use it, language can achieve lots of different things.
3 Words must be carefully chosen so as not to hurt other people.

2 **Taking a closer look**
   a Explain the connections between types of words and what they 'do'.
   b Find two examples for each type of word, e.g. 'loving words': *darling, to kiss, …*

3 SPEAKING **Going beyond the text**
In small groups, practise performing the *poem by illustrating characteristics of the words mentioned through gestures and changing the quality of your voice (louder/softer/lower, etc.). Try not to lose the *rhythm of the poem while doing this.

C2 Making up your own poem

A cinquain ['sɪŋkeɪn] *is a five-*line *poem that is structured according to the rules given next to the example below.*

Painting with words	→ title of poem
Poetry	→ 1 noun
contemplative, rhythmic	→ 2 adjectives
surprising, challenging, unsettling	→ 3 participles (-ing forms)
expresses beauty through words and sounds	→ 1 short sentence
magic!	→ 1 noun: synonym for top noun

Creative writing: Creating a cinquain
1 In pairs, write your own cinquain about an abstract topic (like love, happiness, sadness, disappointment, …) or anything else you feel like writing about.
   Method: Having chosen your topic, start by collecting/brainstorming nouns, adjectives and gerunds related to your topic, then experiment with the words you collected to write your poem.
2 Exchange your collection of words with other pairs and see how many new cinquains you can create.
3 Finally, take turns reading out your favourite cinquains in class.

▶ S13: The stages of writing, p. 135
▶ S14: Creative writing, p. 136

4 Going Places

Download a chronological word list here:  **Webcode** star-33

▶ L29: Comparing and contrasting, p. 191

Find a webtool to create your questionnaire for **1c** *here:*
Webcode star-34

PREVIEW

Main topics
- The benefits of language learning, p. 87
- Going to school in another country, p. 91
- Working abroad, p. 99

Skills in focus
- Viewing, p. 93
- Reading effectively, p. 96
- Writing: proofreading, p. 105

Language in focus
- Spelling and punctuation, p. 104

Chapter Task
- Shooting a video application, p. 106

1 Thinking about the benefits of language learning

a Study the infographic 'The benefits of learning languages' on the opposite page and decide which of the four main benefits (love, intelligence, money, travel) is most important to you personally.

b Compare your findings in groups of four and find out which benefit is most popular among you. Discuss why this is.

c Everyone gets a letter (e.g. A, B, C or D). Find others with the same letter as you and get into new groups. Your teacher will assign your group another benefit of learning English. Together, design a questionnaire to ask your fellow students 3–4 questions about this benefit. **SUPPORT** ▶ p. 118

d Using your questionnaire, each member of your group interviews 1–2 classmates from the other groups and takes notes on their answers.

e Get back into your group (i.e. A, B, C or D), analyse your results and prepare a presentation on them.

f Present your results to class and discuss them.

> In this chapter you will learn about young people who have spent some time in another country. At the end of the chapter, you will shoot a video application for a job abroad. ▶ PREVIEW

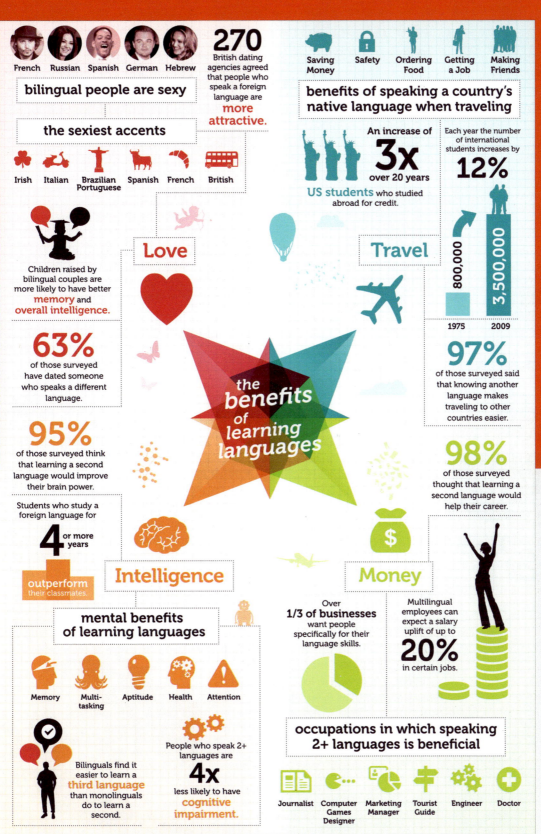

Words in Context

🎧 CD 20
Listen to an audio version of the text on the CD or download it here:
 **Webcode** star-35

LANGUAGE AWARENESS

A **lingua franca** is a language used by people who do not share the same first language. Today, English is the global lingua franca. In different historical periods, however, other languages were used as lingua francas in special contexts or in particular regions. For example, at the time of the Roman Empire, Latin was the lingua franca, and between the 17th and mid-20th century, the lingua franca of diplomacy was French. German once used to be a lingua franca, too: at the turn of the 20th century, German was the language of science.

▶ LA1: Varieties of English, p. 196

▶ Communicating across Cultures, pp. 192–195

▶ Vocabulary, p. 216

The importance of speaking languages

Speaking foreign languages is an essential skill for future personal success in the job market. In the era of the global marketplace, English has become a very important lingua franca, which you can use if you don't speak the native language of a country. It is just as important a skill as being able to use a computer. But how can students advance their English and their intercultural skills at the same time?

Going abroad
School exchanges are one of the best ways for students to make progress with their foreign language skills. But apart from learning the language of the host country, students gain experience of a different culture and environment and develop an awareness and understanding of people from different nations. The students themselves can contribute to mutual international understanding. School exchanges are also a vital opportunity to broaden the horizons of the host families that accommodate the foreign students.
Taking part in a summer camp abroad, for example in the UK or the United States, is another way for young people to develop their foreign language skills. Students take part in a whole range of activities such as canoeing, hiking, dancing or other sports or hobbies.

Working abroad
But there's also an alternative: working as a counsellor at a summer camp is ideal because a young person is given the opportunity to combine language learning and earning money. It also teaches youngsters responsibility, as they are in charge of younger children. Another possibility for students is volunteering. Volunteering in a poor country means meeting new challenges. Volunteers often have unforgettable and life-changing experiences, which can boost their self-confidence and help them develop as a person. There is a wide variety of jobs to do in lots of different places, from building primary schools in Kenya to planting trees in Costa Rica to teaching English to young Taiwanese children.

International friendships
All these possibilities offer young people from different countries and cultures a chance to meet and get to know each other. In many cases it is the beginning of international friendships that last a lifetime. With email and various social media, students are now able to keep in touch easily and perhaps meet again.

The importance of speaking languages

1. **Learning a language**
   Look at the text and make a list of the three most essential ideas of how to improve your knowledge of a foreign language. Try to find two further ideas which are not mentioned in the text and compare your list with a partner.

2. **Collocations**
   a Find as many collocations as possible in the boxes below. In some cases you will have to add an article or a pronoun.

gain
broaden
native
wide
mutual
meet

challenges
variety
horizon
experience
understanding
language

   ▶ L19: Common collocations with prepositions, p. 184

   b Make sentences with at least four of these collocations explaining the advantages of foreign travel.

3. **Synonyms**
   A word which has the same or nearly the same meaning as another word is called a *synonym. Find synonyms used in the text for the following words:
   1 important
   2 possibility
   3 improve

4. **Activate your passive vocabulary**
   Translate the following sentences. The text will help you with the underlined parts:
   1 Viele Jugendliche wollen vor allem ins Ausland gehen, um <u>Fortschritte bei ihren Fremdsprachenkenntnissen zu machen</u>.
   2 Aber ein Auslandsaufenthalt <u>gibt ihnen auch die Gelegenheit, sich als Personen weiterzuentwickeln</u>.
   3 <u>Sie machen Erfahrungen</u> in einer fremden Kultur, die <u>ihren Horizont erweitern</u>.
   4 Einblicke in eine fremde Kultur können zu einem besseren <u>gegenseitigen Verständnis</u> beitragen.
   5 Zeit in einem fremden Land zu verbringen bedeutet, dass man <u>sich jeden Tag neuen Herausforderungen stellen</u> muss.
   6 Aber oft entwickeln sich neue Freundschaften, die <u>ein Leben lang halten</u>.

5. **WRITING An article**
   You have heard about planned cuts in the modern languages department of your school, which will lead to fewer language classes. Write an *article for your school magazine in which you explain the importance of speaking foreign languages.

   ▶ S17: Argumentative writing, p. 139

4 Part A

In a foreign classroom

A1 What a year at a US high school offers

1 **Advantages and disadvantages of a high-school year**
   a Take turns with a partner and pick out five words from the word cloud above. Put them in one of the columns below and describe how they relate to your expectations of attending a US high school as a foreign student.

risk	opportunity	neither

   b Together, think of other risks and opportunities a year at a US high school might offer. Add them to the table.

2 **WRITING An email**
   Your penfriend from England is thinking about going to the USA for a year. He has sent an email to ask you whether you think a year at a US high school is a risk or an opportunity. Write back commenting on his question.
   ▶ LANGUAGE HELP

LANGUAGE HELP
- One cannot underestimate the benefit of …
- One of the main risks facing …
- My advice to you would be to …
- You should consider the following aspects: …
- From what I've heard, …
- A year abroad could …
- a golden/missed opportunity
- … outweigh the risks …

In a foreign classroom

A2 Going to school in another country

Many youngsters spend time at a school in another country. You and your partner will deal with texts written by two teenagers who wrote about their experiences in a foreign classroom.

Partner B: Go to p. 118.
Partner A: Read the following text, which is taken from a report written by British exchange student Emma, who spent some time in Reutlingen. Then work on task **1** on p. 92.

▶ Communicating across Cultures, pp. 190–193

Memories from Reutlingen   *Emma Brighton*

One of my first experiences in Germany involved water, or rather sparkling water. When asking for water in Germany you must ask specifically for still water, something that I was unaware of on my first visit in 2007! My exchange partner seemed horrified when I asked for a glass of water that actually came from the tap, so they constantly
5 gave me orange juice, which they had plenty of in their giant basement!

Every house I visited in Reutlingen had a basement and all of the houses were huge! One exchange partner's house had 4 floors, which accommodated her grandparents as well as her own family. Another thing I noticed was how little TV anyone watched, it was only ever switched on in the evening and this was normally to watch VIVA or RTL. I don't want
10 to sound lazy but television was by far my favourite way of revising my German language skills! But simply being in Germany and experiencing everyday life really improved my language skills. It's amazing how many colloquial phrases and useful words you can pick up in such a short time – things that you could never learn in the classroom but are extremely useful.

15 The moment I entered the exchange school I wanted to be a student there. Everything was so clean, nobody wore a uniform and there was a giant tree growing in the middle of the school! I absolutely loved the fact that there was no school bell, just the sound of gongs playing from speakers. In fact everywhere in Germany seemed to use gongs for announcements including train stations and swimming pools! My friends and I had the opportun-
20 ity to teach part of an English lesson, we found this a bit strange since the entire class seemed practically fluent in English already, so instead the teacher decided that the lesson would best be spent watching Shaun the Sheep – we had no complaints about this! The German students seem to have so much more freedom than we do in the UK. They can leave the school grounds when they don't have lessons, and if their teacher isn't in
25 school then the lesson is cancelled rather than taken by a cover teacher. The teachers actually trusted their pupils, which I feel is something that doesn't tend to happen in the UK.

Undoubtedly the best thing I ever came across in Germany was the Freibad, where I spent the majority of my time. Almost every town in
30 the area had a Freibad but Reutlingen Freibad boasted three huge diving boards, two slides, a wave pool, football pitches and 2 restaurants! I particularly enjoyed one swimming pool which allowed you to sunbathe while having stunning views of the Black Forest. These weren't the only swimming pools in the area either! We visited two
35 other swimming pools during the exchange trip – I had no idea Germans loved to swim so much!

From: the website of UK-German Connection

4 **tap** *Wasserhahn*
12 **colloquial** [kə'ləʊkwɪəl] used in conversation but not in formal speech or writing
22 **Shaun the Sheep** [ʃɔːn] British animated TV series for children
25 **cover teacher** *Vertretungslehrer/-in*

Going Places   Chapter 4

4 Part A

▶ S22: Making and taking notes, p. 148

■ **LANGUAGE AWARENESS**

An **adverb** specifies or changes the meaning e.g. of an adjective, verb, or another adverb. An **intensifier** is a type of adverb that changes the intensity of the word it refers to. It can either strengthen or weaken it; cf. for example:
You look really tired today.
You look a bit tired today.
By using intensifiers, you can be very precise and thus avoid misunderstandings.

▶ LA2: Communication problems, p. 197
▶ LA4: Influencing through language, p. 199
▶ CC 5: Dealing with cultural differences, p. 195

■ **LANGUAGE HELP**
- They are definitely right about …
- They really have a point with regard to …
- When it comes to …, they hit the nail on the head.
- I cannot agree with …
- They are undoubtedly wrong with regard to …
- I cannot go along with their ideas about …

▶ S16: Writing an application, p. 137
▶ Focus on Skills: Proofreading, p. 105
▶ L17: Spelling, p. 184

◀ **COMPREHENSION**

1 **Comparing notes on exchange years**
   a Make notes about Emma's experiences.
   b With the help of your notes, give an oral summary to your partner.

2 **LANGUAGE AWARENESS** The writer of the text frequently uses adverbs to intensify or specify what she is saying, e.g. '… you must ask specifically for still water' (l. 2).
   a Collect other examples from the text.
   b Replace the numbers in the sentences below with suitable adverbs from the ones you collected in **a**.
   When I came to Ireland, I was (1) overwhelmed by the people's friendliness. People would (2) ask me how I was and tell me how brilliant my English was. Of course, later on I realized they were (3) only being friendly. But still, the Irish are (4) very open and friendly people. I (5) enjoyed my time there – it's (6) been one of the best times of my life.

◀ **ANALYSIS**

3 **Intercultural experiences**
   a Being in another country may change your knowledge about the host country and your competence in the target language. Explain these changes with regard to the two texts.
   b With your partner, compare Emma's description of German school life to your experience of school. ▶ LANGUAGE HELP
   c Analyse Friederike's and Emma's texts against the background of the graph below.

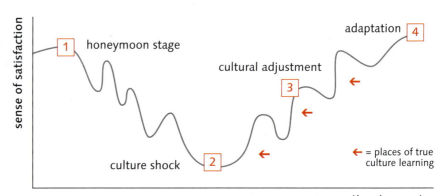

◀ **BEYOND THE TEXT**

4 **WRITING** An email **SUPPORT** p. 119
Like Friederike, you want to study at a British school as an international student. Write a formal email application to the British coordinator of the programme. Proofread your text.

In a foreign classroom

A3 FOCUS ON SKILLS VIEWING

▶ S2: Viewing a film, p. 121

When dealing with visual media such as documentaries, films and clips, you should always find out not just what you can see but also how the information is presented to the viewer. Particularly important are:

- **The setting/context.** Knowing where and when the scene takes place and what is going on is fundamental to understanding the film.
- **Camerawork.** There are various aspects to take into consideration when viewing a film:
  - Perspective: This refers to the angle of the camera from which the action is shot.
  - Movement: The viewer always follows the camera unconsciously. The camera can track a person but it can also zoom in to focus on details.
  - Field size: This refers to the distance between the camera and the subject being filmed. You can show how a character is feeling by zooming in or using a close-up to see their facial expression.
- **Music/background sound.** The choice of music adds to the mood of a film.
- **The speaker or voice-over.** In documentaries there is usually a speaker, who influences the atmosphere by tone and choice of words.

FACT FILE

Low-angle shot The camera looks up at the subject from below.
Eye-level shot The camera is level with the subject.
High-angle shot The camera looks down at the subject from above.
Long shot The camera gives a view of the situation from a distance.
Tilting shot The camera stays still but moves up or down.
Zoom The camera is stationary but seems to approach (zoom in) or moves away (zoom out) from the subject.
Close-up The camera shows the subject close and in detail.
Fade-in/Fade-out the gradual appearance (fade-in) or disappearance (fade-out) of a subject at the beginning or end of a shot

1 Before viewing
The film sequence you are about to watch is from a documentary about a leading British boarding school called Stowe. Before you watch it, speculate how the film-maker might deal with the subject.

2 Viewing for the first time
You will watch the opening sequence of the documentary about Stowe without sound. Concentrate on the setting and the atmosphere created in the film. Note down the things you see and then write down what impression you get of the school.

 DVD 07

3 Viewing for the second time
  a Now watch the sequence a second time concentrating on the way the shots are presented. Look at the Fact File on the right and decide which ones the director uses. Then fill in the table below showing how the director achieves the effect he desires. Use the webcode to download the table.

 DVD 07

Download the table here:
Webcode star-36

Shot	What does the shot show?	What camerawork is involved?	What effect does the shot have?
Shot 1	lawns and a lake with neo-classical buildings in the distance	long shot, then zoom in; fade-out at end	gives an overview of the area showing how green and beautiful the surroundings are
Shot 2			

  b Exchange your results with a partner. Watch the scene again, and check your partner's findings. Rewrite your findings if necessary.
  c The way a series of shots is presented to you affects your attitude to the subject. Describe the effect the director is trying to achieve in this opening sequence.

TROUBLE SPOT
affect sth. (v) = etwas beeinflussen
effect (n) = (Aus-)Wirkung

4 Part A

 DVD 07

4 Viewing for the final time
Now watch sequence with sound. Concentrate on music and speech.
a Describe how the music contributes to the atmosphere.
b Listen carefully to what the speaker says and note down adjectives the speaker uses. Compare your results with a partner. Explain what they show about the director's attitude to his subject.

5 Evaluation
Now that you have examined the opening sequence in all its aspects, discuss how you think the director will deal with his subject – the boarding school Stowe. How does this compare with your answer in task **1**?

A4 VIEWING Life at an elite boarding school

Cara Dörenberg is a 16-year-old from Lower Saxony in Germany who has been at Stowe for a year now. This excerpt from the documentary shows us her life at Stowe.

— COMPREHENSION ◄

1 Before viewing
State what you think life at Stowe is like from what you have seen so far.

2 Viewing for the first time
Watch the sequence and list the topics dealt with.

 DVD 08

▶ S2: Viewing a film, p. 121

— ANALYSIS ◄

3 Examining how material is presented
The excerpt of this documentary can be divided into four main parts:
- inside Cara's room
- in front of the chapel and during the assembly
- the headmaster and inside the classroom
- lunch break at the cafeteria

In groups, concentrate on one of these parts and analyse how the director presents the material.

4 LANGUAGE AWARENESS Making something attractive
Describe how the video uses language to draw an attractive and convincing picture of the school.

— BEYOND THE TEXT ◄

5 Considering the advantages and disadvantages of a public school
a In groups of three, go to the website of Stowe School. Each of you checks out one of these three areas: Academic aspects, Life at Stowe and Admissions, and reports to the others in your group about your findings. Then report back to the class.
b Discuss whether you would like to be a student at Stowe.

In a foreign classroom

A5 LISTENING Hosting exchange students *Hillary Clinton*

Hillary Clinton was US Secretary of State (the equivalent of a Foreign Minister) from 2009 to 2013. She was responsible for relations between the USA and other countries. In this address she talks about hosting foreign exchange students.

► COMPREHENSION

1 Listening for gist
Listen to Clinton's statement and explain in one sentence what she says about hosting exchange students.

2 Listening for information
Listen to Clinton's statement and decide which of the following are correct (there may be more than one correct answer).
1 Young people from around the world travel to the USA in order to
   a learn about American life,
   b become eager exchange students who will look for work in the USA,
   c learn about life around the world,
   d get positive impressions of the USA.
2 The American host families who accommodate exchange students
   a often visit their host students in their own countries,
   b are helping to solve the problems of the world,
   c become richer as the State Department pays them,
   d help build connections across the world.
3 Exchange students return home
   a with better stereotypical views of Americans,
   b with a promise of future leadership in their countries,
   c with positive images of the USA,
   d with the core values of the USA.

3 Listening for detail
Listen again and list three benefits of student exchanges as given by Clinton.

4 LANGUAGE AWARENESS Relating to the audience
Find words and phrases that signify what kind of audience Clinton is addressing.

► BEYOND THE TEXT

5 WRITING Reacting to the speech YOU CHOOSE

a Design a (digital) flyer for Clinton's campaign. Use the webcode to find a webtool that will help you create your flyer.

OR

b CHALLENGE Write a text in which you discuss whether exchange students are also diplomats.

🎧 CD 21
engaged active, busy
share perspectives [pəˈspektɪvz] share ideas
enrich sth. improve the quality of sth., often by adding sth. to it
span *(v)* stretch from one point to another
ripple *(v)* move in very small waves
showcase sth. present sth.
dispel sth. [dɪˈspel] make sth. go away

► S1: Listening for information, p. 120

TROUBLE SPOT
engagiert = **committed, involved**
engaged = *verlobt, beschäftigt, (Telefonleitung) besetzt*

LANGUAGE AWARENESS
In order to be successful and convincing, **good speakers** always try to **relate to their audience** by adapting vocabulary, register and style, e.g. by referring to personal experience to introduce some emotion or by using humour.

► LA4: Influencing through language, p. 199

Find a webtool to help you create your flyer here:
 Webcode star-37

Part A

▶ S6: Reading and analysing non-fiction, p. 127

A6 FOCUS ON SKILLS READING

Effective reading usually comprises three steps:
1 *Before you even start reading, it is helpful to think about what you might expect from a text after reading its heading.*
2 *In the reading process, you use*
   a *skimming for global understanding;*
   b *scanning in order to find specific information.*
3 *If in-depth understanding is what you want, use close reading: Read the text several times and check unknown vocabulary.*

1 What the text is about
The text on the opposite page is titled 'The European Day of Languages'. Consider what the text could be about by deciding which of these statements might be discussed in the text.
1 The EU wants Europeans to speak one language, preferably English, in order to strengthen its role on the world stage.
2 The EU wants Europeans to learn more foreign languages in order to promote intercultural communication.
3 The EU wants to do more to promote languages which are dying out.

■ **TROUBLE SPOT**
The EU wants Europeans to learn/speak …
Not: ~~The EU wants that Europeans learn/speak …~~

2 Skimming and scanning
Explain whether the following questions require scanning or skimming to be answered. Then answer the questions.
1 What happened in Osijek, Croatia?
2 What is the European Day of Languages?
3 What percentage of the world population speak English as their first language?

▶ S4: Skimming and scanning, p. 123

3 The intention of the text
Read the text closely to discover its intention. Then state what text type it belongs to. Collect phrases from the text that support your view.

▶ S5: Identifying text types, p. 124

Logo of the European Day of Languages

96   Chapter 4   Going Places

In a foreign classroom

The European Day of Languages

The European Day of Languages is celebrated annually on 26 September and was founded by the Council of Europe and the European Union. The day serves to recognise the rich diversity of
5 language in the world, encourage monolinguists to take up a foreign language, and celebrate those who have a proficient knowledge of two or more languages. The open and jubilant nature of this day also seeks to challenge the fearful
10 discomfort many experience towards language learning and highlight its social and practical value.

'But everyone speaks English'
On the contrary, only 6% of people in the world speak English as their first language.
15 Moreover, the rapidly globalising world and the financial crisis means that employers are looking for candidates with an edge – a multilingual edge. Although slow, loud English might cut it for tourists ordering paella in Spain, the world of work requires the sophisticated and adaptable individual who has clearly learnt to operate new systems of thought and perspective in learning an additional language. That resentful Spanish waiter who
20 has to listen to English barked at him also represents a wide cultural gulf which can only be narrowed by both sides endeavouring to understand the other. And this begins with language – it is a concrete sign of compassion and commitment to another country and encourages a cycle of cooperation. The celebratory atmosphere of the European Day of Languages therefore embodies the sense of unity that a multilingual world would bring.

25 *What are you capable of?*
In restricting yourself to your mother-tongue, a huge amount of potential might be going to waste. In a world where we are constantly stretching the human mind to its limits with science and technology […], acquiring additional languages is a significant boost for brain power. The process of learning a language makes it easier to learn another – and in switch-
30 ing between two or more languages, scientist Yudhijit Bhattacharjee claims 'it forces the brain to resolve internal conflict, giving the mind a workout that strengthens its cognitive muscles.' In this way, the European Day of Languages also recognises the extraordinary capacity of the linguistic mind. The biological ability to be multilingual might then suggest how vital international relations really are.

35 *How can you get involved?*
EDL is open to everyone. Pupils in a Croatian school in Osijek simply wrote 'I love you!' and 'Thank you!' on posters in several languages. Many have taken the opportunity to invest in a foreign dictionary and start a language from scratch, whereas others have invited a bilingual neighbour over for tea to learn some choice phrases. In the spirit of our
40 multicultural world, perhaps you could organise a class in your school in which bilingual students could lead a taster session, each introducing their language. The choice is yours!

From: www.ukgermanconnection.org

---

4 **diversity** [daɪˈvɜːsəti] *Vielfalt*
5 **monolinguist** [ˌmɒnəˈlɪŋgwɪst] person who only speaks one language
7 **proficient** [prəˈfɪʃnt] advanced
8 **jubilant** [ˈdʒuːbɪlənt] feeling or showing great happiness
10 **discomfort** [dɪsˈkʌmfət] feeling of uneasiness
11 **highlight sth.** *(here)* underline sth.
16 **edge** *(here)* advantage
17 **cut it for sb.** be ok for sb.
sophisticated [səˈfɪstəkeɪtɪd] understanding complex things
19 **resentful** angry
20 **gulf** *Kluft*
21 **endeavour** [ɪnˈdevə] try
22 **compassion** [kəmˈpæʃn] *(here)* deep interest
24 **embody sth.** represent sth.
28 **acquire sth.** [əˈkwaɪə] *(here)* learn sth.
38 **start sth. from scratch** start sth. from the very beginning
41 **taster session** introductory first session

4 Getting involved in a project
Outline some suggestions for how your class could take part in this event.

4 Part A

A7 Why English is so hard

What things do you find particularly difficult about the English language? The following poem deals with one particular difficulty – the plural form. It was first published anonymously in 1896.

We'll begin with a box, and the plural is boxes,
But the plural of ox should be oxen, not oxes.
Then one fowl is a goose, but two are called geese,
Yet the plural of moose should never be meese,
5 You may find a lone mouse or a whole nest of mice,
But the plural of house is houses, not hice.

If the plural of man is always called men,
Why shouldn't the plural of pan be called pen?
If I speak of a foot and you show me your feet,
10 And I give you a boot would a pair be called beet?
If one is a tooth, and a whole set are teeth,
Why shouldn't the plural of booth be called beeth?

If the singular's this and the plural is these,
Should the plural of kiss ever be nicknamed keese?
15 Then one may be that and three would be those,
Yet hat in the plural would never be hose,
And the plural of cat is cats, not cose.

We speak of a brother, and also of brethren,
But though we say mother, we never say methren,
20 Then the masculine pronouns are he, his and him,
But imagine the feminine she, shis and shim,

So the English, I think you all will agree,
Is the queerest language you ever did see.

foot → feet

boot → boots

2 **ox** *Ochse*
3 **fowl** [faʊl] bird that is kept for its meat and eggs, e.g. a chicken
4 **moose** [muːs] *Elch*
12 **booth** [buːð, *AE:* buːθ] *(here)* small tent at a market where you can buy things
18 **brethren** *(old use)* brothers; members of a male religious group

— COMPREHENSION ◀

1 The use of nonsense words
List all the incorrect words like *oxes* (l. 2) in the poem, and write the correct form next to them.

— ANALYSIS ◀

2 The logic of the poem SUPPORT ▶ p. 119
Explain the •poem's line of argument.

3 LANGUAGE AWARENESS **The use of language devices**
Examine which devices the poem uses to put its line of argument across.

— BEYOND THE TEXT ◀

4 Dealing with the English language
a Discuss with a partner whether the poem deals with those trouble spots of English that are relevant to you. ▶ LANGUAGE HELP
b Then discuss with your partner what aspects of English you find easy.
c WRITING Write a new •stanza about some aspect of English. You may integrate your findings from **a** into your poem. SUPPORT ▶ p. 119

LANGUAGE HELP

- The thing that / What annoys me most about English is …
- … seems to be so illogical …
- I have great difficulty spelling …
- The pronunciation and the spelling of a word …
- My pet hate is …
- Some things are quite easy like …
- I can never remember if …

98 Chapter 4   Going Places

Part B: Work and life experience

Work and life experience

B1 VIEWING Summer camps

CCUSA is an international agency that recruits young people to work in summer camps throughout the USA. These young people supervise and look after the camp participants. The following video gives an overview of the camp life at CCUSA.

1 Before viewing
Look at the following stills and guess what activities are offered in these camps and what the camp life might be like.

A  B  C  D

COMPREHENSION

2 Viewing for the first time
  a First, you will watch the clip without sound. Note down what you can see about camp life and camp activities.
  b Compare your findings with a partner.
  c Now watch the video with sound and add as much information about the camp as you can.

DVD 09
▶ S2: Viewing a film, p. 121

3 CHALLENGE Viewing for detail
Watch the video again and write down how life in the camp is different for counsellors and support staff.

ANALYSIS

4 Analysing film techniques
The video wants to convince the viewer to apply for a job in one of the CCUSA camps.
  a Analyse the means the director uses to get the viewer's attention.
  b Discuss which elements you find successful, and which elements you would change.

▶ S2: Viewing a film, p. 121

BEYOND THE TEXT

5 Thinking about working in a camp   YOU CHOOSE

  a Imagine you want to work in a US summer camp. List activities you can offer or you are suitable for, and explain why you could offer them.
  OR
  b Together with a partner make a list of problems that may occur when working at a summer camp and rank the problems from big to small.

Going Places   Chapter 4   99

Part B

B2 Become a volunteer

After watching the video, you and a friend want to convince your parents that a volunteer programme could be a great opportunity for you. Therefore you go to the website of CCUSA (below left) and v•inspired (below right) to find the relevant information.

> **TROUBLE SPOT**
> British versus American spelling
> *counsellor* (BE) = (AE) *counselor*
> *traveller* (BE) = (AE) *traveler*
> *analyse* (BE) = (AE) *analyze*
> *centre* (BE) = (AE) *center*
> *colour* (BE) = (AE) *color*
> *defence* (BE) = (AE) *defense*
> *programme* (BE) = (AE) *program*

CAMP COUNSELORS USA

PROGRAM OVERVIEW

THE BEST SUMMER OF YOUR LIFE
For over 25 years, CCUSA has been placing international participants at the finest summer camps in the USA. Known as the 'Summer Camp Specialists', we take great care in placing every participant at the right camp. Summer camp work is demanding, but the rewards are endless. If you are looking for the adventure of a lifetime, consider becoming a CCUSA Camp Counselor participant.

YOUR ROLE AT CAMP
- Whether you choose to be a counselor or support staff, you will be an ambassador for your country.
- Camp staff are role models to campers and peers 24 hours a day.
- Camp days are filled with activity, requiring commitment and lots of positive energy.
- Successful candidates are outgoing and eager to share themselves.

THE AMERICAN CAMP
Every camp in America is unique; they vary depending on location, environment, activities, facilities and campers. All the camps CCUSA works with are carefully examined and match our high standards, as well as those of the American Camp Association (ACA).

WHY THE CCUSA CAMP COUNSELOR PROGRAM?
- We have over 25 years working with the finest camps in the US.
- Our commitment to place you at the right camp
- Safe, affordable program to immerse yourself in American culture
- Competitive pocket money, free meals and free accommodation
- Excellent experience for your résumé and international friendships to last a lifetime.

ARE YOU ELIGIBLE FOR THE PROGRAM?
- Enjoy working with and being around children.
- Are outgoing, cheerful, flexible, and reliable.
- Are prepared to work for at least nine weeks from May/June to August.
- Will be at least 18 years old by June 1st.

From: the website of ccusa.com

25 **eligible** [ˈelɪdʒəbl] able or allowed to do something because you have the right qualifications, etc.

▶ S21: Mediation of written and oral texts, p. 146

1 **MEDIATION** (English → German) **Answering your parents' questions**
Work with a partner.
  a Before you start reading, write down five questions in German your parents might ask you because they don't really understand the information on the websites.
  b Each of you reads one of the texts and makes notes for your answers in German.
  c Present your German answers to each other.

Work and life experience

4

Volunteer for the National Citizen Service and get yourself an adventure of a lifetime

What is NCS?

National Citizen Service (NCS) is a once-in-a-lifetime chance to challenge yourself, find new friends and make your mark on your community. You'll do outdoor adventure activities like rock climbing, canoeing and archery, develop skills like team building, writing and communication, as well as planning and running a project to benefit your community.

v•inspired and National Youth Agency are delighted to deliver NCS across the North East. We want young people to be empowered to improve both themselves and their communities.

So if you're 15 to 17 years-old, live or go to school or college in the North East, and want to do something worthwhile with your holidays, look no further!

When, where & how?

In the Summer, NCS programmes run from July – August, with regular departure dates. If you have other things on during the holidays – no problem! Just register and we'll get you in the next available spot to suit you and your family's plans. Otherwise, you could wait until the autumn programme – one unmissable week during October half term. Sign up now to be contacted by your nearest NCS delivery organisation.

What does it cost?

Thanks to government backing, the most you'll ever pay is £50, but this could be £10 or even free depending on your circumstances.

Why say yes?

You'll meet incredible people, learn new skills, discover more about yourself and help your community. You'll also get a v30 Award for your work on the community project which looks great on your CV and UCAS statement!

If you're thinking of signing up for autumn, do it now so you can unlock our Early Bird promo to get a free £10 Spotify voucher.

Still not sure? Check out what past NCS grads have to say:

> '... people come away saying it's one of the best experience they've ever had'
> – Claire, North East NCS graduate, 2016
>
> 'It's such an amazing experience, it honestly feels like it's changed my life. Just do it! You'll meet a great bunch of people, go on adventures and make a difference doing a community project which helps people where you live … and it's great for your CV or uni applications. I feel like things have turned around for me! It's like a family'
> – Beth, NCS graduate, 2015

Head to the NCS North East website to find out more.
So, are you ready to say yes to NCS? Sign up now!
From: the website of vinspired.com

---

4 **make your mark** become successful in a particular field
5 **archery** *Bogenschießen*
25 **CV** = curriculum vitae *Lebenslauf*
   UCAS = Universities and Colleges Admissions Service
28 **grad** *(ifml)* = graduate

BEYOND THE TEXT

2 SPEAKING Finding out more information
   a Choose the programme you like better and think of more questions you and your parents might have. Check www.ccusa.com or www.ncsnorth-east.co.uk/about-ncs/ and answer as many of your questions as you can.
   b Present your findings in a one-minute talk in English.

▶ S10: Giving a presentation, p. 130

B3 Nervous about being a camp counsellor?
Lucy Harper

On the internet there are blogs and websites about work in a summer camp. The website 'Secret Diary of a Camp Counselor' allows people to write posts about their experiences in a summer camp. This one is by an English girl who spent a summer working as a camp counsellor.

I was so nervous about being a camp counselor. My main worry was being away from home for so long. I'd never been away from home for more than a week before and although I came across like the independent too-cool-for-school type I'd never had the chance to put my supposed independence into practice.

It was one of my main reasons for wanting to be a camp counselor – I wanted to make sure I'd survive at uni. I'd got into Leeds Uni and that was the other side of the country to where I grew up so I wouldn't be able to just pop home to get my washing done like some of my friends. I also wanted to go to uni with some stories to tell. Absolutely nothing happens in the town where I live so I thought camp would also give me something to talk about. The other thing I was really worried about was getting on with my other camp counselors. Coming from a small town I'd only known the same people all my life. All my friends knew everything about me and accepted me for the way I was and vice versa. I couldn't imagine spending so much time with people I had never met.

- What if we didn't get on?
- What if they didn't like me?
- What if they didn't think I was funny like my friends did?!

If I couldn't make them laugh it was going to be a loooooooooooooong summer! I know my panic was not based on reason. I was going to meet a lot of people during my time at camp and it was pretty unlikely I wouldn't bond with all of them. I think it was more the fact it was going to be an intense environment without really having any face-to-face contact with my friends and family back home that was scaring me. I was so nervous about being a camp counselor I started to worry about all sorts of other things.

---

4 **put sth. into practice** try sth. out in real life
supposed vermutet, angeblich
7 **pop** (v; infml) go quickly
18 **reason** Vernunft
19 **pretty** (infml) very
unlikely unwahrscheinlich
21 **scare sb.** make sb. feel afraid

Work and life experience

- What if the children didn't like me?
- What if I got myself in trouble and got sent home?!

25 [...] I think that just about covers the main things I was nervous about so now let me tell you how it actually was ...

Firstly yes I did miss my family and friends, loads, but the more I got to know the campers I was working with the more it got easier. I was able to email everyone and it was nice to hear the news from back home. In the end though camp was such a little bubble that I
30 started to forget I hadn't checked in with them for over a week!

The other camp counselors were in exactly the same boat with making friends so we all just got on straight away, you don't have much choice. Obviously you find people you get on better with and that's great and also some of them had done camp before so were already in a little group but everyone was friendly. I loved the people I met and it was a
35 great way to prepare me for uni. [...] Similarly some of the children liked me more than others but I wouldn't say there were any that didn't like me at all! [...]

In my experience whatever is making you nervous about being a camp counselor it is probably something you won't care about when you actually start camp. Don't forget you can always ask things at your interview or try and find someone who has been to camp
40 to answer some questions, or just keep surfing this site!

From: the website of Secret Diary of a Camp Counselor, 6 August 2013

29 **bubble** good safe place far from the rest of the world
30 **check in with sb.** contact sb. to say you are ok
31 **be in the same boat** be in the same situation

COMPREHENSION

1 Summarizing
  a List the reasons why Lucy Harper wanted to work in a summer camp.
  b List the fears that Lucy had about working in a summer camp.

2 Understanding her experience
List what Lucy says about her experience working as a camp counsellor.

3 LANGUAGE AWARENESS Working with gerunds
  a In the first two sentences of the text there are two gerunds (-ing forms). Find them and explain why they are used.
  b Find two other gerunds in the text.
  c Write short sentences using gerunds after the following phrases:
    1 My brother is good at …
    2 I don't mind you …
    3 My main reason for …
    4 I had a lot of difficulty …
    5 My best friend really enjoys …

▶ L12: The gerund, p. 177
▶ LA3: Similarities and differences of languages, p. 198

BEYOND THE TEXT

4 WRITING A response
On the blog site there is room for comments below Lucy Harper's text. As you are thinking of applying to work at a camp, write a comment. It can either be a reaction to her text or a question. It should not be more than five sentences long. ▶ LANGUAGE HELP

LANGUAGE HELP
- What struck me was …
- I enjoyed reading this post because …
- What would you recommend me to …?
- How did you go about …?

Going Places   Chapter 4   103

Part B

B4 FOCUS ON LANGUAGE: Spelling and punctuation

When you write a text, it is important that you focus not only on words, style and grammar, but also on spelling and punctuation. This is especially the case in official documents like CVs and applications.

1 Spelling

a Some words seem to remain a mystery in terms of spelling – like *cemetery* ('Friedhof'), *rhythm*, *hear/here* or *bee* ('Biene').
What are your individual spelling weak spots? Make your personal top-three list of the words you always misspell.

b To come to grips with your personal weak spots, you might want to try the following memory tricks:
- Make a sentence in which easy words contain the difficult letters of your weak spot:
An *i*sland *is* land surrounded by water.
There is *a* rat in sep*a*rate.
- Make a sentence in which the first letters of the words inform you about the spelling of your weak spot:
*R*hythm *h*elps *y*our *t*wo *h*ips *m*ove.
- Make a rhyme about your weak spot:
You *hear* with your *ear*.
- Make a picture-word from your individual weak spot:

Use some of the above tricks for the three weak spots you listed in **a**.

c There are, however, some spelling rules that you should remember. Explain …
1 … why the plural of *story* is spelled *stories* but the plural of *toy* is spelled *toys*.
2 … why we have double consonants in *regretted* (but not in *visited*) and in *beginning* (but not in *opening*).
3 … why the final *e* is left out if we add *-ing* to *write*: *writing*.
4 … why the *y* is changed to *i* in *cried* but not in *played*.

2 Punctuation

a Look at the sentences below, and decide how punctuation (e.g. commas, hyphens) might change the meaning of the sentences.
1 I'm sorry I still love you.
2 Let's eat grandpa!
3 I love cooking my family and my pets.
4 You will be required to work twenty four hour shifts.

b Look at the sentences below and decide if they need punctuation, and if so, where.
1 I am waiting for the man who I work with.
2 My mother who teaches at my school is the main breadwinner in our family.
3 I think that he knows who the victim is.
4 From a very young age I knew what career I wanted to pursue.

▶ L17: Spelling, p. 184

'Just ignore the bad spelling. You'll get us all accused of discriminating against people with learning disabilities.'

■ LANGUAGE AWARENESS

English punctuation is quite similar to German punctuation. There are some areas, however, where German and English differ:
- In general, English tends to use fewer commas than German, so it might be useful to stick to the rule 'In case of doubt leave it out'.
- English only separates the main clause and the sub-clause by commas if the subclause comes first.
- English differentiates between defining and non-defining relative clauses, and non-defining relative clauses are not separated from the main clause by a comma.

But make sure to use commas properly to avoid misunderstandings, e.g. *I hate liars (,) like you.*

▶ LA3: Similarities and differences of languages, p. 198

▶ L11: Relative clauses, p. 177

Work and life experience

B5 FOCUS ON SKILLS WRITING (4)
Proofreading

▶ Focus on Skills: Writing, p. 25, p. 42, p. 74

Whenever you write a text, it is important to check the correctness and style of the English you have used and, where possible, to improve the text. This goes for all your work, whether it is an exam, an essay or an application letter.

- Keep a checklist of mistakes you have often made in the past. When reading your text, look for these specific mistakes. Typical mistakes for students include
  a) the *before abstract nouns,*
  b) *missing -s in the 3rd-person-singular present,*
  c) *using present perfect instead of the simple past,*
  d) *using the wrong 'verb + noun' collocation.*
- Do not just look for spelling and grammar mistakes but watch out for style too: make sure your sentences are connected by linking words to make the text flow better.

▶ L4: Present perfect and simple past, p. 169

▶ L15: Linking your sentences, p. 180

1 Proofreading an email
A friend of yours wants you to proofread his email application for volunteer work. Focus first on spelling, then on punctuation, and finally on grammar.

Download this text here:
Webcode star-38

Dear cordinator,

I read your job add and thats why i'm writing this email to you. In your add you say that you want that the applicant has experience to deal with kids. I have two younger sisters, so I am used to taking care of them. I like children
5 very much, and I realy enjoy doing outdoor activities with them!
My mother tongue is german, but I learn english in school since nine years. Moreover from 2009 untill 2010 I have studied one semester at an american high school, so that I almost have a natives' competence. However, I still do mistakes. I can not speak other foreign languages – but if you want me to I am
10 wiling to trie!
I am not a couch potatoe, because I prefer an activ livestyle. Last but by no means least, I am dedicated and hardworking.
Talking all these things into acount, I belief that I might be just the right person for the job, which you are advertising
15 Atached please find my CV.
I am looking forward to hearing from you – kind regards

'I read your college application essay. First of all, the word 'COLLEGE' has two 'L's.'

2 Improving style
Look at the email again and decide how best to improve the style so that it sounds attractive to the person reading it. You can rewrite it entirely if you think that is a solution.

▶ Focus on Style, pp. 180–183

▶ Vocabulary, p. 216

Chapter Task

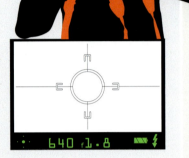

Find a video recording tool here:
Webcode star-39

Applying for a job at a summer camp

In this Chapter Task you will produce an application video in order to become a camp counsellor. Imagine they have asked you to make a 100-second video as part of your application in order to present yourself.

You have 100 seconds …
… to make an impression. The camp organization wants to know why you want to work at a summer camp and what would make you the perfect camp counsellor.
Here are some tips:

1 Plan what you are going to say
100 seconds is not long, so think about what is important to mention. Try to include ideas which you cannot get across in a written application. Make notes first and then plan your 100 seconds.

2 Be creative
Think carefully about where your video will be shot because the setting might also say something about you and your personality (e.g. at your sports training, in a park with your dog).

3 You don't need any special effects
Just film yourself with a camera or even your mobile phone. It would be a good idea to have a friend filming you.

4 Be enthusiastic
Be careful: Don't learn sentences by heart; this will make you seem less confident and natural.
Consider the character traits and features you want to show.
Try and have fun while shooting your video because this will make you look more confident and happy.

5 Get some feedback
Together with a partner, show each other your videos and give feedback. You might want to film it again afterwards to improve the impression you are trying to make.

6 Present your final videos in class
Decide which of you might have the best chance of getting the job.

Chapter Task

Self-Assessment

Look at the tables below. Evaluate how you did when working on the Chapter Task and the chapter itself by giving yourself a grade **A** *(very good),* **B** *(good),* **C** *(satisfactory) or* **D** *(poor). If you aren't completely satisfied with your performance, consult the pages listed under 'Revision and practice' below.*

Download a self-assessment sheet here: **Webcode** star-40

▶ S33: Assessing yourself and giving feedback, p. 160

Analysing a film VIEWING
Evaluate how you dealt with the film about the English boarding school Stowe (p. 94).

Criteria	Revision and practice
1 I found it easy to analyse the different shots in the documentary.	▶ S2: Viewing a film, p. 121 ▶ Workbook, p. 50, ex. 11
2 I appreciated how the music and voice-over contributed to the atmosphere of the film.	▶ S2: Viewing a film, p. 121
3 I understood what the director was able to achieve.	▶ S2: Viewing a film, p. 121

Understanding a text READING
Evaluate how you dealt with the text about the European Day of Languages (p. 97).

Criteria	Revision and practice
1 I used scanning and skimming correctly.	▶ S4: Skimming and scanning, p. 123 ▶ Workbook, p. 60, ex. 4
2 I understood what the intention of the text was.	▶ S5: Identifying text types, p. 124 ▶ S6: Reading and analysing non-fiction, p. 126 ▶ Workbook, pp. 58–59, ex. 3

Working on the Chapter Task
Evaluate how you did when working on your video.

Criteria	Revision and practice
1 I spoke clearly, fluently and freely.	▶ S10: Giving a presentation, p. 130 ▶ Workbook, p. 69, ex. 16
2 I used a lot of different words to present myself.	▶ L18: Using the exact word, p. 184 ▶ L20: One word in German – two in English, p. 185
3 I decided on a suitable setting.	▶ S2: Viewing a film, p. 121
4 I used some camerawork to get the viewer's attention or to underline what I said (e.g. through zooming or close-ups).	▶ S2: Viewing a film, p. 121 ▶ Workbook, p. 50, ex. 11

Working on the topics of this chapter
Evaluate your expertise on the topics in this chapter.

Criteria	Revision and practice
1 I wrote an application letter to work abroad.	▶ S16: Writing an application, p. 137 ▶ Focus on Skills: Proofreading, p. 105 ▶ Workbook, p. 76, ex. 23
2 I know about the pros and cons of spending time abroad.	▶ Texts, pp. 88, 97 ▶ Workbook, p. 46, ex. 3; pp. 47–48, ex. 7; p. 49, ex. 8–9

Focus on Literature 4

| NOVEL pp. 30–35 | SHORT STORY pp. 56–59 | POETRY pp. 80–85 | **DRAMA pp. 108–111** |

Drama

Reading or listening and watching?
- Look at the pictures and talk about your personal experiences of theatres and *plays, e.g. the *atmosphere in the theatre, the plays you watched, what you liked or disliked.
- Discuss the differences between getting to know a play by being in a theatre audience or by reading a *script. Explain which you prefer.

A From page to stage: Performing a script

Multiple Choice *Roger Hall*

Multiple Choice is a *play about a divorced mother who takes her son out of school and teaches him at home because she feels the school is holding him back rather than motivating him. In the following *extract from *Scene Seven, you will meet some of the main characters and see what else they have to deal with apart from the issue of homeschooling.

Read the extract, and try to visualize the situation in which these people are speaking. ▶ A CLOSER LOOK

> **TROUBLE SPOT**
> *play = Theaterstück
> *drama = das Drama als Genre

> **A CLOSER LOOK**
> The **performance** of a *play in the theatre is usually based on a *script written by a professional **writer** (called a *playwright) and is done by *actors and *actresses on a stage.
> So reading the text of a play always means **visualizing the scene** as it might appear on a stage.

(At home. MARGIE sorting out a heap of bills.)
MARGIE: Damn stupid bills – I can't work it out.
PAUL: Want me to help?
5 MARGIE: No. Thanks.
PAUL: Are we in debt¹?
MARGIE: Always. Oh God, how do people manage?
(PAUL looks through the bills.)
10 PAUL: Wow! Visa!
MARGIE: How else could we have got to Alaska? How else can we get to Mexico?
PAUL: Mexico!!
15 MARGIE: Unless you can think of someplace better.
PAUL: No. Wow!
MARGIE: Might have to go to the bank for Mexico. Again.
20 PAUL: How much do we owe altogether?
MARGIE: Oh, Paul, I don't know. The bank, the car, the credit cards. Do you think Visa would take American Express? 25
PAUL: But if we got another loan², it'd only increase the monthly payments. We'd be worse off than ever.
MARGIE: None of your childish logic here, 30 thank you. I don't know. Listen, sorry I mentioned Mexico – don't count on it, huh? (*She pushes bills aside.*) Let's forget this and wallow³ in Dickens. 35
(Door buzzer goes. PAUL answers.)
PAUL: Hello?
(Voice. We can't hear distinctly.)
PAUL: Oh, er, hi …
(Voice continues.) 40
PAUL: OK. (*Presses release button.*) It's Dad.
MARGIE: Your father?
PAUL: Yes.

¹ **be in debt** [det] verschuldet sein
² **loan** money that a bank lends
³ **wallow in sth.** in etwas schwelgen

Drama **LIT 4**

45 MARGIE:	*(panicking)* Jesus Christ, he's supposed to make an appointment for a visit. You shouldn't let him – ohhhh. *(She rushes towards bedroom, rushes back to sweep bills off table. Removes drink and ashtray, too. Just gets into bedroom as GORDON enters. He has a bunch of flowers and a package in hand. He and PAUL shake hands awkwardly.)*	PAUL:	*(embarrassed)* Thanks.
		GORDON:	I wasn't sure if you played or not.
		PAUL:	Soccer, sometimes.
		GORDON:	Oh. Score many points?
		PAUL:	Goals. No.
		GORDON:	Well, you'll have to come up home, take you to see the Patriots[4].
		PAUL:	Yeah.
			(Pause.)
		GORDON:	How's school?
GORDON:	You're growing up.	PAUL:	Er … it's, you know, much the same.
PAUL:	That's the idea.		
(GORDON hands him package, from its shape a football. PAUL unwraps it.)			

From: Roger Hall, *Multiple Choice*, 2012 (first published in 1985)

[4] **the Patriots** ['peɪtrɪəts] American football team

1 Looking at the *scene
a Describe who Margie, Paul and Gordon are, and how you know this.
b Decide which of the adjectives on the right best describes the *atmosphere in the scene, and explain your choice with evidence from the text.

depressing • excited • neutral relaxed • tense

2 Understanding the *action
a The parts of the *script in italics are called *stage directions*. Identify the stage directions in the *extract and point out what kind of information they give the *actors, and how they help a reader visualize the scene.
Draw up a table like this:

*line	stage direction	kind of information
1	At home. M. sorting out …	setting / action
…	…	…
45	panicking	emotion/actor must use suitable gestures, facial expression, voice
…	…	…

▶ S8: Reading, watching and analysing drama, p. 127
▶ RF4, p. 207

TROUBLE SPOT
*actor/actress = Darsteller/in, Schauspieler/in
*character ['kærəktə] = Romanfigur, literarische Figur

b Explain how – besides stage directions – the actors might know how to act on the basis of the dramatic *script, e.g. in ll. 10–35, ll. 57–74. Add a few stage directions of your own.

3 SPEAKING Staging a *scene
In pairs, choose a part of the scene and practise performing it – either the beginning before the door buzzer goes (1), or the second part, when Gordon speaks to Paul (2).
a Before *actors start rehearsing their roles, they try to find out as much as possible about their characters, e.g. their age, their looks, how they feel in a situation, their relations with each other. Discuss these aspects with your partner with regard to the characters you choose. Make notes.

LIT 4 Drama

b Make a list of things you can do to express dramatic meaning in your part, e.g. certain gestures, movements, positions on the stage, *tones of voice, etc.

c Act out your part. Switch roles with your partner to find out who can act out which role better. Then prepare to present your performance to the class.

4 Discussing *genres
In class, sum up and discuss what makes a *dramatic text different from that of a *novel, a *short story or a *poem.

5 Talking about *drama
You have come across quite a few terms to do with drama while dealing with the *extract from the *play Multiple Choice. Find the words that match the numbers in the following text. Use the webcode to download a copy of the text.

Find the gap text here:
Webcode star-41

> Plays are written mainly to be (1), not read. (2) and actresses play the parts of certain (3). Before going on (4) with their performance, they need to practise, or (5) their parts, individually and all together, and make sure they are able to dramatize the main (6).
> The (7) in the *script help them to know how the *playwright imagined the *scene.

B Understanding dramatic conflict

*The following *extract is the immediate continuation of the one above. Read it, always trying to 'see' and 'hear' what may be happening on stage.*

(MARGIE sweeps in, having groomed herself quickly, and manages a dignified entrance.)
MARGIE: Gordon.
GORDON: Listen, sorry to have called without checking first, but I was in town and I – here. (Hands her flowers.)
MARGIE: Thank you.
GORDON: I don't think I'd have recognized Paul.
MARGIE: Well, it's been a long time.
GORDON: (Controlling himself.) Yes. One of the reasons I called was to suggest Paul might like to come up to Boston for a weekend.
PAUL: Er …
GORDON: Whenever suits you. You don't have to decide now. But I thought while I was in town, perhaps we could go out for a meal. Or a movie. Just you and me.
MARGIE: (Correcting.) 'You and I'.
PAUL: Er … yes … er …
MARGIE: Perhaps your father and I could talk alone for a bit.
PAUL: Sure. Yes. (He goes through to room.)
(MARGIE waits until PAUL is out of earshot[2].)
MARGIE: You're supposed to make an appointment.
GORDON: Whenever I have, you've always managed to break it. This way, I thought at least I'd have a chance of seeing Paul.
(She tries to cool down.) […]
GORDON: How's he doing?
MARGIE: Great. He's a great kid.
GORDON: You still read to him?
MARGIE: Oh yes! Every night. Right now it's Nicholas Nickleby[3].
GORDON: Yeah? I saw it on TV. Some of it. You were always reading to him. Even on holiday; through Europe.
MARGIE: Well, it paid off[4]. He reads anything he can get his hands on now.
GORDON: I bet.

---

[1] **groom yourself** make yourself look neat
[2] **out of earshot** too far away to hear what is said
[3] **Nicholas Nickleby** *novel by Charles Dickens (1812-1870)
[4] **pay off** sich lohnen

110 Focus on Literature

Drama

LIT 4

	MARGIE:	That fool of a school complained he was reading too much! That's one of the reasons why I took him –	MARGIE:	I wasn't happy with the way things were going at school so I ... I took him out. I'm teaching him at home.
50	GORDON:	What?		
	MARGIE:	Nothing.	GORDON:	Oh my God.
	GORDON:	'Took him ...' Took him to what? To a psychologist?	MARGIE:	He wasn't learning any –
	MARGIE:	No, no, nothing like that.	GORDON:	What are you trying to do, ruin his life? I mean in the first place it's against the law, isn't it?
55	GORDON:	Margie, I'm entitled[5] to know.		
	(Pause, longish.)			

From: Roger Hall, *Multiple Choice*, 2012 (first published in 1985)

[5] **be entitled to sth.** have a right to sth.

1 Looking at the *scene
Make a list of the topics Margie and Gordon talk about and add a very brief summary of what they say about them.

2 Investigating why ▶ A CLOSER LOOK 1
a Analyse the *extract for signals of dramatic *conflict between Margie and Gordon, and add notes on the conflict to your list using a different coloured pen.
b Examine the development of *tension in the *dialogue and draw a line graph to illustrate it.

3 FREEZE-FRAME Visualizing the moment ▶ A CLOSER LOOK 2
a In pairs, decide on one important moment in the *dialogue that you consider suitable for a freeze-frame.
b 'Perform' your freeze-frame to another pair. Take turns and try to identify the exact moment chosen and say why it is important.

4 SPEAKING Performing a *scene
Imagine Paul enters the room at the precise moment his father learns of his mother's homeschooling arrangement. In small groups, make up a short sequel in which all three *characters argue about Margie´s decision. Rehearse your scene and perform it to the rest of the class. You can use the webcode to record your performances.

5 WRITING Beyond the text YOU CHOOSE

a 'There is no school equal to a decent home and no teacher equal to a virtuous[6] parent.'
Mahatma Gandhi (1869–1948)
Write a comment on homeschooling referring to Gandhi´s statement as well as the excerpts from *Multiple Choice*.

OR

b Imagine Paul used to go to your class and you heard that he is now being taught at home. Write a letter to his mother trying to convince her that Paul should come back to school.

▶ **A CLOSER LOOK 1**
Dramatic *conflict is an important *plot element, which fuels the *tension between *characters in a *play and influences their behaviour up to the *resolution of the conflict at the end of the play. It should not be confused with conflicts in real life.

▶ **A CLOSER LOOK 2**
A **freeze-frame** is the performance of one 'frozen' moment in a *play in which the *actors hold still in one position – neither speaking nor moving – which represents that particular moment.

Find a recording tool here:
Webcode star-42

▶ S17: Argumentative writing, p. 139

[6] **virtuous** [ˈvɜːtʃuəs] *tugendhaft*

Focus on Literature

Support and Partner Pages

> **LANGUAGE HELP**
> - column
> - stick figure
> - arrange sth.
> - bar chart
> - arrow
> - pull on a rope
> - put sth. in an upright position

Find the list of words here:
Webcode star-43

Chapter 1 — The Time of Your Life

A2 FOCUS ON SKILLS: Speaking   p. 16

4 Monologues – Partner B
  a Listen to your partner's talk. Keep track of the time (two minutes!).
  b In a monologue, describe the picture on the left to your partner. Tell him/her what you think it is trying to convey. Try and talk for at least two minutes.
  ▶ LANGUAGE HELP

A4 Teen loses a leg, not his dream   p. 19

5 Zach as a role model? – Support
The following questions might help you to collect ideas:
  - What special personality traits or characteristics should a role model have?
  - What makes Zach Hanf special?
  - Why could Zach be a role model for other teens, what could they learn from him? Consider other teens with disabilities and teens in general.
  - Or: why do you think that Zach isn't the right role model for other teens?

Use your answers to structure your text in paragraphs.
Now go back to the Check-up on p. 19.

A6 FOCUS ON LANGUAGE: Pronunciation   p. 21

3 Pronunciation practice – Partner B
  a Use the webcode to download a list of words. Your partner will read some words to you.
  b Mark the words you have heard, then compare lists. Where did your partner have difficulty pronouncing the words?
  c Now read the following words aloud (only once!), leaving a short pause after each word:
    plays – bag – myth – fried – batter – food – thumb – love – bad – peas.
    Your partner will tick the words they hear on a worksheet.
  d Then compare your list with your partner's results.

B4 Dare to be daring   p. 26

1 Mediation (German → English) – Support
  1 Before summarizing the text in English, it is important for you to understand the main points of the text. The following questions may help you. Note down your answers – in English!
    - Who is 'Generation Ratio'?
    - What is special about 'Generation Ratio'?
    - What role does fear play for this generation?
    - Why is security so important to them?
    - What does the author say about freedom? What relationship is there between freedom and age?

Support and Partner B

2. Be careful when using your bilingual dictionary. Many German words have more than one meaning in English. Carefully read all the translations and have a close look at the context before choosing the translation. One example: Which translation of *Sicherheit* is more appropriate in this context – *safety* or *security*? How do you know?
3. You won't find all the words in your dictionary (and in a test situation, you won't even be allowed to use one). So you will have to paraphrase, which means explaining a word in English. If for example you don't know the English equivalent of *Bücherfanatikerin*, consider how you would explain it in German, e.g. 'eine Frau, die viel und voller Begeisterung liest'. Then translate your explanation into English.

Now go back to task **2** on p. 26.

▶ S25: Using a dictionary, p. 151

▶ S23: Dealing with unknown words, p. 149

B5 Choices   p. 27

1 Understanding the speaker – Support
  1 Answer the following questions:
    - Why does the speaker want to cut down some of the young trees?
    - Why doesn't she cut down the first tree she comes to?
    - Why doesn't she cut down the other trees?
  2 Discuss your answers with someone who hasn't used the support option.
  3 Then complete the following text: The speaker wants a clear view of … from the window of her house. She wants to … because they are in the way, but when she discovers …, she decides …

Now go back to task **2** on p. 27.

2 Examining choices – Support
  a Explain the speaker's choices and their consequences by completing the chart on the right.

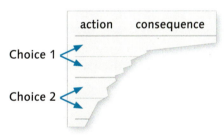

Now go back to task **3** on p. 27.

Chapter 2   Communicating in the Digital Age

A1 The connected generation   p. 40

2 Interpreting image and meaning – Support
Complete the following sentences about the cartoon:
  - In the first panel, the man is holding the woman by the arms and …
  - He seems to be very …
  - His mouth …
  - The woman looks very …
  - She is leaning …
  - In the second frame the woman is leaning …
  - The man checks … and reads that …
  - Now he looks …

Now go back to task **3** on p. 40.

Support and Partner B

A4 Conversation – a vanishing skill? p. 44

1 Looking for the main ideas – Support
  a 1 Begin by dividing the text into sections. Look for signal words that suggest a break in the argumentation *(but / on the other hand …)*.
     2 Find a headword that fits each of your sections. If you can't find one word that fits, try re-organizing your sections.
     3 Use each of the headwords you have chosen as the centre of a circle in your mind map. Surround them with the major points from each of the sections of the text.

Now go back to task **1b** on p. 44.

B1 Parental spies p. 47

▶ S13: The stages of writing, p. 135

4 Writing – Support
Before you begin writing, organize your ideas. An outline can be helpful:
  1 The Samanis' situation
  2 How they dealt with the situation
  3 Why it was easy for Mr Samani to protect his daughter
  4 How I feel about the Samanis' way of managing the situation
     a My reaction
     b Reasons (e.g. reference to Ms Barker's statement)
  5 Conclusion (e.g. recommendations for other families)

B2 Teenagers and their parents: two sides p. 47

1 Working with infographics – Partner B
Look at the table below showing the results of a survey published in 2017 about parents controlling their teenage children's online behaviour (1060 parents of 13- to 17-year olds living in the USA). Work on task **a**.
  a Match the percentages A–E to the statements 1–5.

A	61%	1	used parental controls for teen's online activities
B	60%	2	looked through teen's phone calls / messages
C	48%	3	checked which websites their teen visited
D	39%	4	used monitoring tools to track teen's location with his/her mobile phone
E	16%	5	checked their teen's social media profile

Support and Partner B

b Listen to what your partner tells you about what American teenagers experienced online. Then tell him/her what is true using the information from the infographic below:

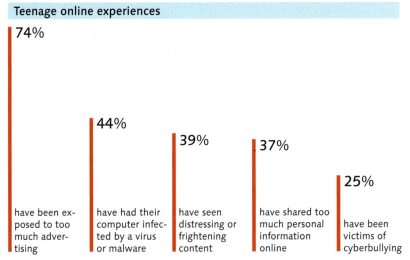

Teenage online experiences

- 74% have been exposed to too much advertising
- 44% have had their computer infected by a virus or malware
- 39% have seen distressing or frightening content
- 37% have shared too much personal information online
- 25% have been victims of cyberbullying

From: Brüggen et al., *Jugendmedienschutzindex*, 2017

c Tell your partner what you think is true in task **a**. Ask him/her for the right figures.

Now go back to task **2** on p. 48.

Chapter 3   Living in the Global Village

A3 The Fairphone – the world's first fair-trade smartphone   p. 67

3 Listening for detail – Support

b 1 Look at the task again and work out what information you are looking for. You are looking for ways the Fairphone project is trying to 'improve the current situation'. What does that mean exactly?

2 Here are some notes to help you. Before listening for a second time copy down the problems in the box on the left and then complete the notes by writing down the solutions while you listen.

The current situation – the <u>problem</u> with the production of smart phones	Improving the situation – Bas van Abel's <u>solution</u>
There is a dark side to the production of mobile phones.	Educating people …
Workers face poor working conditions.	Offering …
Minerals come from areas where there is war.	Looking …
Phone users do not understand how their phones work.	Making a phone which …

Now go back to task **4** on p. 67.

Support and Partner B

A5 A vision of the future in China   p.71

6 Creative writing – Support

    b Try to imagine the situation. All the workers' possessions are inside the closed factory, and the company owes them money. Consider what possible actions they might take: will they break into the factory or will they start to go away? What will happen next in either case?
Once you have decided how the crowd will react, look at the text again to check the narrative perspective: is it a first-person narrator ('I') or a third-person narrator ('he')? From whose perspective should it be narrated? Make sure your continuation of the story keeps to the same style.

B2 Junk raft completes voyage to Hawaii   p.73

1 Writing a summary – Support

In the text, there are seven main ideas you need to communicate in your summary. Choose the seven most important facts in the text from the list below.

- name of text, type of text, author, date and source
- main idea: junk raft trip across to Hawaii
- quote from Eriksen 'It's awesome!'
- the reason for the trip
- how the raft was made
- how (and what) they communicated
- where they docked in Hawaii
- the hardships they faced
- the speed they sailed at
- what they swapped with Roz Savage
- their plans for the future

Now go back to task **2** on p.73.

2 Examining quotes – Support

    b This text contains three quotes from Marcus Eriksen, all taken from different times.

      1 First find the three quotes and look at how the author got the quotation and when. Decide whether the quotations are used:
- to provide an eye-witness account of an event
- to convey someone's feelings in his or her own words
- to provide an expert's opinion about something
- to give a contrasting opinion
- to give the text a feeling of authenticity
- to pull the reader into the text

      Several of the above are possible. When choosing, write down why you have chosen the particular reason.

      2 Now write a general statement about the author's intention in writing the article. What is she trying to do? In your answer, don't repeat the quotes, but mention each one by giving line numbers, then state how each quote helps the author achieve her intention.

Now go back to task **3** on p.73.

Support and Partner B 3

B6 Whatever happened to the hole in the ozone layer? p.76

Partner B: Read the text below about ozone.

The hole in the ozone layer

Chlorofluorocarbon (CFC) is any member of an organic compound containing carbon, chlorine, and fluorine. CFCs were first created and manufactured in the 20th century. They were used in aerosol sprays (e.g. deodorants), refrigerators, air conditioning and fire extinguishers because of their special chemical properties. In the 1970s it was discovered that CFCs destroy ozone when they come into contact with it. The large-scale production of CFCs in large range of products led to a high concentration of CFCs in the atmosphere, which had a massive impact on the ozone layer, especially over Antarctica, where a hole started to appear every September.

1 Ask your partner for the following information about ozone:
- what it is
- where it is found
- what function it performs
- how it is measured

2 Answer your partner's questions about CFCs.

Now go back to the text on p. 76 and read it in order to find out what has happened to the ozone layer.

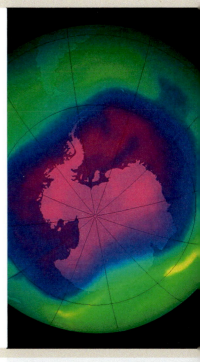

B7 How international cooperation reduced CFC production p.77

2 Comparing findings – Support

1 Before continuing with this support section, look carefully again at the operator word in task **2** on p. 77. The word *compare* is asking you to point out things which are the same – so look for similarities – and for things that are different – so look for differences.

2 In task **1** of **B6** (at the top of this page) you found out that CFCs were phased out by many countries working together over a period of 20 years. Check whether the notes you just made contain this idea.

3 Decide how to structure your answer. Start with a general statement to describe the text and the graph, and then describe how they are similar and how they are different. Below are some phrases to help you.
- The text and the graph both describe …
- The text mentions …
- The graph depicts …
- The graph supports the opinion in the text that …

Now go back to task **3** on p. 77.

▶ Verbs for Tasks, p. 224

4 Support and Partner B

Chapter 4 Going Places

Lead-in p. 86

1 Thinking about the benefits of language learning – Support

c A good questionnaire requires simple questions with short answers. The following formats could be useful if you are uncertain:
- Yes/no questions, e.g. 'Do you think there are student jobs for which you need English?'
- Either/or questions, e.g. 'Is it better to learn a) French or b) Spanish?'
- Single-choice questions, e.g. 'How important is language learning for you? A) very important B) important C) rather unimportant D) absolutely unimportant'

Now go back to task **d** on p. 86.

Find a webtool to create your questionnaire here:
 Webcode star-34

A2 Going to school in another country p. 91

Partner B:
The following is a text written by German exchange student Friederike, who spent a year at a school in Cheshire. Read the text, then work on task **1** on p. 119.

A foreign exchange student from Germany
Friederike v. Raumer

One of the first things I noticed after arriving in Britain was the accents, or rather, the fact that my accent did not match theirs. I had learned English with the help of American TV and had apparently started to sound American myself! But after a week the accent had gone and now people tell me I sound British.

My host family consisted of a mum and dad, two kids and a cat, and they live in a big house with a garden, which was quite different to anything I was used to as I had only ever lived in city flats.

One of my favourite things about Britain is pop culture. I love watching TV (or, as they call it, the „telly"), and it really helped me understand the culture. The family I stayed with likes watching stand-up comedy programmes, and there is no better way to learn a language than through comedy!

I loved getting to attend a secondary school in Knutsford in Cheshire. It was different to my school back in Germany in so many ways, but the most obvious difference was the dress code. Not only do students have to wear a school uniform, they are also not allowed to dye their hair or wear make-up or nail polish. It felt very weird to suddenly have to wear a uniform – I had never even tied a necktie before! At my school in Germany we are allowed to wear pretty much whatever we want, and one of my friends even had green hair for a while. When I told the British students about this they were absolutely shocked!

Another thing I really liked was the food. My friends had warned me about the notoriously bland and overcooked English food, but I found it to be quite the opposite! I got to try English classics like sticky toffee pudding, pies, curries, and Jammy Dodgers (a jam-filled biscuit), and all of them were delicious. My favourite was the sandwiches, of which the Brits eat more than 3.5 billion every year. One British stereotype I found to be true is that they drink a lot of tea. The kettle is always on, and

15 **weird** [wɪəd] strange
16 **necktie** Schlips
22 **sticky** klebrig

Support and Partner B

there is no problem that cannot be solved with a good cuppa – a tradition that I adopted right away.
Unpublished manuscript, 2018

27 **adopt sth.** make sth. (a custom etc.) your own

1 Comparing notes on exchange years – Support
 a Make notes about Friederike's experiences.
 b With the help of your notes, give an oral summary to your partner.
Now go back to task **2** on p. 92.

▶ S22: Making and taking notes, p. 148

4 Writing an email (p. 92) – Support
The typical structure of an emailed application includes the **five 'S's**:
- **S**alute: You greet the person you are writing to. Quite often, you do not know the person's name. In an email, it is then ok to write for example *Dear coordinator* or *Dear Sir or Madam*. Do not write *Hello* or *Hi*. The line after the salutation starts with a capital letter.
- **S**pecify: Say why you are writing and what you are applying for.
- **S**elf-presentation: In at least two paragraphs you explain what makes you a suitable candidate. You can describe past experiences, language skills and other relevant skills.
- **S**ummary: Wrap everything up in one summarizing sentence like *I, therefore, believe that I am the ideal candidate for …*
- **S**igning off: Finish your email with a sentence like *I look forward to hearing from you soon* and a phrase like *Yours faithfully / Yours sincerely / Sincerely yours* (AE). Do not forget to type your name.

Moreover, use long forms *(we do not)* instead of contractions *(we don't)*. Avoid exclamation marks and emoticons such as ☺.

A7 Why English is so hard   p. 98

2 The logic of the poem – Support
One of these sentences summarizes the idea behind the poem. Decide which one, and then support it with arguments.
 1 Rhyming nouns should use the same plural forms.
 2 There should only be one way of forming a plural.
 3 Plural pronouns are easier to form than plural nouns.
 4 The formation of English plurals is not always logical.
Now go back to task **3** on p. 98.

3 Dealing with the English language – Support
 c Use a structure like the one below:

We say __ if it is present tense.	[e.g. *take*]
But if it's past, it's __. You see?	[e.g. *took*]
So now __, in a past sense,	[e.g. *make*]
should then be __. Don't you agree?	[e.g. *mook*]

Skills File

Listening and viewing skills
S1 Listening for information 120
S2 Viewing a film **P** 121

Reading and text skills
S3 Marking up a text **P** 122
S4 Skimming and scanning **P** 123
S5 Identifying text types **P** 124
S6 Reading and analysing non-fiction 126
S7 Reading and analysing narrative prose 127
S8 Reading, watching and analysing drama 127
S9 Reading and analysing poetry 128

Speaking skills
S10 Giving a presentation 130
S11 Communicating in everyday situations **P** 132

S12 Having a discussion **P** 133

Writing skills
S13 The stages of writing 135
S14 Creative writing 136
S15 Writing a formal letter or email 136
S16 Writing an application **P** 137
S17 Argumentative writing 139
S18 Writing a review 141
S19 Writing a report **P** 143
S20 Writing a summary 144

Mediation skills
S21 Mediation of written and oral texts **P** 146

Study and language learning skills
S22 Making and taking notes **P** ... 148
S23 Dealing with unknown words . 149
S24 Learning new words **P** 149

S25 Using a dictionary **P** 151
S26 Using a grammar book **P** 152
S27 Working with visuals **P** 153
S28 Working with charts and graphs **P** 154
S29 Working with cartoons **P** 156
S30 Doing project work 157
S31 Using search engines **P** 158
S32 Learning languages with electronic devices 159
S33 Assessing yourself and giving feedback 160
S34 Finding and developing your individual language learning skills **P** 161

P A task allows you to practise the skill.

> *Download the suggested answers to the Skills File PRACTICE tasks here:*
> **Webcode** star-65

Listening and viewing skills

▶ S1 Listening for information

When you are listening to English, you may find yourself in a situation where you have to listen for specific details: you may be listening to an announcement at an airport or at a railway station, to the weather forecast, etc. At other times, you need to get the gist of something, e.g. when you are watching a *film or a *play in English and you want to roughly understand what is going on.

In everyday situations you can't usually listen to the same thing twice, so you need to be able to identify relevant information right away. Be aware of what you are listening for:
- If you want to find out what the general or main topic is, you are *listening for gist*.
- If you need some specific information, then you are *listening for detail*.

If you are listening for detail, ask yourself what exactly you need to understand, e.g. weather words like *sunny, dry, cloudy, chance of rain,* etc. or place names, numbers of platforms, times, etc. While listening, watch out for these keywords.

If you are listening for gist,
- don't worry if you do not understand every word;
- watch out for 'signpost expressions' that help you to follow somebody's (e.g. a public speaker's) train of thought, e.g. *on the one hand, … of course, the most important argument is …;*
- try to anticipate what will come next.

> **TIP**
> Often you can ask others who have listened to the same announcement, etc. for clarification.
> In a conversation, you can ask the other person to repeat or rephrase what they have said.

S2 • Listening and viewing skills

▶ S2 Viewing a film

Watching a *film can make you laugh, cry, feel angry or scared. Knowing some of the techniques used to achieve such responses will increase your understanding of how films work.

Films can, in part, be analysed in the same way as *fictional or non-fictional texts, because films usually tell a story or, in the case of documentaries, they present information.

Step 1: Before viewing, look at the information available (film poster, DVD cover, stills, TV magazine info, etc.) to find out what kind of film you are going to watch. Is it a documentary or a feature film, such as a thriller, drama, science-fiction film or a comedy?

Step 2: While viewing, try to keep track of the *plot. Take notes on how the *characters act and what the *setting is like or note down what information is presented.

Step 3: After viewing, write down what effect the film or a particular scene has had on you. Your spontaneous reaction will often help you to find out which elements of the film you want to pay special attention to when watching it again.

■ **LANGUAGE HELP**

- The film is about … / shows … / tells the story of …
- The music intensifies/fades as … / creates/builds tension/suspense/joy/…
- The actor's body language and facial expressions add to the feeling of …
- In this scene the music and lyrics / the props support the plot / underline the feeling of …
- The soundtrack/lighting/editing establishes/reinforces the mood of the scene.
- The camera movement creates a feeling of …
- The camerawork/soundtrack helps to … / underlines / emphasizes …
- The close-ups reveal his emotional state.
- The props in her room characterize her as a … person.

The effect a film has on its viewers is not just created by *what* is presented (plot, characters and setting, information), but also by *how* the story is told or the information is presented. Films achieve their effects through their specific camera work, their editing (i.e. the way the individual *scenes are joined) and their soundtrack (music and sounds). Here are some examples:

What you see		Possible effect
The camera seems to be looking through the eyes of the character or is looking directly over his or her shoulder. One character's face is shown in close-up, while the other characters are presented through long or medium shots.		▶ The character's emotions are revealed and you identify with that character.
A character is shown through a low-angle shot.		▶ The character appears bigger. He or she seems to be dominant, i.e. to have power over the other characters in this scene.
A character is shown through a high-angle shot.		▶ The character appears smaller. He or she seems to be inferior, i.e. to have less power than the other characters in this scene.

Reading and text skills • S3

Two or more characters are shown through eye-level shots. 	▶ The characters appear to be on the same level.
The scene is rather dark. People and objects cannot be clearly distinguished. The soundtrack is eery or moves towards a *climax.	▶ The viewer may feel tense or scared.
There are short shots and lots of cuts. *Flashbacks (showing past events) or flash-forwards (showing future events) are used.	▶ The *action is fast-paced and exciting.
The camera takes a steady position.	▶ The action appears slower.
The music is uplifting, pleasant or catchy.	▶ The viewer feels relaxed and in a good mood.

PRACTICE

Watch an excerpt from the film *The Truman Show* (1998). Afterwards, take notes and/or talk to a partner about the impression you get of Truman Burbank, the *protagonist, in this scene. Then analyse what techniques created this impression. ▶ DVD 10

Find a transcript of the excerpt here:
 **Webcode** star-45

Actor Jim Carrey as Truman Burbank in *The Truman Show*

Reading and text skills

▶ S3 Marking up a text

When working with photocopied texts or printouts, you can mark up important information so that you can find it more easily when you are working with the text again, e.g. when you are writing about it or preparing for a test.

Step 1: As you read the text, bear in mind what information you are looking for. You may want to read the task/question again.

Task:
a) Sum up the following text.
b) Analyse the *stylistic devices used in the text.

Time to **embrace** the e-book?

When electronic books first came onto the market, some thought it spelt the end for the printed page.
But following a flurry of headlines, and prophesies of doom

original expectations have not been met
choice of words: great excitement

S4 • Reading and text skills

Step 2: When you find the relevant information in your text, mark it by underlining, highlighting or circling the relevant words or passages. Only mark keywords.

> **TIP**
> 1. Use different colours for different tasks.
> 2. Also mark words which show that a different opinion or a contrast is being introduced to help you understand the logical structure of the text.

Step 3: Finally, add headings or keywords in the margin or summarize passages with short phrases or sentences.

from the publishing industry, the <mark>revolution</mark> in downloadable literature <mark>failed to materialise</mark>.
However, despite scepticism from some technology experts that the tactile satisfaction of the paper book has not been successfully replicated, it now seems that the <mark>e-book is starting to take off</mark>. […]
Two literary professionals put the e-book to the test over the last few weeks, with surprisingly positive results. 'You <mark>forget about the technology</mark> if the story is good,' says author Naomi Alderman.
'It just becomes invisible.' […]
While Hughes admits that 'there is a visceral quality that you miss with an old book,' it is the <mark>question of space</mark> that pleases her most.
'I find that <mark>my books breed overnight</mark>,' she says. 'I can control my environment now.
I'm not going to live in this ever-expanding library.'
What is <mark>slowing the take off</mark> of the e-book, says Alderman, is that the book has become a '<mark>celebrity object</mark>'.
'People are fetishising the paper <mark>book</mark>, they are <mark>fetishising</mark> literature,' she says.
But with over 25,000 classic books, whose copyright has run out, available for download from the website Project Gutenberg, Alderman is emphatic about the impact e-books will eventually have.
"They represent <mark>a democratisation of literature</mark> even more important than the public library,' she says.

From: *BBC Radio 4*, 7 August 2008

now: e-books getting more successful

people don't mind e-books

e-books take up less room
personification: books seem to be alive and to multiply

paper books are cherished (→ choice of words)

e-books make reading affordable for everyone

PRACTICE

Do tasks a) and b) (cf. p. 122). Write about 50 words for each task and decide whether the marked-up words/phrases were helpful or whether you would have marked different ones.

▶ S4 Skimming and scanning

Skimming *(reading for gist)* and scanning *(reading for specific information)* are both time-saving reading techniques, particularly when working with long texts.

SKIMMING
Suppose you are doing research on a certain subject. Your internet search has led you to several texts that could be relevant to your topic – but you are not sure yet. Reading each text closely in order to find out will take a lot of time …

Reading and text skills • S5

Step 1: Look at the following elements to get a general idea of what the text is about:
- headings and subheadings,
- pictures and captions,
- the first and last sentence of each paragraph (one of them is usually the 'topic sentence', which states the main idea of that paragraph),
- the last paragraph, which often contains a summary of the text.

Don't worry about unknown words.

Step 2: Summarize in your own words what the text is about. If you can do so without problems, your skimming was probably successful.

SCANNING

You are looking for specific information on a newspaper page, e.g. the price of a ticket, a certain figure or date, or somebody's name – and you are in a rush.

Step 1: Choose a few keywords or phrases related to the information you are looking for. When looking for ticket prices, for instance, they might be words or *symbols like *price, £, fee, ticket* or *reservation*.

Step 2: Look quickly at the page and search for your keywords. You can use your finger to guide your eyes. Only stop when you notice one of your keywords or a related word.

Step 3: Read the passage or paragraph containing your keywords more closely. If the information you need is not there, continue scanning.

PRACTICE

a Skim the text 'Junk raft completes voyage to Hawaii' (Chapter 3 'Living in the Global Village', Text **B2**, pp. 72/73). What is the main idea of the text?

b Scan the text and find out what they managed to achieve.

▶ S5 Identifying text types

In lessons and exams you will often be asked to analyse texts. Start by identifying the text type, then proceed to analysing the text systematically.

Basically there are two types of texts: *fictional texts (i. e. literary texts, *Dichtung*, ▶ S7–9) and *non-fictional texts (*Sachtexte*, ▶ S6). However, a text may also contain elements of several different text types.

Step 1: Skim the text or a section of it to get a general idea of its content. Sum up in one or two sentences what the text is about. Try to find out where and when the text was published.

The text talks about the real world, expresses the writer's personal opinions, criticizes something or tries to persuade its readers.	The text shows a world that was created in the mind of its *author. The *setting, the *characters and the events that happen in it may or may not seem realistic.
▶ **non-fictional text**	▶ **fictional text**

Skills File

S5 • Reading and text skills

Step 2: Examine the text more closely. Look at
- the content and the purpose: is the text meant to inform, persuade, entertain, …?
- the style or *tone of the text: is the language formal or informal, simple or complex?

Use the table below to identify the text type.

Non-fictional texts		Fictional texts	
Text type and examples	*Contents and purpose*	*Text type and examples*	*Contents and purpose*
Expository texts feature story, news story, summary, etc.	comprehensive and detailed information no personal opinion	***Poetry** ballad, sonnet, shape *poems, etc.	expresses an insight into some aspect of life, usually through the use of *rhyme, *rhythm and *imagery
Descriptive texts travel book, *biography, etc.	description of actual places, objects, events or people contains the writer's observations and impressions	***Drama** comedy, tragedy, etc.	creates a *plot through *dialogue and/or *monologues
Argumentative texts editorial, letter to the editor, review, *speech, etc.	discussion of problems and controversial ideas opinions, the pros and cons of an issue clear line of argument	***Narrative prose** *novel, *short story, etc.	tells a story from a certain perspective (narrative *point of view)
Persuasive texts *speech, advertisement, etc.	use of *stylistic devices to persuade or convince the reader		
Instructive texts manual, recipe, etc.	instructions to the reader use of imperatives and the passive voice		

PRACTICE

Using the information above and noting down characteristic features, identify these text types:
1. 'Teen loses leg, not his dream' (Chapter 2 'The Time of Your Life', Text **A4**, p. 18)
2. 'Greyhound Tragedy' (Chapter 2 'The Time of Your Life', Text **B2**, p. 22)
3. 'Dare to be daring' (Chapter 2 'The Time of Your Life', Text **B4**, p. 26)
4. 'Whatever happened to the hole in the ozone layer' (Chapter 3 'Living in the Global Village', Text **B6**, p. 76)
5. 'Memories from Reutlingen' (Chapter 4 'Going Places', Text **A2**, p. 91)

▶ S6 Reading and analysing non-fiction

Analysing a text is more than just saying what it is about. It means looking at how the content, structure and language interact in order to achieve a certain aim.

Step 1: Find out what type of text you are dealing with (▶ S5), what its purpose is and what aspect (or aspects) of the text you are expected to examine.

Attitude	What a writer thinks about a subject is often expressed by adjectives and intensifiers: something may be said to be '*completely* irrelevant', '*absolutely* brilliant', etc. The use of comparatives and superlatives has the same effect (e.g. 'easily the most convincing argument is …').
Argumentation	Discourse markers like *on the contrary, on top of that, additionally* or *in conclusion* can help you trace how the writer develops his or her argument. Rhetorical questions, colourful adjectives, emotional *images or *stylistic devices such as *repetition, *alliteration or enumeration can be used to convince or persuade the reader.
Stylistic devices	To make the most important information stick in the reader's mind, the writer may use techniques such as rhetorical questions or repetition. The writer can also point out specific aspects by using expressions like *one should not forget that …*
Mood	The writer may try to evoke feelings like fear, anger or sympathy in the reader.

Step 2: Decide whether the text achieves its purpose. Then write your analysis or make notes to prepare an oral report of your findings.

> **LANGUAGE HELP**
>
> - The text/paragraph deals with … / focuses on … / is aimed at … / tries to … / presents …
> - The mood/tone indicates … The repetition of … emphasizes/underlines/stresses …
> - The imagery has a … effect on the reader. The style of language suggests that … / explains precisely … / is used ironically. The arguments are supported by …
> - The writer is impartial/biased / draws the reader's attention to …
> - The writer succeeds in informing/persuading/convincing the reader by using …

'Think of an essay as a collection of tweets, only joined together.'

S7–S8 • Reading and text skills

▶ S7 Reading and analysing narrative prose

*When reading *narrative prose like *short stories and *novels it helps to remember the following:*

- Read long texts (e.g. novels) at a speed you are comfortable with. Don't worry about unknown words as long as the flow of your reading is not slowed down too much and you can still make sense of what you are reading. (▶ S23)
- With short texts (e.g. short stories), you should sometimes slow down and read between the lines. Usually, the shorter the story, the more you will find the meaning by looking very closely at the text. (▶ p. 59)
- Especially when reading a novel, keeping a reading log can help you keep track of what is happening. Make notes on the *plot and the *characters, or write down your reactions to what you have been reading. That way you will be able to participate in classroom discussions more easily.

When you analyse a short story, a novel or any other narrative text, you will have to pay attention to
- the *characters* (▶ p. 33),
- the *narrator and the *point-of-view (▶ p. 58),
- the *plot* and the *story* (▶ p. 59),
- the *setting
- and the *atmosphere.

▶ Focus on Literature: Narrative Prose – the Novel (pp. 30–35)
▶ Focus on Literature: Narrative Prose – the Short Story (pp. 56–59)

▶ S8 Reading, watching and analysing drama

*Plays are written to be performed. Therefore, when you read a play, you will enjoy it more if you imagine what it would look and sound like on a stage. If possible, say the *lines out loud and perhaps even find someone to act them out with.

Before *watching a play* in a theatre, familiarize yourself with the list of *characters (usually found at the beginning of the printed play or in the theatre programme) in advance. This will help you follow the play much more easily.

When you talk about and *analyse a play* in class, you will be looking at the following aspects:

- ***Monologues and *dialogues:** In a play, there is no *narrator. The audience has to construct the *plot from what the characters say (to each other or to themselves) and do.
- **Language:** The language in a play is often particularly expressive or dramatic, since it must inform about motives, plans or background, characterize the *characters, create *tension or *humour, etc.
- **Structure:** A play is traditionally divided into *acts which consist of one or more *scenes (referred to as 'Act 1, Scene 2', etc.). Sometimes there is a prologue that introduces the play and an epilogue that wraps up or comments on the *action at the end of the play.
- ***Stage directions:** In the written play the *playwright gives a few hints regarding how the *actors should speak the lines, or when they should enter or exit the stage.

> ■ TIP
>
> *play* = Theaterstück
> *drama = Drama (i.e. text form, e.g. *modern drama* or *Elizabethan drama* (i.e. the plays produced during the time when Queen Elizabeth I reigned)
> *playwright, dramatist* = Stückeschreiber/in, Dramatiker/in
> *character* = Figur
> *actor, actress* = Schauspieler/in

Find tools to support your reading projects here:
 Webcode star-46

Reading and text skills • S9

- **Actors and their acting:** The director and the actors bring the words and the stage directions to life. Since there are usually only few stage directions, there is room for creative interpretation.
- **Stage *props and lighting:** Props, i.e. the objects used on stage by the actors during the play, can take on *symbolic meanings. The way the stage is lit helps create a certain *atmosphere or mood.

▶ Focus on Literature: Drama (pp. 108–111)

▶ S9 Reading and analysing poetry

*Poems often use *images and formal elements to convey a message. Recognizing these aspects and analysing how they contribute to the overall effect and message of the poem will also help you appreciate it.

Here is a poem by the English poet Roger McGough (born 1937), followed by a step-by-step guide:

Poem for a dead poet
Roger McGough

He was a poet he was.
A proper poet.
He said things
that made you think
5 and said them nicely.
He saw things
that you or I
could never see
and saw them clearly.
10 He had a way with language.
Images flocked around
him like birds,
St Francis he was,
of the words. Words?
15 Why he could almost make 'em talk.

From: Roger McGough,
Holiday on Death Row, Jonathan Cape, 1979

Step 1: Read the poem two or three times (aloud, if possible) to get a feeling for it. Then try to summarize in one or two sentences what it is about and who is speaking to whom.

The poem by Roger McGough is about a dead poet. The speaker reflects on the powers of the unnamed poet to discover and express truths others could not see.

> Find tools to work with and create poetry here:
> **Webcode** star-47

Skills File

S9 • Reading and text skills

Step 2: Examine the structure of the poem:
- Does it have *stanzas ('Strophen')?
- Is there a *rhyme scheme – are there rhyming words within a *line (internal rhyme) or at the end of lines (end rhyme)?
- Does the succession of stressed and unstressed *syllables create a certain *rhythm?

The poem consists of 15 lines. There is no rhyme scheme. When you read the poem out loud you notice a certain rhythm is created by the repetition of words, e.g. in l. 1: 'He was a poet he was', or l. 14: 'of the words. Words?'. Alliteration like 'proper poet' (l. 2) adds to the rhythmic quality. …

Step 3: When reading the poem several times, certain words or lines may catch your attention because they seem particularly difficult, meaningful, or melodious. Look out for *stylistic devices such as
- complex or simple sentences,
- contrasts or *repetitions,
- a refrain,
- *imagery (*metaphors, *similes and *symbols),
- sound effects like *alliteration or *assonance.

The first two lines state that the dead person was a real ('proper') poet. Reasons are given in the next three stanzas. They show the same structure: first it is said which powers the poet had (ll. 3–4; ll. 6–8, l. 10), then this reason is elaborated on (ll. 5, 9, 11–12). A simile is employed in ll. 11–12 to express the poet's special powers. The speaker compares him to St Francis who is said to have talked to birds and other animals.
The diction is rather simple and colloquial, which is also shown by the phrase 'you or I' (l. 7).
In the very last line, however, the adverb 'almost' questions the effectiveness of his poems. …

Step 4: Having identified the relevant formal and stylistic elements, think about the effect they have on you.
- Do they possess symbolic meaning?
- How do they emphasize the overall message of the poem?

The poem expresses the idea that it is not enough to be good with words and deal with difficult issues. If people cannot understand the message and the imagery of the poem, the poet has accomplished nothing. …

When you are asked to write an analysis, use your notes and the language help below to produce a coherent text, keeping to the order of steps 1–4.

LANGUAGE HELP

- **Step 1:** The poem by … deals with / is about …
  In the poem … describes / reflects on …
  The poet speaks to / addresses the topic of …
  The title reminds the reader of … / refers to …
- **Step 2:** The poem is made up of … / consists of … lines / stanzas. The rhyme scheme is … / There is no consistent rhyme scheme. The word … rhymes with … The use of … creates a certain rhythm. Line … runs into line … which emphasizes …
- **Step 3:** The poet employs specific images, such as metaphors or similes, in order to …
  The diction/register is simple/colloquial/formal, which intensifies the feeling of … The most prominent stylistic device used in the poem is …, which serves to …
- **Step 4:** All in all, … The overall effect is …
  The poem aims at showing / illustrating / conveying / expressing the idea that …
  For me, the main/central message is …

▶ Focus on Literature: Poetry (pp. 80–85)

Speaking skills

▶ S10 Giving a presentation

Whether in school, at university or at work, presentation skills are extremely useful and important. For a presentation to be successful, it has to be carefully prepared and well delivered.

PLANNING YOUR PRESENTATION

Step 1: Find out about the general framework for your talk.
- How much time will you have?
- What kind of equipment (blackboard, flip chart, video projector, …) will be available to you?

Step 2: Research your subject and make notes (▶ S22) in English.
- Although you may be tempted to use German sources (texts, websites, …), you will have to turn them into English if you want to use them in your presentation, and this will take more time than using sources in English in the first place.

Step 3: Decide what kind of information you need and how you can structure it in a logical way. Leave out any irrelevant information.

Step 4: Think of ways to make your talk interesting and easy to understand for your audience.
- Visualize facts and figures by using charts, visuals, diagrams, etc.
- Add interesting details, funny aspects or examples to keep your audience's attention.

Step 5: Decide whether you want to give out a handout or support your presentation through electronic media, a poster, transparency or other means of presentation.
- Ask somebody to check your handout. Make sure that posters, transparencies, etc. can be read easily.
- Before the actual presentation, test any electronic media you are planning to use.

> ■ TIP
>
> When designing a poster or wall display, remember the following:
> - Make it visually attractive and informative.
> - Headings should be clear and legible.
> - Complex information should be visualized, e.g. through diagrams.
> - There should be a good balance between visuals and written information.
> - There should be some structure or line of thought that guides the reader through the various sections of the poster/display.

Step 6: If you are working in a team,
- decide who is going to present which parts,
- check that the different parts make one coherent presentation,
- make sure that everybody takes part in the presentation.

S10 • Speaking skills

PREPARING YOUR PRESENTATION

Step 7: Prepare your notes, e. g. on index cards.
- Check unknown words. Look up the pronunciation of new and difficult words in a dictionary (▶ S25).

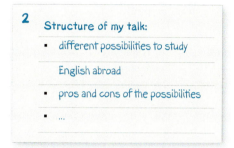

- Write down only keywords or short phrases, not complete sentences.
- Number the cards so that you don't get confused.

Step 8: Practise your presentation in front of friends or a mirror. (If you're doing a team presentation, practise as a team.)

GIVING YOUR PRESENTATION

Step 9: Get your listeners' attention.
- Refer to interesting, funny facts or tell anecdotes which lead to the topic of your presentation.
- Give an overview of your presentation and explain its topic and structure.

> **LANGUAGE HELP**
>
> Hello everybody. My talk today is going to be on … After that I will tell you more about …
> First I will give you a general idea of … At the end of the talk I will explain why … and give you some examples.

Step 10: Speak slowly and clearly and make sure you speak loudly enough.
- Try to speak freely and don't read out complete sentences.
- Stand in front of the audience and try to keep eye-contact with your classmates.
- Keep your presentation simple. Avoid extremely long sentences and using too many figures or new words. Remember that your audience can only listen to your presentation once.

Step 11: Round off your presentation by
- summarizing the most important facts/aspects,
- thanking your audience for their attention,
- asking them if they have any questions.

> **LANGUAGE HELP**
>
> So, as I have pointed out, … That was my/our presentation on …
> It is important to keep in mind that … Thank you for listening. I hope you enjoyed my/our presentation. Do you have any questions?
> Also …

Find tools to practise your speaking skills here:
 Webcode star-48

Speaking skills • S11

▶ S11 Communicating in everyday situations

Talking to people in everyday (and especially in intercultural) situations isn't always easy, as the following example shows.

You are staying with an Irish family. One day, when you come home from school, the mother of your host family asks you some questions.

Host mother:	Do you like your school at home?
You:	Yeah, sure!
Host mother:	Oh, that's nice. What are your favourite subjects?
You:	I don't know.
Host mother:	Oh, well … Maybe you will enjoy school here too. Have you already met some of your new teachers?
You:	No.
Host mother:	Er … Would anyone like some more bread?

This conversation isn't 'flowing' and the mother finally gives up. Following certain rules, however, will make things much easier and communication more successful. Compare the following conversation with the version above:

Host mother:	Do you like your school at home?
You:	Yes, it's okay. Of course I don't like all my teachers.
Host mother:	Oh, but that's natural. What are your favourite subjects?
You:	Sorry, what are 'subjects'? I don't know the word.
Host mother:	Oh, subjects … like English, Maths, Science …
You:	Oh – now I understand. My favourite subject is History. But I like Maths too.
Host mother:	I am sure you will enjoy school here too. Have you already met some of your new teachers?
You:	No, not yet. But I will meet some of them tomorrow, when classes start. …

The following steps will help you communicate easily and smoothly:

Step 1: Evaluate the communicative situation and decide what *register you should use. For instance, when talking to a teacher or head teacher you will probably want to use a more formal *style of language than when talking to other young people at a party.

> ■ **LANGUAGE HELP**
>
> **Formal:** Excuse me, do you know …
> Excuse me, can you tell me …
> Could you help me, please?
> Hello. Nice to meet you.
> Good morning. How do you do? (I'm) pleased to meet you.
>
> **Less formal:** Hi! I'm new here. My name is …
> Hi there. Is it okay if I sit here?
> This is a great concert, isn't it?
> Great day today, isn't it?

Step 2: Start the conversation in a friendly way. Start talking about something you have in common, e.g. the situation you are in together, etc.

Step 3: Keep the conversation going:
- Show that you are interested in talking to the other person.
- Avoid one-word answers – you might appear impolite or uninterested.
- Involve the other person in the conversation, e.g. ask him or her questions or add new aspects to the conversation.
- Avoid topics which might be too personal: religion, politics, illnesses, etc.
- If there is something you don't understand, don't be shy – ask questions.
- If you don't know certain words or phrases, use paraphrases or ask your partner for help. (▶ S23)

■ LANGUAGE HELP

Sorry, I didn't get that. Could you repeat that, please?
Did I get that correctly? Do you mean that …?

I don't know the correct word in English, but what I mean is …
What do you call …?

Step 4: Round off the conversation:
- Say goodbye in a friendly way.
- Say thank you if you were offered/given help.
- Refer to a future meeting if that has been planned.

■ LANGUAGE HELP

Formal: I hope to see you soon. It was nice talking to you. It has been a pleasure meeting you. Have a nice day. Thank you very much. Thank you for your help.

Less formal: Bye then. See you later. Until tomorrow.

PRACTICE

Find a partner. Imagine that you are meeting at a friend's party, but you don't know each other. Talk with your partner for five minutes.
Afterwards, give each other feedback: How comfortable did you both feel during your conversation? Were you bored? Were you interested in what your partner had to say? Did you both take an equal part in the conversation?

▶ S12 Having a discussion

In a (classroom) discussion you exchange ideas and opinions with others. Since you have to react to what the other participants in the discussion are saying, you should prepare for it so that you have useful words and phrases ready.

PREPARING THE DISCUSSION

Step 1: Prepare the topic of the discussion. Research aspects you are interested in and make notes. If it is a controversial topic, think about your own position or opinion and note down your reasons for thinking the way you do. In a role-play you may have to take a position which is not really your own.

Step 2: Organize and structure your notes. Make sure that you have the relevant facts ready during the discussion and do not have to look for them. (▶ S22)

Step 3: Think about your initial statement on the topic. This will ease your way into the discussion.

Speaking skills • S12

HAVING THE DISCUSSION

Step 4: State your point of view on the topic, e.g. give your prepared statement.

Step 5: Listen to what others have to say. When you answer or say something, make sure to refer back to their statements and arguments, for example showing which of their arguments do not convince you and why not.

■ LANGUAGE HELP

Stating your opinion	Agreeing	Disagreeing
• In my opinion/view … • As far as I'm concerned … • Well, I'd say … • It's a fact that … • The way I see it, … • Personally, I think … • If you ask me … • It seems to me that … • I think/feel/reckon/believe … • First of all … / To start with I'd like to point out that … • There can be no doubt that … • Nobody will deny that … • I'm absolutely convinced that …	• I quite agree. • I couldn't agree with you more. • That's true/right. / That's just it. • Quite!/Exactly!/Precisely! • Certainly!/Definitely! • You're quite right. • I agree entirely/completely. • I think so too. • That's just how I see it / feel about it. • You've got a good point there. • That's exactly how I see it. • Yes, indeed.	**Polite disagreement:** • I'm afraid I don't quite agree there. • I'm not so sure, really. • Do you really think so? • Well, that's one way of looking at it, but … • I'm not convinced that … • Well, I have my doubts about that. **Strong disagreement:** • I doubt that very much. • That doesn't convince me at all. • I don't agree with you at all. • I disagree entirely. • It's not as simple as that.

Step 6: At the end of the discussion, try to summarize your point of view or your main arguments.

PRACTICE

Think about the pros and cons of spending a term in an English-speaking country. Make notes, then find a partner and discuss the issue, using as many phrases as possible to state, agree with or contradict opinions.

▶ CC3: Expressing your opinion politely, p. 193

Writing skills

▶ S13 The stages of writing

If you make your writing concise and to the point, your readers will find it easier to follow your thoughts. You should carefully plan and draft your text and then revise what you have written. This takes some time, but your texts will greatly profit from it.

Planning stage
Allow enough time for this stage. Think about these questions:
- What topic are you going to write about?
- What precisely are you expected to do (describe/outline/analyse/…)?
- Who are you writing for?
- What text type is required? (▶ S5)
- What criteria apply to this kind of text?

You should
- do any necessary research on your topic (▶ S31),
- collect ideas and arguments concerning your topic,
- order or rank these ideas and arguments,
- write an *outline* (see the tip on the right).

Drafting stage
Now write the first version of your text:
- Add *topic sentences* and *linking words* to your outline.
- Start new paragraphs for new ideas.
- Elaborate on your ideas or provide suitable examples.
- Think of an *ending* for your text, then write an *introduction* that prepares the reader for that ending.

Revision stage
Finally, you or somebody else should take a critical look at your draft. Proofread it several times, each time focusing on a different aspect:
- Does the text read well, is it logical, coherent and complete?
- Check different aspects of your text: content, *style, grammar, vocabulary, idiomatic expressions, spelling and punctuation.
- Write a second draft of your text. Don't hesitate to change whole passages or rearrange the structure of your text if your analysis or your feedback advises you to.

> **TIP**
>
> In an outline, the most important ideas should be farthest to the left:
>
> *Title*
> I. *Main idea 1*
>   A. *Important fact*
>   1. *Supporting fact*
>   2. *Supporting fact*
>   a. *Example or detail*
>   b. *Example or detail*
>   B. *Important fact*
> II. *Main idea 2*
>
> All 'main ideas' are of equal importance, as are the 'important facts', etc.
> Use keywords when writing an outline.

LANGUAGE HELP

How can you avoid using the same words over and over again?
Look at your notes and underline keywords. Then collect other words with the same meaning.
Example: 'Could <u>smartphones</u> be a <u>valuable</u> <u>tool</u> for <u>learning</u> in <u>school</u>?'
Useful synonyms:
smartphones = modern cell phones, mobile phones
valuable = helpful, useful, respected, treasured
tool = instrument, device, gadget
learning = studying, education
school = places of learning, classrooms
Use your new words in the introduction, adding a thesis.

How can you present your arguments convincingly?
Use powerful verbs: *analyse, look at, examine, discuss, focus on*.
Examples: 'In this essay I will focus on three problems caused by smartphones.' 'This essay examines the effects of smartphones on young people in our society.'

Writing skills • S14–S15

▶ S14 Creative writing

Creative writing can be really fun. As a starting point and for inspiration, you can take an existing text, most often a literary text.

For instance, you may be asked to
- fill a gap in a story, add a *scene to a *play, continue or write an ending for a story,
- put yourself in somebody else's position and write from that person's perspective, e.g. take the *point-of-view of a literary *character and write that character's diary entry.

The better you understand the initial text or character, the more convincing and successful your own text will be. When continuing a given text, you should
- keep the *tone of the original text,
- stick to the original's *form* and *style,
- make sure your *plot fits that of the original,
- make the *characters* act and speak in a way that matches the way they act and speak in the original,
- show a good understanding of the cultural background, such as *setting and cultural phenomena.

When you have been asked to write a particular type of text (e.g. a diary entry, a formal letter, an *article for a school magazine), make sure you include the formal and stylistic elements typical of that type of text.

▶ S15 Writing a formal letter or email

When applying for a place at university, asking for information from a company or organization, etc., your mail or letter should follow certain formal rules.

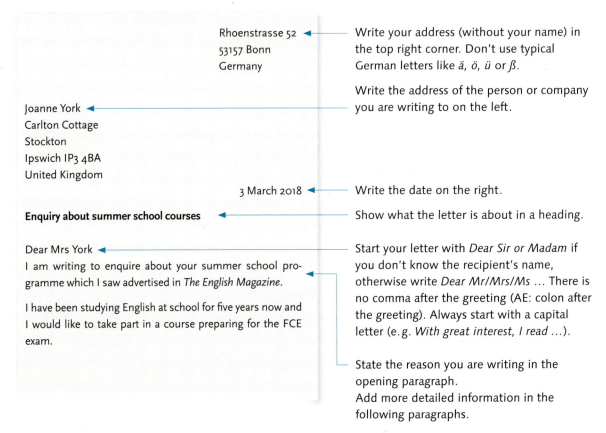

Could you please tell me if you offer any courses for that level this summer? It would be helpful to know about dates, application procedures and the cost of the course. In addition to that I would like to know if accommodation would be cared for by your school or if I would have to organize that myself. ◄──── Use long forms (*I am / We are / I would*) rather than short forms (*I'm / We're / I'd*) and abbreviations.

Any additional information about your school would be very welcome.

Thank you for your help. I look forward to hearing from you soon. ◄──── If you are asking for information or a favour, thank the recipient in advance.

Yours sincerely, ◄──── Finish your letter with *Yours faithfully* if you don't know the recipient's name, otherwise write *Yours sincerely* (AE: *Sincerely, Sincerely yours* or *Yours truly*).

Verena Stricker

Verena Stricker ◄──── Type your name at the end of the letter, leaving space for a handwritten signature.

When writing a **formal email**, it is not necessary to include the recipient's address or the date in the body of your email, as they appear automatically in the header.
- Open and close your mail the same way you would when writing a formal letter.
- Do not use emoticons, smileys, etc.
- Type your name and contact details at the bottom.

A **letter to the editor** follows most of the conventions of a formal letter or email. Note the following, however:
- Nowadays, letters to the editor are very often sent by email. Watch out for contact information on the magazine's or paper's website.
- Your letter should be brief.
- Start like this: *Sir or Madam* (i.e. leave out *Dear*).
- Omit the closing remarks (*Yours faithfully/sincerely*).
- Don't forget to give your name, address and phone number.

▶ S16 Writing an application

If you want to apply for a holiday job or a position in a company (e.g. an internship), you should send them a cover letter and a CV (curriculum vitae).

The cover letter
The cover letter for an application follows the rules of a formal letter (▶ S15). Since you are presenting yourself, it is important to avoid mistakes and to use formal language. State in what ways you are suited for the position you are applying for. Show that you have collected information about the company you are writing to and that you have a real interest in the position advertised. Mention what documents you are enclosing. At the end of the letter, express hope for a reply or an invitation to an interview.

Writing skills • S16

The CV (AE: résumé ['rezəmeɪ])

Your CV gives information about you, about your education, qualifications, etc. to the person you are applying to.

A CV should be clear and effective – remember the KISS rule ('Keep it short and simple'). Use a clear and easy-to-read font, highlight particularly relevant information, and don't forget to check your CV for spelling mistakes.

CURRICULUM VITAE
Lukas Meister

Rheinuferstrasse 2, 53158 Bonn, Germany
Telephone: +49(0)201 000 8177 Mobile: +49 178 000 4235
Email: Lukasmeister@mail.de

Personal statement
I have always enjoyed working with visual media, i.e. films, photographs, etc. and with computers. Being creative, I enjoy developing ideas to solve problems.
English is my favourite subject at school and I expect to improve my language skills further and to become a more independent person by spending time in the UK.

Education
2011–date	Secondary School: Alfred-Krupp-Schule, Essen
2007–2011	Primary/Elementary School Gartenstrasse, Essen

Qualifications/skills
IT skills	Excellent knowledge of MS Word, PowerPoint, Excel, web design, photoshop
Language skills	German native speaker; good written and spoken English, basic French
Technology	Winner of the gold medal 2013 for 'school inventors' in the 'Junior Ingenieur Akademie' (school engineering course)

Work experience
May 2017	Placement: two weeks at local IT company, organized by my school

Hobbies and interests
Member of school drama club, member of school computer club, basketball in after-school club. I enjoy listening to and playing music and making films.

References
Available on request

- Give your personal details: name, contact details, nationality, etc.
- Add a personal statement explaining why you are suitable for the specific place or job.
- Show the stages of your education so far (schools, exams, etc.).
- List your qualifications and present your key skills, especially those the employer is looking for.
- Give information on any work experience.
- Write something about your hobbies or interests.
- Note down that references are available on request.

S17 • Writing skills

PRACTICE

Read the job advert below. Then write an application, consisting of a cover letter and your curriculum vitae, for the position of film production assistant. (You may also make up a person applying for the job.)

> A position is available to assist in the production and processing of online videos explaining and demonstrating technical solutions to common problems around mobile phones. A rough outline of the video storyboards can be seen at fixphone.com. Hours are flexible.
>
> Candidates will need to have the creativity to generate simple but effective solutions to presenting ideas in audio-visual media. Good IT skills and a mature approach to working independently are essential.
>
> Contact: Peter Miller
> fixphone.com
> Easton Vale, Seven Acres Lane
> Nottingham
> NG1 5ZA
> Great Britain

▶ S17 Argumentative writing

When writing a comment or any other type of argumentative text, you have to structure your text clearly and argue in a logical manner in order to convince your readers.

PLANNING STAGE

Step 1: Read the task carefully. You are expected to react to a text you have read or to a statement or a thesis you have been given, for example:

'Now that e-books are on the market, the printed book won't survive.' Write a comment.

- I like the smell of books.
- How much do e-books cost?
- …

Brainstorm ideas about your topic and start making notes.

Step 2: Write down the arguments pro and con that come to mind.

Pro: The printed book will not survive.	Con: The printed book will survive.
1. E-book readers can store thousands of books. I don't need bookshelves, don't need to carry lots of books with me on holiday. …	1. Many people enjoy holding a real book made of paper in their hands and they like the smell of books.
2. An e-book reader can do everything the traditional book can, but it has lots of additional functions: you can save comments, look up words in a dictionary with one click, etc. E-books are a bit cheaper than …	2. You can borrow books from friends or give a book away as a present once you have read it.
	3. An e-book reader has to be charged from time to time.

139

Skills File

Writing skills • S17

Step 3: Arrange your arguments in a logical way, following either of these two patterns:

A Present the arguments for and against in separate paragraphs:	**B** Answer each argument immediately with its counter-argument:
1. Introduction	1. Introduction
2. Arguments pro	2. Argument 1 ▶ counter-argument 1
3. Arguments con	3. Argument 2 ▶ counter-argument 2
4. Conclusion	4. Argument 3 ▶ counter-argument 3
	5. Conclusion

Always plan to finish with the argument that supports your position most strongly, because this is the one the reader will remember most.

1. *My position: pro, i. e. the printed book will not survive.*
2. *Line of argument: structure B (argument → counter-argument)*
3. *Argument 1: Many people like traditional books. → Counter-argument 1: They will get used to e-books once they know more about them.*
4. *Argument 2: People say that normal books are cheaper since they can be borrowed from friends.*
   → Counter-argument 2: E-books are a bit cheaper than printed books and can also be exchanged with others for a limited time.
5. *Argument 3: Critics point out that e-books need electricity. → Counter-argument 3: But e-books have more to offer than traditional books.*

WRITING STAGE

Step 4: Write your introduction. Refer to the topic and state your point of view.

These days the e-book is becoming more and more popular. Several companies sell their own e-book readers and advertise them both on the internet and in shops. Many people fear that the traditional printed book will go out of fashion and that e-books mean the end of the printed book.

Step 5: Present your line of argument, following either structure A or B (see above). Use discourse organizers.

Many people claim that they like printed books because they enjoy touching paper and hearing the rustling of the pages. However, this preference for traditional books may be due to the fact that e-books have only been around for a relatively short time. Once people start using e-books they will …
When I first saw an e-book reader, I, too, thought that reading books on such a gadget would not be fun, but …
A frequently used argument against e-books is that they are more expensive – that you cannot borrow them from friends and read them for free. That may be true, but it's a fact that e-books are cheaper than printed books. This is because they don't have to be printed, packed, shipped or displayed in shops. And not only are e-books cheaper, they also help protect the environment, because their carbon footprint …

> **TIP**
> Your arguments will appear more convincing if you
> 1. quote authorities, experts or statistics,
> 2. refer to your personal experience whenever possible,
> 3. present facts: *It can't be denied that …, It's a fact that …, It goes without saying that …*

▪ LANGUAGE HELP

Use these expressions to make your comment more coherent and easier to read:
- **Contrasting:** *on the one hand – on the other hand / whereas … / however …, Contrary to what most people believe / to public opinion, … While / Although …*
- **Listing arguments:** *first of all, first(ly), second(ly), …*
- **Adding and elaborating:** *additionally, on top of that, furthermore*
- **Reasoning:** *That is why / because …, One reason for this is that …*
- **Concluding:** *To sum up, … – In conclusion, … – All in all, … – I would like to finish by pointing out again that …*

Skills File

Step 6: Write a conclusion. Sum up your arguments and round off your comment by restating your thesis, but do not give new information and do not use the same phrases that you used in the introduction.

Weighing up the pros and cons, it becomes clear that e-books can do everything that traditional, printed books can do. Gradually, people will get used to this technology and will lose their reservations. In the long run, printed books will not survive this process.

▶ S18 Writing a review

When writing a review of a book or a *film you give your reader information (*author/director, *plot, *characters, *actors, …), but you also express your opinion about the book or film in question.

PREPARING YOUR REVIEW

Step 1: Read the book or watch the film you want to write about. Make notes of anything that you find especially interesting, good or bad.

Step 2: Add to your notes by writing down important information about the book or the film, then structure your thoughts and ideas.
You can use a mind map or a grid like the one below, which is for a film review.

Header ('Kopfzeile')
  Title
  Running time
  Your rating
  Year
  Director
	'Juno'
	92 minutes
	***** (= excellent)
	2007
	Jason Reitman

Introduction
  Basic information/type of film
  Characters
	– teen comedy, but with a serious topic: teen pregnancy/abortion
	– Juno (aged 16), her boyfriend Paulie, childless couple Mark and Vanessa

Main part
  Plot (be careful – perhaps your readers don't want to be told the ending before they have read the book or watched the film themselves)
  Cast
	– 16-year-old Juno MacGuff (Ellen Page) gets pregnant by her friend Paulie Bleeker (Michael Cera)
	– doesn't want to have an abortion. Decides to have the baby adopted, finds childless couple Mark and Vanessa (Jason Bateman and Jennifer Garner)
	– …

Comments Your own opinion, e.g. on the plot, the actors, the *dialogue, special effects and the 'message'	– very funny (but insightful!) dialogues, witty script – Ellen Page plays Juno excellently – great soundtrack – film addresses a serious topic (abortion vs. adoption), even though the film is so funny – film stresses people's responsibility for their unborn children – …
Conclusion Summary of your opinion	– highly amusing teen comedy with characters you will like and a clever, witty script – funny and moving at the same time – highly recommended!

Writing skills • S18

WRITING YOUR REVIEW

Step 3: Put your ideas/thoughts into a coherent text.

Start with a *header*.	Film review: 'Juno' – a great teen-comedy on a serious topic 2007 – running time: 92 minutes – rating: ***** (excellent)
In the *introductory paragraph*, give some basic information.	The teen comedy 'Juno', directed by Jason Reitman, is a highly amusing film with a clever and witty script, a wonderful cast and a deeper meaning.
In the *main part* give a short summary of the plot first. Use the present tense. Avoid general words or expressions like *good* or *really bad*.	Ellen Page stars in her first main performance as 16-year-old Juno MacGuff, who becomes pregnant by her school mate Paulie Bleeker (Michael Cera). Since she doesn't want to have an abortion, Juno decides to have the baby adopted. She finds Mark and Vanessa (Jason Bateman and Jennifer Garner), a couple wishing to be parents. But as Juno gets to know Mark and Vanessa better, she starts to doubt that they would be the perfect family for her unborn child. At the same time, Juno's family and friends start to be more supportive concerning the baby. …
Then *comment* on the positive or negative aspects of the film/book.	The script, which was written by Diablo Cody, contains dialogues which are both clever and extremely funny. Due to the excellent script, the viewer is entertained and amused, even though the dialogues are deep throughout the film. Ellen Page does a great job as unconventional Juno, so that her performance is bound to stay in the viewers' minds long after they have left the cinema. The supporting cast are convincing too, especially Michael Cera as Bleeker. Director Jason Reitman uses a great soundtrack and has created colourful, vivid scenes. Probably the greatest aspect about the film is that it addresses the issue of teenage pregnancy and abortion in an appropriate way, without being moralizing. …
Finish your review by *summarizing* the main aspects and by giving a *recommendation* whether the film (the book) is worth watching (reading).	'Juno' is a great teen comedy that convinces not only through the characters but also through the many funny, yet moving moments. Highly recommended!

Find useful phrases for writing a film review here:
Webcode star-49

Skills File

S19 • Writing skills

▶ S19 Writing a report

A report gives factual information about an event in a formal and objective way so that readers can easily understand it.

Step 1: Gather as much information about the event as possible. Try to find answers to the '5 Ws': *Who? What? Where? When?* and *Why?* Sometimes, the question *What is the consequence?* should be answered as well.

Step 2: Order the information. Put the answers to the 5 Ws at the beginning. Add details later on.

Step 3: Make your report sound formal:
- Whenever possible, use the passive to report what happened.
- Avoid direct quotes.

> ■ **LANGUAGE HELP**
> XY is believed/thought to have been ... Police confirmed that ... It was reported that ... Many people were left without ... The missing person was last seen ... He was considered to have ... It could be established that ... An undisclosed source revealed that ... According to reliable sources ... An eye-witness stated that ... Bystanders claim that ...

Make your report sound objective:
- Avoid writing about your personal thoughts and feelings.
- Only include information that is unbiased and reliable. When quoting witnesses, focus on facts and leave out any offensive expressions.

Step 4: Write your report in the simple past. Use a new paragraph for each new aspect.

PRACTICE

Imagine you are a journalist writing a report on the Friederike winter storm, which hit Europe in January 2018. Write the report by following steps 1–4 above and using the language help given below.

> ■ **LANGUAGE HELP**
> hit Europe – (death toll) rise to x – cause travel delays – cancel long-distance train services – power cut – sustain injuries – blow roof tiles off buildings – debris – be blown to the other side of the road

Writing skills • S20

▶ S20 Writing a summary

When you work with written or spoken texts, you are often asked to summarize the text or certain aspects of it. To do this, you need a proper overview of the text, its content and its message. Then you have to decide what to include in your summary and what to leave out. The following steps and rules can guide you.

THE PLANNING STAGE

Step 1: Listen to or read the text carefully. Either make notes (▶ S22) or mark the most important words and phrases (▶ S3). Find out which text type you are dealing with (▶ S5).

Step 2: Listen to or read the text again and try to answer the '5 Ws' (Who? What? Where? When? Why? Perhaps also *What is the consequence?*). To get a better understanding of the text, you may also want to use the reading strategies explained in ▶ S7 and S9.

Step 3: Decide which passages of the text (marked orange in the example from Chapter 2, p. 40, below) contain essential information that needs to be part of your summary and which passages can be left out. Take your time to check which parts of the text contain examples, numbers, comparisons, quotes, *imagery, direct speech, etc. – these parts do *not* belong in a summary.

What?	**A2 The comeback of the written word** *Gideon Spanier*
What?	Texting, emails, tweets and other forms of text-based communications on a mobile device are now more popular than making phone calls or talking face to face.
Who?/Where?	The average Briton sends 50 mobile text messages a week, double the number four years ago, which will confound those who thought the SMS was a dying technology.
(comment)	Social media and email are also taking up more of our time – an average of 90 minutes a week (although that might seem impossibly low to some smartphone addicts).
What? (examples/numbers)	Among the 16- to 24-year-olds, 96% use some form of text-based communication each day to keep in touch with friends and family, 90% send texts and 73% use social media but only 67% make voice calls.
What? When?	Indeed, the overall amount of time that Britons spent making voice calls on both mobile and landlines fell for the first time last year, sliding 1%.
Who? (*repetition)	These are just some of the surprising findings from media regulator Ofcom's Communications Market Report, an authoritative annual guide that was published today. Watching video and playing games were meant to have taken over our life in the digital age but it turns out that words still matter. If anything, the power of text has increased, which should give hope to anyone who cares about reading – or believes in the future of journalism.
Why?	New technology lets us communicate in a pithy and highly effective way in real time, hence the popularity of the text message, the tweet and the live blog. At the same time, digital now allows us easy access to the biggest [collections] of documents and books [...]
What?	From: 'The joy of text – it's words that matter in mobile age', London Evening Standard, 18 July 2012

S20 • Writing skills

THE WRITING STAGE

Step 4: Write your summary in your own words.

1 Write an introductory phrase, mentioning the essential aspects, such as the title, *author, topic, main message and source of the text.

The text 'The comeback of the written word', written by Gideon Spanier and published in the 'London Evening Standard' on 18 July 2012, deals with the rise of text-based digital communication.

> ■ LANGUAGE HELP
> The story/text is about …
> The text deals with …
> In the text the reader gets to know …
> The topic of the text is …
> The article shows …

2 Use the present tense. Don't copy the original text – use your own words.

In his article, Spanier illustrates the continued importance of the written word in digital media and points out that text-based communication has become more common than talking to people on the phone or in real life.
Spanier quotes the Ofcom's Communications Market Report recently published in Britain, which shows that the majority of Britons use …
So although people had feared that the written word would go out of fashion …

3 Round off your text by restating the main message or *action.

All in all, the text focuses on … and points the reader's attention to the fact that …

Step 5: Check your summary. Does it contain the most important facts and ideas from the original text? Have you left out examples, unnecessary details, etc.? Have you checked the spelling, punctuation, tenses, etc.?

Mediation skills

▶ S21 Mediation of written and oral texts

Not everybody speaks and understands both German and English. So you may sometimes find yourself in a situation where you have to help people understand each other – where you have to mediate between speakers of German and English. How and what exactly you mediate depends on the context.

You and your English friend Steven, who speaks very little German, are planning to spend part of the summer holidays together, but you haven't decided yet on what to do and where to go. While you are still looking for ideas, you have come across an interesting website:

RAUS VON ZU HAUS –
WEGE INS AUSLAND FÜR JUNGE LEUTE
[…]

Was macht man bei einer internationalen Jugendbegegnung?
Bei einer internationalen Jugendbegegnung wird ein politisches, gesellschaftliches, geschichtliches oder religiöses Thema oder ein bestimmtes Projekt bearbeitet. Die Themenvielfalt ist riesig, z. B. Europa, Menschenrechte, Jugendkulturen, Mitbestimmung, Medien, Umwelt usw. Zumeist ist für
5   jede/n etwas dabei. Es gibt auch Jugendbegegnungen im kulturellen (Tanz, Theater, Film, Musik, Kunst), im sportlichen (z. B. Akrobatik) und sogar im Berufsbereich (z. B. Austausch zwischen Kochlehrlingen aus verschiedenen Ländern). […] Es gibt eine gemeinsame Arbeitssprache (z. B. Englisch), die ihr ansatzweise beherrschen solltet, oder es stehen euch Gruppendolmetscher/-innen zur Verfügung. Meistens übernachtet ihr gemeinsam in einer Gruppenunterkunft z. B. in Jugendher-
10 bergen, Jugendgästehäusern, auf einem Campingplatz usw. […]

Kosten und Anmeldung
Da internationale Jugendbegegnungen häufig vom Bund, der EU oder von den Jugendwerken (z. B. Deutsch-Französisches Jugendwerk) gefördert werden, müsst ihr zumeist nur einen geringen Teilnahmebeitrag zahlen. Die Anreise kann individuell oder in der Gruppe erfolgen. Z. T. sind die
15 Reisekosten im Teilnahmebeitrag inbegriffen.

From: www.rausvonzuhaus.de/Jugendbegegnungen

You send Steven the link to the website, who then asks you for more specific information: 'Do you know what we can do there? Will it all be in German? How much does it cost? Where will we sleep?'

S21 • Mediation skills

How to proceed	Example
Step 1: Analyse the communicative situation. Who are you talking or writing to? What text type are you expected to produce – an informal letter or email, an *article for a school magazine, …? Adapt your *style and *register.	- You are writing to a friend the same age as you. - Therefore you can use informal language. (If you were mediating to your head teacher, for instance, you might use more formal language.)
Step 2: - Will you speak or will you write? (Speaking allows you to use gestures and other non-verbal means of communication.) - What text type are you dealing with? (▶ S5) - What does the person you are mediating to need to know and why?	- Perhaps you will type the information while you are chatting online or you will send Steven an email. - The text is an informative text from a website advertising a programme for young people. - Steven has four distinct questions.
Step 3: Select the necessary information from the original text and communicate it in the target language. - What specific information is your communication partner looking for? Do they need any extra explanations on aspects they don't understand because they have a different cultural background? - What can you leave out? The mediated text will usually be considerably shorter than the original text because you do not need to explain every aspect of the original text. - What aspects (e.g. aspects that are culturally distinct) have to be explained in more detail? - How can you express the relevant information in the other language, e.g. by paraphrasing? (▶ S23)	*It's about a meeting of young people from many different (apparently mainly European) countries. Participants work on a topic related to politics, history or some other relevant field. There are also cultural and sports activities.* *The programme will probably be in English, but there will also be people who can translate.* *I can't find specific information on the cost, but the leaflet says that the programme is not very expensive, because it is partly paid for by the EU or other organizations.* *We would stay in youth hostels or sleep in tents.*

PRACTICE

Look for an official description of your school, e.g. on your school website. Based on this, write a short article for an English school magazine in which you portray your school for students interested in an exchange.

Study and language learning skills

Under this heading you will find many skills which you have been taught for several years, not only in English, but also in other subjects because they are of general importance like, for example, doing project work. Some of them, however, more or less exclusively refer to languages, like e.g. dealing with unknown words or learning new words.

In Sekundarstufe II, your task will be to advance these skills, to develop individual language learning strategies and to improve them. In order to do so, you might e.g. assess your products, become aware of your learning strategies, keep track of and avoid your pet mistakes.

▶ S22 Making and taking notes

When you are organizing information and putting your own thoughts on paper in short form, you make *notes* ('Notizen machen', 'Stichwörter notieren').

When you are listening (e.g. to a presentation) and write down keywords and ideas, you take *notes* ('mitschreiben', 'protokollieren').

Step 1: Watch out for keywords. They contain the information you need to get the gist of what you have read or heard and to answer a question.

Step 2: Write down the most important information only (as in the example on the right). Do not write complete sentences. Use abbreviations and *symbols, but always use the same ones so that you can understand your notes later. Mark any open questions.

Step 3: Go through your notes again and add to them if necessary.

> **Communication**
> - communication = transmitting information
> - means of comm.: writing, speech, forms of art, etc.
> - conventions: some behaviour is rude, i.e. speaking loudly in public; in conversations
> - silence = strange > small talk
> - these days: technological advances (??)

■ **TIP**

If you haven't set up your own system of abbreviations and symbols, you can use the following ones:

the same as	=	for example	*e.g.*
not the same as	≠	important	*impt.* or *!*
about the same as	≈	not	*x* or *ô*
and	+	with	*w.* or *w/*
and so on, et cetera	*etc.*	without	*w/o*
becomes / will be	–>	open question	*??*
between	*b/w*		

PRACTICE

You have to deliver a one-minute speech on the topic of communication. Check whether you find the notes given above sufficient. If not, add to them. Then give the speech.

S23–S24 • Study and language learning skills

▶ S23 Dealing with unknown words

When you hear or read a word you don't know, there are ways of finding out what it means. Equally, when you need to get your message across in speaking or writing and don't know a particular word, there are ways around that problem.

Reading and listening
- Use the context, the title or headings, subtitles or pictures to work out the meaning of the word.
  transmit = send
- If you know part of the word, you may be able to infer the meaning of the word.
  non-verbal = opposite of 'verbal'
  knowledge (from 'to know'): things someone knows
- Watch out for similarities between the unknown word and other words you know.
  facial: from 'face'
  gestures ≈ German 'Gesten'
- Beware of 'false friends'!
  acts = German 'Handlungen' (not 'Akten')

When you communicate, you exchange (i. e. transmit and receive) verbal or non-verbal information. Thoughts or messages can be conveyed through speech, visuals, written interaction or people's behaviour, i. e. facial expressions or gestures. Communication has been defined as acts in which information about people's wishes, attitudes, perceptions, knowledge or affective states are passed on.

> **TIP**
> When reading or listening to a text, you do not have to understand every single word.

Speaking and writing
When you cannot think of a particular word in a conversation or when writing a text, you can get the meaning across by paraphrasing:
- Use *synonyms (words with the same meaning as the unknown word) or antonyms (words which mean the opposite):
  It's the same as 'to send'. (→ to transmit) / It's the opposite of 'to send'. (→ to receive)
- Use a phrase or a relative clause to explain what the unknown word means/does/is used for.
  It's the movements people make with their hands. (→ gestures)

▶ S24 Learning new words

When learning a language, increasing your vocabulary is at least as important as mastering the grammar. You can extract new and useful words and phrases from any text you read.

Depending on the main topic, a text usually contains a number of words that belong to a specific word field. A good way of learning words in context is to make a network of all the words related to that word field.

> **TIP**
> Never learn new words as isolated items or German-English translations. Always connect new words to ones that you already know and use them repeatedly, otherwise you will forget them quickly.
> The more active you are when learning new words, the better. Reading and saying new words out loud is better than just reading them.

> **LANGUAGE LEARNING SKILLS**
> In the process of learning English you have been introduced to many different **ways of dealing with unknown words and learning new words**. Your task now is to find your individual way of dealing with this job:
> - Do you learn new vocabulary best by writing it down in a little booklet?
> - Do you prefer electronic devices?
> - Do mind maps work better for you than lists?
> - Are you able to ignore unknown words if you can still get the gist of a text without looking them up?
> - Can you use other foreign languages to explain unknown words?

Study and language learning skills • S24

Step 1: Skim the text and decide which topic or word field is particularly prominent. In the example text on the right, this could be *Teenagers and mobile phone use*. Underline all the words and expressions in the text that belong to this topic. On a separate piece of paper, start a mind map with the topic in the centre.

Step 2: Now add words and phrases to your mind map, both from the text and from memory. Think of
- *synonyms, e.g. cell phone (AE) = mobile phone (BE), access the internet = go online,
- antonyms, e.g. go online – go offline,
- collocations, e.g. (to) increase substantially,
- graphic symbols or drawings,
- examples (which you can add in brackets), e.g. mobile devices (cell phones, tablets),
- terms belonging to the same word family, e.g. wireless (Wi-fi),
- possibly German equivalents, e.g. connectivity = 'Netzwerkfähigkeit'.

Step 3: Practise your new words and phrases by saying them out loud and by writing them down. Prepare a one-minute *speech in which you use as many words and phrases from your mind map as possible.

Step 4: Revise your vocabulary from time to time, first at short intervals, then longer ones – first the next day, then again a few days after, then two weeks after that, etc.

Smartphone adoption among American teens has increased substantially and mobile access to the internet is pervasive. One in four teens are "cell-mostly" internet users, who say they mostly go online using their phone and not using some other device such as a desktop or laptop computer.

These are among the new findings from a nationally representative Pew Research Center survey of 802 youths aged 12–17 and their parents that explored technology use. Key findings include:
- 78% of teens now have a cell phone, and almost half (47%) of those own smartphones. That translates into 37% of all teens who have smartphones, up from just 23% in 2011.
- 23% of teens have a tablet computer, a level comparable to the general adult population.
- 95% of teens use the internet.
- 93% of teens have a computer or have access to one at home. Seven in ten (71%) teens with home computer access say the laptop or desktop they use most often is one they share with other family members.

"The nature of teens' internet use has transformed dramatically – from stationary connections tied to shared desktops in the home to always-on connections that move with them throughout the day," said Mary Madden, Senior Researcher for the Pew Research Center's Internet Project and co-author of the report. "In many ways, teens represent the leading edge of mobile connectivity, and the patterns of their technology use often signal future changes in the adult population."

Mobile access to the internet is common among American teens, and the cell phone has become an especially important access point for certain groups:
- 74% teens aged 12–17 say they access the internet on cell phones, tablets and other mobile devices at least occasionally.
- 25% of teens are "cell-mostly" internet users – far more than the 15% of adults who are cell-mostly. Among teen smartphone owners, half are cell-mostly.
- Older girls are especially likely to be cell-mostly internet users; 34% of teen girls aged 14–17 say that they mostly go online using their cell phone, compared with 24% of teen boys aged 14–17. This is notable since boys and girls are equally likely to be smartphone owners.
- Among older teen girls who are smartphone owners, 55% say they use the internet mostly from their phone.

From: www.pewinternet.org 2013

S25 • Study and language learning skills

PRACTICE

The example text on p. 150 (right column) also contains some expressions belonging to the word field *Doing a survey*. Do steps 2 and 3 and create a mind map for that word field. Add some words from memory.

Find more tools to practise new words here:
 Webcode star-50

▶ S25 Using a dictionary

Using a bilingual dictionary

Use a bilingual dictionary when you are looking for a translation.

For instance, you may want to write about the positive effects of globalization and need the English words for 'Handel' and 'handeln'. Look them up in the German-English section of your bilingual dictionary.

- The running heads at the top of each page help you find the right page quickly (top left-hand corner: first entry on page, top right-hand corner: last entry at bottom of page).
- 'Handel' and 'handeln' are the headwords.
- The numbers show that the headword may have different meanings.
- The notes in *italics* help you to find the particular meaning you are looking for.
- Examples and collocations are found below the headword.

In the English-German part of your bilingual dictionary you will find
- the pronunciation of every headword,
- irregular verb forms, the comparison of adjectives, etc.

In addition, there are infoboxes with more information on usage.

Handel
1 ≈ *Wirtschaftszweig* business / ˈbɪznəs/
2 ≈ *Kaufen und Verkaufen* • *allg* trade /treɪd/; *mit Waffen, Drogen* traffic /ˈtræfɪk/: *der Handel mit Luxuswaren* the **trade in** luxury goods
3 **im Handel sein** be* available

handeln
1 *mit Waren* deal* /diːl/: *Er handelt mit Gebrauchtwagen.* He **deals in** used cars.
2 ≈ *feilschen* haggle /ˈhægl/: *Ich habe mit ihm um den Preis gehandelt.* I **haggled** with him **over** the price.
3 ≈ *vorgehen* act /ækt/: *Wir müssen handeln, ehe es zu spät ist.* We must act before it is too late.
4 **von etwas handeln** be* about something

deadly /ˈdedli/ (**deadlier**, **deadliest**)
1 *allg* tödlich
2 *BE* • *umg* todlangweilig

deal /diːl/ *Verb* (**dealt**, **dealt** /delt/)
1 (*playing cards*) geben, austeilen (*Spielkarten*)
2 *mit Drogen* dealen
▶ **deal in** /ˈdiːl ɪn/ WIRTSCHAFT handeln mit
▶ **deal with** /ˈdiːl wɪð/
1 ≈ *erledigen* sich kümmern um; fertig werden mit
2 ≈ *zum Inhalt haben* handeln von

From: *Schulwörterbuch English G21,* Berlin: Cornelsen, 2011

■ TIP
Whether using a print or an online dictionary, make sure it gives you enough information on correct usage. You may want to check with another dictionary whether the word you have chosen is the right one in the given context. Many online dictionaries help you with the pronunciation of words by allowing you to listen to sound files.

■ TIP
Learner dictionaries usually have a reference section, e.g. notes on grammar and *style, samples of typical texts such as letters of application or CVs.

Using an English-English dictionary

Sometimes a monolingual dictionary can prove more helpful than a bilingual dictionary because it doesn't only give equivalents of words in another language, but also definitions and example sentences.

Study and language learning skills • S26

That way, an English-English dictionary helps you to improve your vocabulary. It also allows you to correct mistakes and to improve your grammar skills.

In order to choose the right meaning from those given, always read the whole entry.

The information on usage and style helps you to avoid using the wrong *register.

Looking at the examples of common collocations and idioms can help you avoid false friends.

Many dictionaries provide more specific information on typical error areas.

Information on grammar helps you avoid some grammar mistakes, e.g. countable vs. uncountable nouns. In order to check for grammar errors like tenses or word order, refer to a grammar book.

> **alien** /ˈeɪliən/ *adj., noun*
> *adj.* **1** ~ (to sb/sth) strange and frightening; different from what you are used to **SYN** hostile: *an alien environment* • *In a world that had suddenly become alien and dangerous, he was her only security.* **2** (*often disapproving*) from another country or society; foreign: *an alien culture* **3** (*disapproving*) not usual or acceptable: ~ **to sb/sth** *The idea is alien to our religion.* • *Cruelty was quite alien to him* **4** connected with creatures from another world: *alien beings from outer space*
> *noun* **1** [NAmE also ˌnon-ˈcitizen] [*law or technical*] a person who is not a citizen of the country in which they live or work: *an illegal alien* ⊃ compare RESIDENT ALIEN **2** a creature from another world: *aliens from outer space*
>
> From: *Oxford Advanced Learner's Dictionary*

PRACTICE

Use your bilingual or English-English dictionary to correct the mistakes:

1 Formal or informal? Correct the second part of the sentence:
   I'd really like to give you a hand, but I am presently occupied.
2 Beware of false friends!
   Because of her fantasy she can tell the most wonderful stories.
3 What does 'economic' mean?
   My new car is very economic.
4 Countable or uncountable?
   He gave me a lot of useful advices.

Find more online dictionaries here:
🖱 **Webcode** star-51

▶ S26 Using a grammar book

A grammar book is useful for correcting mistakes and improving your grammar. (Lexical errors such as wrong expressions, false collocations, etc. are best looked up in a dictionary ▶ S25.)

Step 1: Always analyse your tests or any homework marked by your teacher. Keep track of your mistakes and find out which areas of grammar are your weak spots.

Step 2: Find your problem area (e.g. 'word order', 'tenses') in the contents page of your grammar book or in the index pages at the back of the book.

Step 3: Study the relevant entry. Read both the rules and the examples.

Step 4: Use your grammar book actively:
- Create your own grammar cards and use them to revise your grammar points.
- Do some exercises on the topic.
- Look for examples of the grammar point in question in the texts you are working with. Say the rule out loud, perhaps using your grammar card.

> ■ **TIP**
> Many grammar books allow you to test yourself. On the basis of your results, they tell you which areas you need to work on and provide suitable exercises for your weak spots.

> ■ **TIP**
> When you create grammar cards, give them a clear layout which allows you to quickly take in the card. Examples, rules and problem areas should stick out so that you can easily memorize them. Use colours or other markers to highlight particularly relevant information.

S27 • Study and language learning skills

PRACTICE

In your latest test the following sentences have been marked as wrong. Say why – which aspects of grammar will you have to study more closely?
1 I met my brother <u>yesterday in town</u>.
2 At the moment everybody <u>talks</u> about Johnny Depp's latest movie.
3 There are so <u>much</u> people in town today.

▶ S27 Working with visuals

Visual material, e.g. photos, posters, drawings or sketches, can illustrate what is said in a text. They may also convey messages non-verbally, without the help of any text. Advertisements mostly use a picture together with a slogan or text to catch the viewer's attention. This is how you get the most information out of the material you are working with. Here, a poster is used as an example.

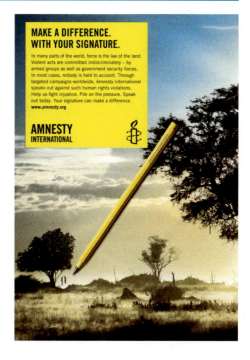

Step 1: Get a first impression: Read the heading or caption, then find out what the general topic is.
Check the source of the poster and, if possible, when and where it was published. Start making notes.
Notes
- *Heading: 'Make a difference. With your signature.'*
  = appeal to people to sign a petition
- *Source: Amnesty International*

■ LANGUAGE HELP
This poster (picture/photo/drawing/sketch) is about/shows/provides proof of/gives information on/introduces the topic of/conveys the impression that/…

Step 2: Describe the poster systematically, e.g. from foreground to background, from top to bottom, or begin with the dominant •image and describe it in detail. Make notes of the most important aspects.

■ LANGUAGE HELP
In the centre/foreground of the poster/photo/picture/… one can see … The poster shows a picture of … Underneath that, a … can be seen. In the drawing there are … The biggest part of the photo shows …

Yellow box with text in upper left corner:
- *Heading (imperatives) in capitals at the top*
- *Text with more details*
- *'Amnesty International' + logo (candle and barbed wire)*

Background photo:
- *Savannah (Africa?) with a few trees*
- *In the distance, two tiny figures can be seen hanging from a tree.*
- *Yellow pencil that appears to be lying on top of the photo*

Step 3: Analyse the poster. Look at the colours, the effect on the viewer, … Who is addressed and why? What may be the artist's/photographer's intention? Draw conclusions about what the poster is trying to do, whether it does so effectively and how it goes about it.

- *The yellow box draws attention to the explanatory text.*
- *The two imperatives look/sound insistent.*
- *The pencil is pointing at the two hanged figures, making it immediately clear what the petition is about.*
- *Amnesty International logo*
- *Contrast between the colours of the photograph and the yellow colour of the box and of the pencil*
- *Photo does not reveal its gruesome detail at first sight*

Step 4: Evaluate the poster by answering a concluding question: Does it achieve its aim?

- *Very effective – catches and holds viewer's attention.*
- *Clear appeal by two imperatives and picture of pencil*
- *Informative text*

PRACTICE

Describe and analyse the poster, following the steps outlined above. Write a short text.

LANGUAGE LEARNING SKILLS

Working with visuals (▶ S27), **charts and graphs** (▶ S28) and **cartoons** (▶ S29) are skills that you are familiar with, also from other subjects. What is special about them in English is that you need to use the English language to describe, analyse and interpret this material, and this implies using specific words and structures – 'I can see …' is not adequate anymore. So make sure to learn and practise the relevant vocabulary and structures.

▶ S28 Working with charts and graphs

Charts and graphs visualize complex information. There are different types of charts and graphs: pie charts, bar charts, line graphs or tables.

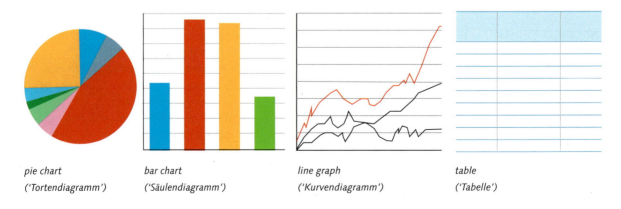

pie chart
('Tortendiagramm')

bar chart
('Säulendiagramm')

line graph
('Kurvendiagramm')

table
('Tabelle')

Suppose that in the course of your research you find the chart below.

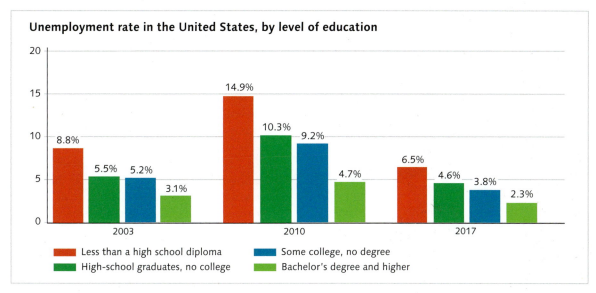

From: *statista.com*

Analyse the chart in three steps:

Step 1: Identify the type of chart or graph you are dealing with. Give the source.

- *bar chart*
- *source: statista.com*

Step 2: Describe the graph/chart: what is it about? What does it refer to? What information does it give?

- *unemployment rate broken down by education*
- *chart shows the different unemployment rates of people with different levels of education*

> **LANGUAGE HELP**
> The bar chart / pie chart / graph is about … / It deals with … / It is taken from …
> The pie chart compares the size / number of … / It shows the different … in … It is divided into … sections which show …
> The graph shows the relation between … and … … has the largest / second largest … / is twice / three times as big as … A huge majority / minority is … There are more than / nearly twice as many … as there are …

Step 3: Draw conclusions from the chart/graph.

- *chart shows that those who have a better education, i.e. those with a Bachelor's degree and higher, are less likely to be unemployed than those without a high-school diploma; the unemployment rate among people with less than a high school diploma peaked in …*

'This red line documents the change in this red line over a period of time.'

Study and language learning skills • S29

PRACTICE

Look at the chart below. Copy the text, filling the gaps in the text with words from the list at the bottom. You do not need all the words.

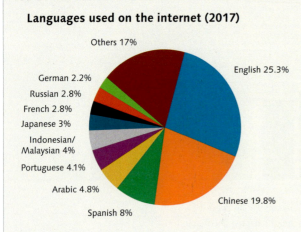

Languages used on the internet (2017)
- Others 17%
- English 25.3%
- German 2.2%
- Russian 2.8%
- French 2.8%
- Japanese 3%
- Indonesian/Malaysian 4%
- Portuguese 4.1%
- Arabic 4.8%
- Spanish 8%
- Chinese 19.8%

From: *statista.com*

The … chart shows the different internet users by language. The chart is … into eleven different …, each of which represents a different language group of internet users. It is obvious from the chart that users of English and … use the internet most – their slices added make up almost … of the internet users worldwide. The percentage of German internet users is 2.2 …, and there are about … as many speakers of Arabic who use the internet.

---
bar • per cent • pie • twice • three times
half • slices • divided • double • line • taken
Chinese • others

▶ S29 Working with cartoons

*Cartoons are humorous or satirical drawings that often deal with a topical event or issue. They usually do not state the point they are supposed to make directly. The following steps will help you to describe and analyse a cartoon systematically.

Step 1: Topic / First impression

Note down your first impression. What is the cartoon (which you can also see on p. 43) about?

Two people – a man and a woman – are sitting at a table.

> ■ **LANGUAGE HELP**
> This cartoon is about/shows/provides proof of/deals with …
> What is striking/captivating/… when first looking at the cartoon is the fact that …
> The most prominent feature is …

'I'm so glad you agreed to meet in person. There are some things that just can't be said in 140 characters.'

Step 2: Description

Describe the cartoon systematically. What people, events or trends does it refer to? Mention any labels, speech bubbles or captions.

The man and the woman are holding hands. They are looking into each other's eyes and are smiling happily, …

> ■ **LANGUAGE HELP**
> In the centre/foreground/background, at the top/bottom of …
> On the left/right of the cartoon …
> Underneath there is …
> The caption reads …

Skills File

S30 • Study and language learning skills

Step 3: Analysis

Analyse the cartoon. Does it have a caption? Are the *characters or the issues presented in a positive or negative light? How is this done? What point is the cartoonist trying to make?

The cartoon mildly criticizes the widespread use of modern media, i.e. mobile phones and social networking sites, in personal relationships. The cartoon conveys its message through humour and exaggeration.

LANGUAGE HELP

The cartoon may be meant to show … It is very eye-catching because of its use of … It speaks to the observer directly by …
The layout / use of colour / … is criticizing / making fun of …
The cartoon shows …
It conveys its message through … / brings its message across by …

Step 4: Evaluation

Say whether you think the cartoon is effective or not and give reasons, using your background knowledge about the cartoon's topic.

The cartoon addresses an important aspect of our digital age and its influence on personal relationships. I think it does this quite effectively. The exaggeration is amusing, but despite the humour, the criticism of …

PRACTICE

Describe and analyse the cartoon on p. 129.

▶ S30 Doing project work

A project is a complex task usually done by a team, involving several hours of work and often resulting in a written or oral product, e.g. a wall display or a presentation. Project work typically proceeds along the following stages.

Step 1: Agree on the topic of your project or look closely at the topic assigned to your group. When is your deadline? Decide what has to be done and who in your group will do what (e.g. do research on the internet or prepare a poster) and by when. How can everybody contribute to the project? What is each member of your group especially good at?

Step 2: Plan your work. What are your specific aims? Decide what kind of information you need and where you can find it. How do you want to present your results – in a display, a presentation, a web page, a class magazine? Agree on a schedule, including regular group meetings at which all group members give status reports and problems are discussed.

Step 3: Research your topic. Collect material on the internet, go to a library, conduct interviews, write to organizations, etc. Save time by skimming material (▶S4) and make notes (▶S22). Be selective.

Step 4: Once you have collected enough material, organize what you have found and start writing your text. Begin with a rough sketch of what the finished product (your presentation, wall display, class magazine, etc.) should look like. Did your teacher ask for anything specific?

TIP

When doing research,
- only use information found on reliable websites (▶S31),
- make sure the information collected allows you to look at the topic from all sides; do not limit yourself to one single point of view;
- make your own notes instead of copying and pasting.

Study and language learning skills • S31

Step 5: Check your written and visual material. Is it well organized and clear? Is the English correct? Give your text to somebody else in your group to check again. Then arrange your information and visual aids (a poster, a diagram, etc.).

Step 6: Practise your presentation and present your project. (▶S10)

Step 7: After your presentation, assess your work. With your group, discuss what went well and what you could do better next time. (▶S33)

> Find more tools to help you with your project here:
>  **Webcode** star-52

▶ S31 Using search engines

Searching the internet for information can be very frustrating, simply because there is so much out there that it is difficult to find exactly what you need. Here are some ways to make your research more effective.

How can you limit the number of hits so that you will find useful information more quickly?	• Brainstorm which keywords would most likely appear in the perfect article for your search quest. Combine them to get the most exact results. Typing in 5–7 keywords is better than just two or three. The more specific the word(s), the better the results. • Linking keywords with OR produces results with either keyword. • Putting a minus symbol in front of a keyword excludes all websites with that keyword from the results.
Once you have found a suitable website, how do you find your keyword(s) on that site?	Press the control key (*cmd*, *Strg* or *Ctrl* on your keyboard) + *F*. A small search window will open. Type in your keyword and press the enter key (return key).
How can you find the original source of a quote?	Enter the full quote or parts of it, using quotation marks. This way you will only find websites with that exact phrase.
How can you determine whether a website provides reliable information?	• Domain names ending with *.gov* or *.edu* indicate that the information is likely to be accurate. Sites of scientific institutions are usually also reliable. • Personal blogs or the homepages of interest groups are more likely to be biased. You should read them with caution. • Check for cross references: does the website quote other sources which support the information given? • Beware of commercial sites that require payment.
How can you use search engines to check whether a certain expression is proper English?	• Set the preferences (settings) on your search engine to English-language websites only. This will lower the risk of accessing sites written by non-native speakers of English. • Enter the phrase you want to check: if the number of results is only a few hundred hits, it is probably not correct English or at least it is not commonly used. If the number of results is high, though, the phrase seems typical and therefore acceptable.

PRACTICE

'Do smartphones have a negative effect on your health?' Use the internet to find arguments for a discussion. Which terms would you expect on a website with useful information? Try out different sets of keywords and compare the number of hits and the order in which the top entries are listed.

S32 • Study and language learning skills

▶ S32 Learning languages with electronic devices

You probably use various electronic devices and digital media in different spheres of life already – maybe even to improve your English. The following will give you some ideas on how to do so sensibly and on how to make the most of the digital media you use.

When using digital devices, you should always ask yourself whether they provide the special help and support you need. Don't expect them to do the trick and miraculously expand your language skills: learning a foreign language needs time and effort, whether it's done with or without electronic devices.

When using electronic devices to improve your language skills, you can make use of their benefits to different degrees:

LEVEL 1
You simply use an electronic device instead of using a printed text or writing things by hand. The device may be the medium at hand, which is comfortable to use and possibly also more fun, but there is no extra value in it.

LEVEL 2
You use an electronic device because it offers extra (support) functions, e.g.:
- You watch an American series online because it is not dubbed and you get a lot of language input through the original version.
- You use an electronic dictionary rather than a printed one because it is faster and you can also listen to the pronunciation.
- You rehearse your English presentation and record it digitally because then you can check it or get others to assess it.
- You type your homework out on your computer, not only because it's easier to read a printed text than your handwriting, but also because it can be revised much more comfortably. Plus, you can use the spell-check function.
- You learn your new vocab via an app. It keeps track of the words you want to learn and presents them to you again and again until you've memorized them – and there is no cheating!
- You revise grammar via an app that offers you special exercises for your individual weak spots.

It is only you who can make use of the extra functions an electronic device offers. If you decide to ignore the spell checker or the recommendations of your app, they cannot help you!

LEVEL 3
You use digital devices for a completely different working and learning process. For example, if you work on a project as a team and you cannot meet regularly, you can save it in the cloud and give each team member access to the documents. Thus, you can all work on your product at different times and in different places. You can use chat-functions to add remarks and ideas for improvement or you can revise your product in a correction circle.

Study and language learning skills • S33

▶ S33 Assessing yourself and giving feedback

Feedback from others helps you to find out about your strengths and weaknesses. In turn, giving others feedback also helps you to develop your self-assessment skills. In addition, you can learn alternative strategies by observing how your classmates deal with a task.

Evaluating your own work involves looking at what you know (i.e. what you have learnt), how you go about learning English (i.e. your study and language skills) and how you interact with others (i.e. your team skills). Here are some tips:

- Be honest with yourself. Don't pretend there is nothing to improve in order to avoid extra work.
- Think of ideal examples and compare yourself and your work with them. What would an 'ideal student' do?
- Test yourself, e.g. by preparing a one-minute talk on a particular subject.
- Set yourself clear and specific goals. Set yourself a deadline by which you want to have accomplished a certain goal.
- Always remember what you can do well and let that motivate you.

> **■ TIP**
> When checking for grammar or lexical errors, pay attention to aspects that are particularly relevant for the kind of text you are dealing with. For example, when giving feedback on a picture analysis, check whether the present progressive is used to say what the people in the cartoon or picture are doing.

When you assess the work of others, keep the following in mind:

- Refer to a feedback sheet or checklist, or write down what you would ideally expect to find in your partner's work, e.g. 'A good formal letter includes the following elements …'. Or simply ask your partner what he or she wants you to focus on.
- Read your partner's text or watch his or her presentation carefully, focusing on one or two aspects only, e.g. 'Is the writing interesting?', 'Does the text have a convincing structure?'. Using different colours, mark the elements in the text that have been written well and those which need improvement.
- Start with something encouraging. Be positive: point out the strong points in your partner's work, not just the mistakes.

> **■ LANGUAGE HELP**
> You did a good / an excellent job. What I really like about your work/text is …
> I can see you put a lot of effort into your work.
> That's a promising start. Your text contains quite a few / a lot of good elements; however, …
> Your text meets many of the relevant criteria such as …

- Make your tips as specific as possible. Say 'Use topic sentences at the beginning of a new paragraph' rather than just 'Work on your structure'.

> **■ LANGUAGE HELP**
> You might want to focus more on …
> Why not try to … instead of …
> If you changed/rewrote the beginning/conclusion/ the passage where you …, your text would sound even more convincing/ professional/emotional/…
> I think it would be a good idea to … Maybe you could … in order to …

- Take turns discussing your findings with your partner. Ask your partner to explain what you do not understand in his or her feedback. If there is anything you cannot agree on, consult your teacher, a grammar book or a dictionary.
- Use the feedback from your classmate(s) or your teacher to revise your first draft.

▶ Levels of the Common European Framework of References for Languages (inner front cover)

S34 • Study and language learning skills

▶ S34 Finding and developing your individual language learning skills

You have used some or many of the skills and strategies presented in S1–S33 since you started learning English. In the years to come you will need to customize them for yourself in order to support your language learning process at school, after school and/or maybe for other languages.
There are three important steps to take. Be honest with yourself.

STEP 1: Where am I?
Here you have to take stock and review your language skills and learning process. In order to do so, you should reflect on yourself, look at your results and achievements in English, consider the results of self- and peer evaluation that you have done or been given, and maybe even ask your teacher where you stand with learning English. Do you know how to actively learn English and improve on your results? Or have you just passively gone with the flow?

STEP 2: Where would I like to be?
Would you e.g. simply want to avoid some of your pet mistakes, to be better at speaking or to receive a better mark for your essay? Do you wish to be well-prepared for the next written test, to hand in a fitting application for a job, scholarship or exchange year or do you simply want to survive the Abitur in English? Set yourself reachable goals.

STEP 3: What are the next steps?
Now that you've decided what you'd like to achieve, you will have to consider when and how to do so. What are the precise methods and strategies you can use in order to reach these goals? What can you do? And within what period of time?
- If you have to enlarge your vocabulary, what is your strategy (e.g. using an electronic app or rather reading and writing more texts)?
- If you have problems with mediation, is it because you have difficulties getting ideas into English or rather because you don't know enough about English text types like email, formal letter, leaflet etc.? Should you rather practice explaining things in English or applying the correct text features?
- If you are not very successful in presentations, is it due to a lack of communicative skills or are you unsure about the choice of content to present? Should you e.g. practice how to identify relevant content or how to get it across in front of an audience?

PRACTICE

Consider your own weak spots and your strengths in English, then fill in the table below. You might want to look at older tests or assignments or you could ask a partner or your teacher for help.

	What I'm good at in English	Why I'm good at it	What I'm bad at in English	What I could do to get better
1.				
2.				
3.				
4.				

Preparing for a Speaking Exam

SE1   Finding out about the exam 162
SE2   Monologues. 163
SE3   Dialogues/Interacting 164

Download model answers to the tasks here: **Webcode** star-66

▶ SE1 Finding out about the exam

Some tests you have to sit in class can take the form of a speaking exam. Just as with written tests, there are many ways to prepare for them.

Step 1: You need to find out what kind of speaking exam you will be confronted with. The following overview will help you to identify your specific exam situation.

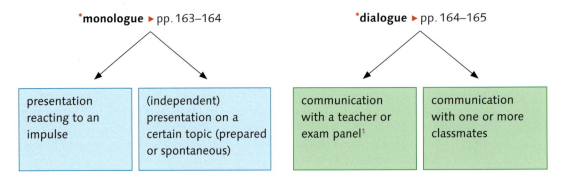

monologue ▶ pp. 163–164   *dialogue* ▶ pp. 164–165

- presentation reacting to an impulse
- (independent) presentation on a certain topic (prepared or spontaneous)
- communication with a teacher or exam panel[1]
- communication with one or more classmates

Your exam could also be a combination of the formats mentioned above, e.g. a monologue followed by a dialogue on a connected theme.

Step 2: Other aspects you will need to pay attention to are:
- Partners: If there are partners, are they chosen beforehand, or is it up to you to choose someone? Can you practise with your partner(s) to prepare for the test?
- Format: What form does your exam task take? Which prompts/stimuli do you get?
- Time frame: How long is the exam? How long are the different parts? Who is responsible for time management?
- Preparation time: Do you know the topic in advance? Can you prepare at home? Do you only get preparation time at school right before the exam? How much?
- Use of media: Are you expected to use different forms of media, e.g. a transparency, a poster, a computer presentation, etc.?
- Marking: How will your exam be marked? Your examiner will usually assess a combination of content and language aspects (including pronunciation, presentation and interaction skills).

---

[1] **exam panel** [ɪgˈzæm ˌpænl] *Prüfungskommission*

SE1–SE2 • Preparing for a Speaking Exam

Step 3: You should find your own way of collecting everything that is connected to the exam in a special (electronic) file. This could include information on marking schemes, past exams, collections of relevant topics, and phrases and tips to help you to perform well in the exam. Even more importantly, you should make the most of every opportunity to speak English!

PRACTICE

Make an outline of the specific speaking exam you will have to face. If you aren't sure about all the aspects, ask your classmates and your teacher.

▶ SE2 Monologues (= zusammenhängendes Sprechen)

One part of your speaking exam may be a monologue. You might be confronted with a prompt/stimulus to which you will have to respond spontaneously. The prompt/stimulus could come in the form of a quotation, a short text, a list of written questions, a picture, statistics or a cartoon.

PRACTICE 1

a Make a mind map for each of the six forms of prompt/stimulus mentioned above (quotation, short text, etc.). Collect words, phrases and even sentences to describe, analyse or comment on them.
▶ S6, 27, 28, 29

b `YOU CHOOSE` Make notes on one of the three prompts below. Describe, analyse and comment on it for at least two minutes. The phrases you collected in **a** might help you.

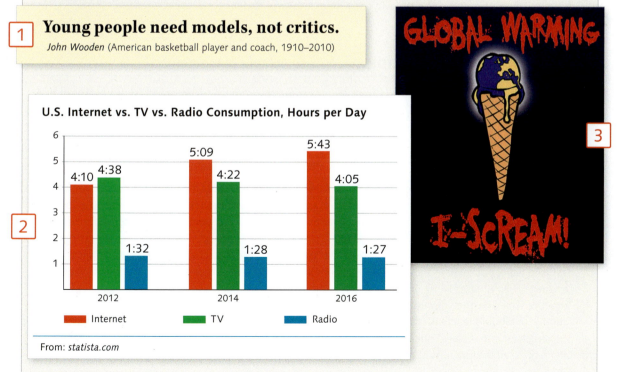

1 **Young people need models, not critics.**
John Wooden (American basketball player and coach, 1910–2010)

Preparing for a Speaking Exam • SE2–SE3

Your exam monologue might also be a presentation on a given topic which you can prepare beforehand.

PRACTICE 2

a Order the following steps of a presentation *chronologically and add other useful tips or phrases. Copy them into your folder.

A
Deliver your presentation: Don't simply read out what you have prepared. Try to connect with the audience, pay attention to your body language and how you speak.

B
Analyse your topic: What exactly are you asked to do? Which sub-aspects are included? What do you and your audience already know about the topic?

C
Practise your presentation: Rehearse what you want to say and how you want to say it. If possible, present it to a friend or family member.

D
Collect information on your topic: Make notes. If you are allowed to, research your topic using different sources.

E
Prepare your presentation: Check important phrases, prepare index cards or other forms of media you want to use.

b Signposting is a very helpful strategy for all forms of presentation. By using 'discourse markers' like *first of all, finally, next, I would like to come to my conclusion, what is more important than the first argument is …*, you are letting your audience/listeners know exactly where you are in the overall structure of your talk. Collect more of these phrases and copy them into your folder.

▶ SE3 Dialogues/Interacting (= an Gesprächen teilnehmen)

There will most certainly be an interactive or dialogue part to your speaking exam. It can be in the format of a conversation, a discussion, an interview or a role-play.

PRACTICE

a Together with a partner, try to define special features of the four formats given above (i.e. conversation, discussion, interview, role-play). Refer to specific aspects, such as whether you are allowed to give your personal opinion, whether you have to take over a role, which special phrases and sentence forms are necessary, etc. Use a dictionary if you need one.
b Any kind of communication consists of so-called 'speech acts'. Look at the speech acts A–J on the opposite page, put them in a logical order (there might be more than one solution) and match the Language Help phrases 1–10. Copy the finished table into your folder.
c Together with a partner, discuss a topic you are interested in, e.g. 'Should smartphones be banned at school?' or 'Should teachers communicate with students via online social networks?'. Use as many of the phrases given as possible. Time yourself.
d On the basis of **b**, start a list of useful phrases and match them with relevant speech acts. Add to the list whenever possible.

SE3 • Preparing for a Speaking Exam

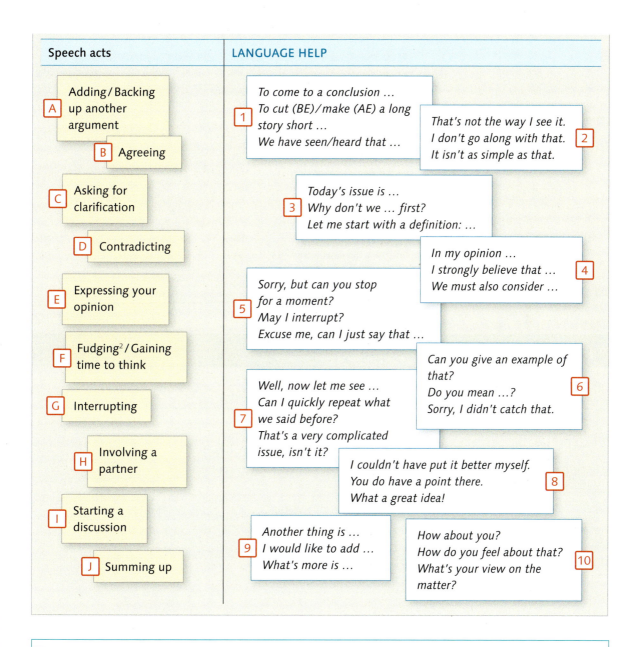

Speech acts	LANGUAGE HELP
A Adding / Backing up another argument	1 To come to a conclusion … / To cut (BE) / make (AE) a long story short … / We have seen/heard that …
B Agreeing	2 That's not the way I see it. / I don't go along with that. / It isn't as simple as that.
C Asking for clarification	3 Today's issue is … / Why don't we … first? / Let me start with a definition: …
D Contradicting	4 In my opinion … / I strongly believe that … / We must also consider …
E Expressing your opinion	5 Sorry, but can you stop for a moment? / May I interrupt? / Excuse me, can I just say that …
F Fudging[2] / Gaining time to think	6 Can you give an example of that? / Do you mean …? / Sorry, I didn't catch that.
G Interrupting	7 Well, now let me see … / Can I quickly repeat what we said before? / That's a very complicated issue, isn't it?
H Involving a partner	8 I couldn't have put it better myself. / You do have a point there. / What a great idea!
I Starting a discussion	9 Another thing is … / I would like to add … / What's more is …
J Summing up	10 How about you? / How do you feel about that? / What's your view on the matter?

■ TIPS FOR THE TEST SITUATION

- Be well prepared and you are halfway there: You should be informed about the test situation and should have practised and memorized enough phrases and sentences to be able to overcome problems and awkward silences.
- Be on time for the exam.
- If you are allowed preparation time, make notes that you will be able to understand quickly in the exam.
- Use the time you are given for every part of the exam wisely. Don't rush, but don't talk too slowly. If some words simply don't come, try to paraphrase them or use simpler words.
- Be polite and responsible: In a dialogue situation you are not only fighting for yourself, but also with and for your partner. He/She is relying on you as much as you are on him/her.

---

[2] **fudge** (infml) avoid giving a clear answer

Language Practice

Focus on Grammar
L1   The tenses: verb forms 166
L2   Simple present and
       present progressive.......... 167
L3   Present perfect simple and
       present perfect progressive 168
L4   Present perfect and
       simple past................. 169
L5   Simple past and
       past progressive 170
L6   Past perfect and
       simple past................. 171
L7   *Will*-future and
       going to-future 172
L8   The passive 173
L9   Conditional sentences. 175

L10   Indirect speech............. 176
L11   Relative clauses 177
L12   The gerund 177
L13   Participle constructions 178

Focus on Style
L14   Formal and informal English .. 180
L15   Linking your sentences 180
L16   Emphasis 183

Focus on Vocabulary
L17   Spelling 184
L18   Using the exact word 184
L19   Common collocations with
         prepositions 184

L20   One word in German – two
         in English 185
L21   Verbs of reporting.......... 186
L22   Germanisms 187
L23   Suffixes.................... 187
L24   Prefixes................... 188
L25   Opposites................... 189
L26   Using the right expressions
         for *lassen* 189
L27   Using the right expressions
         for *wollen* 190
L28   Using the right expressions
         for *sollen*................. 190
L29   Comparing and contrasting ... 191

Download the answers to the Language Practice tasks here:
 Webcode star-67

Focus on Grammar

▶ L1   The tenses: verb forms   DVD 11 (Auxiliary verbs)

TEST YOURSELF

Read the table carefully. Then complete the sentences below with the correct form of the verb (active or passive).

	Tense	Active	Passive
Talking about the present	Simple present Present progressive	*I ask* *I am asking*	*I am asked* *I am being asked*
Talking about the present <u>and</u> the past	Present perfect (simple) Present perfect progressive	*I have asked* *I have been asking*	*I have been asked*
Talking about the past	Simple past Past progressive	*I asked* *I was asking*	*I was asked* *I was being asked*
	Past perfect (simple) Past perfect progressive	*I had asked* *I had been asking*	*I had been asked*
Talking about the future	*will*-future (simple) *will*-future progressive	*I will ask* *I will be asking*	*I will be asked*
	going to-future	*I am going to ask*	*I am going to be asked*
	Future perfect	*I will have asked*	*I will have been asked*

1 He never (go) to the hairdresser. (simple present)
2 They (watch) by the police for half an hour. (present perfect simple)
3 You (not eat) meat, do you? (simple present)
4 I (not write) a text message yesterday. (simple past)
5 She (walk) around for about ten minutes. (present perfect progressive)

Make a timeline with the tenses, and write sentences about yourself in each tense next to the timeline.

L2 • Focus on Grammar

▶ L2 Simple present and present progressive   DVD 12 (Present progressive)

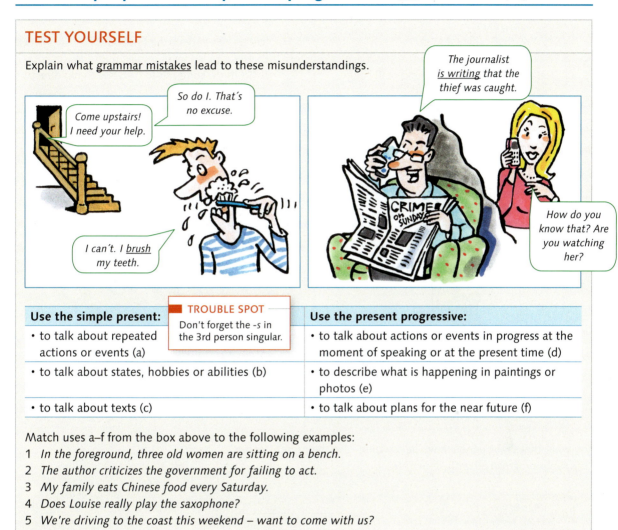

TEST YOURSELF

Explain what grammar mistakes lead to these misunderstandings.

Use the simple present:	**TROUBLE SPOT** Don't forget the -s in the 3rd person singular.	Use the present progressive:
• to talk about repeated actions or events (a)		• to talk about actions or events in progress at the moment of speaking or at the present time (d)
• to talk about states, hobbies or abilities (b)		• to describe what is happening in paintings or photos (e)
• to talk about texts (c)		• to talk about plans for the near future (f)

Match uses a–f from the box above to the following examples:
1 In the foreground, three old women are sitting on a bench.
2 The author criticizes the government for failing to act.
3 My family eats Chinese food every Saturday.
4 Does Louise really play the saxophone?
5 We're driving to the coast this weekend – want to come with us?
6 The exhibition halls are currently being renovated.

a A German student has written an email to introduce herself to her British host family. Unfortunately, the tenses are not always used correctly. Look for her mistakes and correct the verbs where necessary.

> Dear Mr and Mrs Busby,
> My name is Jana. I am 17 years old and I am living in Hamburg. I have an older brother, a younger sister and a dog. Hamburg is very close to the sea, so I am going sailing very often with my family. I usually like the strong wind when I sail, but this summer there is so much rain that I am not always enjoying our sailing trips. (It rains right now, too, that's why I sit at my PC and write emails.) I also play tennis in my free time and I am often listening to music. For me it is very exciting to travel to Britain because I have never been abroad before.
> Yours sincerely,
> Jana

Focus on Grammar • L3

b Some verbs, e.g. *think*, *look*, *see,* can be used in the simple form or the progressive form, but with different meanings. Choose the right form of the verb in brackets in the following sentences, then translate the sentences into German:

1a I (think) that's a great idea.
2a She can't come to the phone – she (have) a shower.
3a Don't talk to Harry – he (look) really angry.
4a (you/see) that small house behind the trees?

1b Hey, what (you/think) about?
2b Her family (have) a small house in Rockport.
3b In the second photo, the boy (look) directly into the camera.
4b Is it true that Samantha (see) Roger?

▶ L3 Present perfect simple and present perfect progressive

TEST YOURSELF

Explain the difference between the uses of the present perfect simple and the present perfect progressive.

Jessica **has walked** for five hours.

Ralph **has been** walking non-stop for two hours.

Say what these four people have been doing. Use the present perfect (simple or progressive) with *since* or *for*.

■ TROUBLE SPOT
Ich **kenne** Milena seit zehn Jahren.
I've known Milena for ten years.

Remember:
since + point in time
for + period of time

I started going to dancing lessons two months ago.

1 Lara

I started doing a yoga course in May.

I began working for my uncle's firm one year ago.

2 Amira

Example: *Lara has been going to dancing lessons for two months.*

Last October I began preparing for my trip to Asia.

3 Chris

I began training for the swimming competition three months ago.

Last week I started studying for the test.

4 Thomas

L4 • Focus on Grammar

▶ L4 Present perfect and simple past

TEST YOURSELF

Explain what grammar mistake leads to this misunderstanding.

Speech bubble (man): I played the piano for eight years.

Speech bubble (woman): Really? Why did you stop?

Use the present perfect:	Use the simple past:
• to say that something has happened (but not when it happened). • to say that something has happened in the past and has an influence on the present or is still going on.	• to say that something happened at a particular[1] point of time in the past or during a particular period in the past, • to report a series of actions or events in the past.
Examples of signal words and phrases: *already, never, ever, yet, all my life, all day, since 2017, for three years.*	Examples of signal words and phrases: *yesterday, last week, a year ago, at 8 o'clock, in 2017, When …?*

a Complete the sentences with the present perfect or simple past and explain your choice.
1. (you/see) Cathy this morning? – Yes, in fact I (see) her just a few minutes ago.
2. We (be) best friends since we (meet) in kindergarten. I don't think that will ever change.
3. No, I (never be) to Edinburgh, but I (visit) my uncle in Glasgow last summer.
4. Queen Elizabeth II, who (reign) since 1952, is second only to Queen Victoria, who (reign) for over 63 years.
5. Justin (become) a member of the book club last year, but he (not read) one book since then.
6. I (love) fantasy novels ever since I (discover) *Harry Potter* while I was still in primary school.

b Translate the dialogue between the police officer and the suspect into English.

Polizist:	Wann sind Sie vorgestern nach Hause gekommen?
Verdächtiger:	Ich bin vorgestern um 19:00 Uhr nach Hause gekommen.
Polizist:	Haben Sie seitdem irgendwelche Besucher empfangen?
Verdächtiger:	Nein, niemand ist seitdem vorbeigekommen. Gestern Abend habe ich mich so einsam gefühlt, dass ich schon darüber nachgedacht habe, bei meinen Nachbarn zu klingeln.
Polizist:	Die vier Polizisten, die gestern Abend in Ihrer Wohnung auf Sie gewartet haben, haben das übrigens auch getan.

c Imagine you are applying for your dream job. Make notes on what you could say about yourself, your interests and your experience that could qualify you for this job. Then write a text in which you present yourself as a candidate. Mind your tenses! ▶ S16: Writing an application, p. 137

[1] **particular** [pəˈtɪkjələ] *bestimmt*

Focus on Grammar • L5

▶ L5 Simple past and past progressive

TEST YOURSELF

There was a blackout at 8:05 pm last Tuesday. Answer the questions below the pictures, then explain the difference between the two situations.

What was Ted doing when the lights went out?

What did Ted do when the lights went out?

> **Use the past progressive:**
> - to say that an action was in progress at a specific time in the past, e.g. when another action started or interrupted it:
>   *Ted was watching TV when suddenly the screen went dark.*
>   The second action is expressed in the simple past.
> - to describe the background situation in a story or report.

a Write five sentences about actions that were interrupted by another action.
Example: *I was having a nightmare when my alarm clock rang.*

b Complete the text below with the simple past or the past progressive of the verbs in brackets. Decide which form fits each gap best. There are seven places where the past progressive would be better than the simple past.

1 Jimmy Preston (get) more and more nervous. **2** The 16-year-old schoolboy from Connecticut (stand) backstage in a New York City theatre, waiting for his call to go on stage. **3** He (read) his text once again. **4** Jimmy (have to) speak a powerful monologue, and he (want) to get it right. **5** He (play) the role of an ex-soldier from the Iraq War. **6** In the play the ex-soldier (describe) the psychological problems he (suffer) now he was back home from Iraq.
7 The lights in the theatre dimmed. It was time for Jimmy to go on stage. He quickly (move) forward, looking confused, like the soldier whose role he (play). **8** Jimmy started his monologue: 'My symptoms didn't appear straightaway. Then everything (hit) me all at once. I had nightmares. I couldn't sleep …'
9 Two months ago Jimmy and the other actors, his mates from the school drama club, (rehearse) because they wanted to put on the play *Voices in Conflict* for parents and friends at their school. **10** When they (get) ready for the first night, their head teacher suddenly (ban) the drama project. Some parents didn't like the school putting on an anti-war play. **11** The story (reach) the newspapers in New York and shortly afterwards the drama club got an invitation to perform there. **12** Back on the New York stage Jimmy's nerves had gone and he (do) his monologue confidently: 'I can't seem to find happiness in anything …'

c Write a scary story. Tell the story in the simple past with the past progressive when necessary.
You can start like this:
One Saturday night I was walking home from a party. It was raining and the wind was getting stronger with every minute, so I started to run. Suddenly …

L6 • Focus on Grammar

▶ L6 Past perfect and simple past

TEST YOURSELF

Explain the difference between the two situations described by the sentences below:

When the police arrived, the bank robber had fled.   *When the police arrived, the bank robber fled.*

Use the past perfect:
to express that an action happened before another action in the past.

a Combine the sentences with the conjunctions given in brackets. Make sure the time sequence is correct by using the past perfect (simple) for one of the verbs.
1 Liz dressed up nicely. She went to her friend's party. (before)
2 Tom came home. He switched on the TV. (after)
3 I read a scary story. I couldn't sleep well last night. (because)
4 Sandy repaired Peter's bike. She gave it back to him. (when)
5 Tahara booked her flight to Paris. She packed her suitcase. (as soon as)

b Complete the text about Bruno Mars with the correct verb forms (simple past or past perfect).

1 Bruno Mars (be) born as Peter Gene Hernandez in 1985 in Honolulu, Hawaii. **2** His parents (be) professional musicians who regularly (play) music from the 1960s and 70s in concerts with the whole family. **3** Before he (start) singing Elvis Presley songs in these shows as a young boy, he (watch) his family many times on stage, so he (know) exactly how to enthuse[2] the audience. **4** In order to pursue a musical career, he (move) to Los Angeles after he (finish) high school. **5** He (be) well prepared to write songs that combined the energy of Motown and Doo-Wop music because he (listen) to this kind of music throughout his childhood. **6** After he and some friends (found) the production team 'The Smeezingtons', they (create) a number of songs for other musicians. **7** By the time Bruno Mars (start) his own solo career in 2010, he (already write) several hit singles, among others Travie McCoy's 'Billionaire'. With millions of sold records, various awards and worldwide concert tours, Bruno Mars has now become one of the most successful musicians of our time.

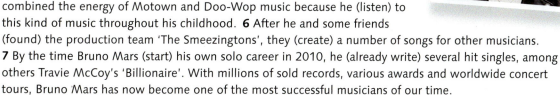

c Together with a partner, tell a story about a really bad day. Explain what happened and why things didn't go well. Take turns. Use the simple past to tell the story and use the past perfect to talk about actions that preceded the mishaps[3].

---
[2] **enthuse** [ɪnˈθjuːz] *begeistern*   [3] **mishap** *Missgeschick*

Focus on Grammar • L7

▶ **L7 Will-future and going to-future**   DVD 13 (Future tense)

TEST YOURSELF

Explain the difference between the two situations and why the speakers are using different future forms.

In many situations, the *will*-future and the *going to*-future can be used interchangeably[4]. In some cases, however, you must choose which form to use:

Use the *will*-future:	Use the *going to*-future:
• to talk about future events that cannot be influenced: My birthday *will be* on a Sunday this year.	• to talk about personal plans and intentions: We*'re going to fly* to Boston in the Easter holidays.
• to make general statements about the future: World population *will continue* to rise until 2050.	• to express personal views about future events in a particular situation: Rihanna's new single *is going to storm* the charts.

Special uses of the *will*-future:	
• to express willingness, offers and unplanned, spontaneous[5] decisions:	'I need a pocket calculator for this.' – 'Wait a sec, I*'ll fetch* you one.'
• to express unwillingness:	'I *won't help* you, so don't ask me again!'
• to (indirectly) give someone an order:	'*Will* you please *stop* talking? I'm trying to concentrate.'

a Make complete sentences using the correct verb form for the future:
1. tomorrow / thunderstorms / on Sunday / sky / clear
2. in 2050 / Germany's population / ca. 71 million
3. Rob and Sue / have a party / on Saturday
4. When / you / 18 years old?
5. Sam / take part / competition for young film-makers
6. sneak preview / new James Bond film / Saturday at 11 pm

---

[4] **interchangeable** *auswechselbar, austauschbar*   [5] **spontaneous** [spɒnˈteɪnɪəs] *spontan, ungeplant*

L8 • Focus on Grammar

b What do you say in each of these situations?
1. 'I have no idea how to use this ticket machine.' – <u>You:</u> 'No problem, … show you.'
2. When you come back from break, someone is sitting on your chair. – <u>You:</u> '… get up? This is my seat.'
3. 'If you're so upset about his decision, why don't you talk to him about it?' – <u>You:</u> 'It's no use, … change his mind.'
4. You see someone approaching the entrance, carrying lots of boxes. – <u>You:</u> '… open the door for you.'
5. <u>You:</u> 'I'm really sorry, but I can't go on holiday with you.' – 'Why not?' – <u>You:</u> 'My parents … let me.'
6. You are working in the school library. Two kids at your table have been laughing and making jokes since they arrived. – <u>You:</u> '… be quiet? Other people are trying to work here!'

c Think ahead: What will your life be like after you have finished school? What are you going to do after you have finished school? Make notes and add the correct forms of the future. Then interview a partner about their future plans and tell them about your own plans and expectations.

▶ L8 The passive

TEST YOURSELF

Make complete sentences from the headlines.

THREE KILLED IN CAR ACCIDENT   **WATER DISCOVERED ON MARS**   **PAINTINGS STOLEN FROM MUSEUM**

Use the passive:
- when the person who does something is unknown or unimportant:
  All the sandwiches *have been eaten*.

The passive consists[6] of a form of **be** followed by the **past participle.**
The passive progressive is formed with *being*:
At the moment the car *is being looked at* by the mechanic.

The preposition **by** ('von', 'durch') is used to say who or what does or causes the action:
This picture was painted *by* a 12-year-old girl.

In contrast to their German equivalents[7], some English verbs can form a **personal passive** with (mostly a person as) a subject. These verbs include: *advise, allow, tell, follow, help, join, offer, promise, recommend* ('empfehlen'), *thank, give, show*:
We were given the necessary information. ('Uns wurden … gegeben.' / 'Man gab uns …')
I have been promised a new computer if I pass my exams.
We were told the true story about the first Thanksgiving.

a Rewrite these sentences in the passive (leave out the subjects):
1. Employers created over 80,000 new jobs last year. *Over 80,000 new jobs were created last year.*
2. Every year, publishers publish about 80,000 new titles in Germany.
3. Warner Bros.[8] released the first part of *The Hobbit* in 2012.
4. They will open a new cinema in Broad Street next year.
5. Film-makers have adapted F. Scott Fitzgerald's novel *The Great Gatsby* for the cinema four times.
6. Viewers must wear special glasses to watch a film in 3D.

---

[6] **consist of sth.** *aus etwas bestehen*   [7] **equivalent** [ɪˈkwɪvələnt] *Entsprechung*   [8] **Warner Bros.** *US-amerikanische Filmgesellschaft*

173

Language Practice

Focus on Grammar • L8

b Official notices and rules are typically written in the passive. Read the following text about Cotham School in Bristol and use the passive to write down the rules the students have to follow.

> 1 Students must show respect towards others. *Respect must be shown toward others.*
> 2 Students must wear the school uniform at all times. They must remove outdoor clothing, such as coats, hats, gloves, etc., in classes and assemblies.
> 3 The school rules do not allow the students to wear make-up or jewellery except for one pair of stud[9] earrings.
> 4 Students must switch off their mobile phones and keep them in their bags when they are in school. They may not bring MP3 players, iPods or headphones for mobile phones to school.

c Use the passive to write about the rules at your school.

d Translate the German sentence parts into English using a passive form with the person as subject.
Example: *(Dem Schüler wurde erlaubt)* ... to use his mobile phone in school.
   The student was allowed ...
   1 *(Ihr wurde geraten)* ... to have her car's brakes repaired.
   2 *(Man gab uns)* ... the keys to our rooms.
   3 *(Man sagte uns)* ... to stay calm when sighting a bear.
   4 *(Den Schülern wurde empfohlen)* ... to do internships[10] in different companies.
   5 *(Den Organisatoren wurde gedankt)* ... by the participants of the course.
   6 *(Der Dame wurde geholfen)* ... to enter the bus.

e Active or passive: Complete the text about Bethany Hamilton with the correct verb forms. Pay attention to the tenses. Sometimes more than one tense is possible.

1 Bethany Hamilton was born into a family of surfers in Hawaii in 1990. She (teach) surfing at a very young age by her family, and at the age of eight she (enter) her first surf competition, which she easily (win). **2** Bethany (become) really passionate about surfing. **3** In order to have more time to surf, she (begin) homeschooling after she (finish) sixth grade at school, because the nearest high school was a 40-minute ride from her home. **4** However, Bethany's dream (threaten) dramatically when the 13-year-old girl (attack) by a 14-foot tiger shark[11] while she (surf) off Kauai's North Shore. **5** She (lose) her left arm and over 60% of her blood in the attack and had to undergo surgery[12] several times afterwards. **6** Yet, she (recover) with an unbelievably positive attitude. **7** Just one month after she (attack) by the shark, she went back to the ocean to surf.
8 The way back onto the surfboard was not easy for her: She had to learn to paddle and balance with only one arm, and a handle had to (add) to the surfboard so she could hold onto it.
9 But managing everyday life and walking through the streets with only one arm also became challenges she had to cope with. Just three months after the attack, Bethany (return) to surf competitions.
10 And one year later, a book with the title *Soul Surfer* (publish) that (tell) the story of her way back onto the surfboard. **11** Seven years later, this book (make) into a movie that (bring) her story to an even larger audience. **12** With all she has gone through, Bethany has become an example of inspiration and hope for many people who (suffer) similar strokes of fate, and a large number of people (touch) by her positive message.

---

[9] **stud earring** *Ohrstecker*   [10] **internship** [ˈɪntɜːnʃɪp] *Praktikum*   [11] **shark** *Hai*   [12] **surgery** [ˈsɜːdʒəri] *Chirurgie; hier: Operation*

L9 • Focus on Grammar

▶ L9 Conditional sentences DVD 14–15 (*if*-clauses: second/third conditional)

TEST YOURSELF

Conditional sentences are used for expressing conditions and drawing conclusions[13]. They can be used to talk about events and situations in the present, future or past.

Match these descriptions to the conditional sentences a–d in the table below.
1. talking about something that is improbable or not true now or in the future
2. talking about something that didn't happen in the past and its consequences for the past
3. talking about something that can actually happen in the present or future
4. talking about something that didn't happen in the past and its consequences for the present.

	facts	conditional sentences
a	The next ICE arrives in Bonn at 11:05.	If we take the next ICE, we can be in Bonn by 11:05.
b	Nelson Mandela died in 2013.	If Nelson Mandela was still alive today, he would make a good UN Secretary-General.
c	Lara sprained her ankle[14] and couldn't run in the race.	If Lara had been able to compete, she might have come in first.
d	I was offered a job at Microsoft in 1980, but I turned it down.	If I had accepted the job offer, I could be a millionaire today.

Conditional 1 (*if* + present | main clause: *will*-future or *can/may/should/must* + infinitive)
If I *miss* the bus, I*'ll take* a taxi.

Conditional 2 (*if* + past | main clause: *would/could/might* + infinitive)
If I *missed* the bus, I *would take* a taxi.

Conditional 3 (*if* + past perfect | main clause: *would have/could have/might have* + past participle)
If I *had missed* the bus, I *would have taken* a taxi.

Conditionals 2 and 3 can be **mixed**: If I *had missed* the bus, I *would be* late now.

---

a Draw your own conclusions from the facts by making conditional sentences.
  Look at the examples in the table above if you need help.
  1. 'Don't forget your umbrella – it's raining out there!' *If you don't take …*
  2. Most plants need water at least once a week. *If it doesn't rain …*
  3. Christian has been offered an interesting job, but the pay is very low. *If the pay …*
  4. Bill Gates's father wanted his son to study law, but Bill ignored his father's wishes. …
  5. The plot[15] to assassinate Hitler in July 1944 failed.
  6. Every year the sea level rises about three millimetres, threatening coastal cities.
  7. Can't you walk faster? The train leaves in ten minutes!
  8. Donna doesn't invest much time in her schoolwork – maybe that's why her grades aren't so hot.

■ **TROUBLE SPOT**
No *will* or *would* in the *if*-clause!

b Prepare ten interview questions for your partner. Ask your partner the questions and answer your partner's questions. Use questions with the first, second or third conditional.
  What will you do if …?   Where would you go if …?   How would you have felt if …?
  …

---

[13] **conclusion** [kənˈkluːʒn] *Schlussfolgerung*   [14] **sprain your ankle** *sich den Fuß verstauchen*   [15] **plot** *Komplott, Verschwörung*

Focus on Grammar • L10

▶ L10 Indirect speech

TEST YOURSELF

How would the man in the cartoon on the right report the results of his conversation with the priest?
Begin: *I asked him …, and he told me …*

Use indirect speech:
- to report what somebody says or said.

If the reporting verb is in the past (e.g. *said, told sb., asked*), there is usually a 'backshift' of tenses, i.e. the tense in indirect speech is changed from present to past (e.g. *is* ▶ *was*):
'I'm studying maths.'
▶ She says she *is* studying maths.
▶ She said she *was* studying maths.

To report yes/no questions you need the conjunctions *if* or *whether*:
'Are you finished?'
▶ He asked *if* we were finished.

To report commands and requests, use an infinitive construction:
'Wait here!' – They *told us to wait* here.

At last, the mystery of the Mayan[16] calendar revealed[17].

a Put the following sentences into indirect speech. Be careful not to change the meaning of the sentences.
1 'I don't like the smell coming from the kitchen,' said Linda.
2 'Have you done your homework, Jasper?' asked Jasper's dad.
3 'You will be rewarded with a cake for your work,' the headmaster announced.
4 'Linda came here yesterday,' the assistant confirmed.
5 'I had shown 15 different sweepers to the man before he decided to buy a pair of socks,' the shop assistant complained.
6 'Don't go there after dark,' Jean's mother warned.

■ **TROUBLE SPOT**
In English we do not use a comma before indirect speech.

b Report what the people below have said – not every word – using suitable reporting verbs from the list.

admit • advise • apologize (for doing) • complain • explain • invite
promise • suggest (doing) • warn (sb. not to do)

1 Michelle: 'Come over to my place when you've finished your homework.'
2 Robert: 'I'm telling you: don't eat fish in that restaurant.'
3 Lara: 'Well, you're right. Linda really does look best in the green skirt.'
4 Mum: 'I'm sorry, but I really don't have the time to go to that meeting. I'm too busy.'
5 Steve: 'To be frank, I've never liked that armchair we got for our wedding. It's awful.'
6 Lena: 'I'll come over tomorrow afternoon and help you make the sandwiches.'

[16] **Mayan calendar** ['maɪən] *Kalender der Maya*   [17] **reveal sth.** *etwas enthüllen*

L11–L12 • Focus on Grammar

▶ L11 Relative clauses   DVD 16 (Relative pronouns)   ▶ L15: Linking your sentences, p. 180

TEST YOURSELF

Fill the gaps with the correct relative pronouns where necessary.
1 *The taxi driver … drove too fast has to pay a fine.*
2 *Isn't that the artist … paintings were stolen from the museum?*
3 *The book … you gave me is great.*
4 *You should send her lilies[18]. They are the flowers … are the most suitable for this occasion.*

Use relative clauses:

- to help identify the person or thing we are talking about.

The relative pronouns **who/that** are used to talk about persons: *the girl who/that …*
The relative pronouns **which/that** are used to talk about things: *the shop which/that …*
The relative pronoun **whose** ('dessen', 'deren') is used to say that something belongs to someone:
The first three people whose names are drawn win a free holiday.

If the relative pronoun is the object of the relative clause, it can be left out.
Lilly is the girl [who] I met at the library. – Here's the smartphone [that] you've been looking for.

Commas are used to separate a 'non-defining relative clause' from the rest of the sentence.
The actor Charlie Chaplin, who was born in England, made most of his films in Hollywood.

a Translate the German sentence parts into English.
   1 This is the job *(von dem Jane jahrelang geträumt hat).*
   2 I need to buy a present *(das einem dreijährigen Jungen gefallen würde).*
   3 A Bernese mountain dog is the kind of dog *(der am besten zu deiner Familie passen würde).*
   4 Look, there is the boy *(dessen Bild heute in der Zeitung ist)*!

b Use relative clauses to define these words:
   1 adventure 2 idol ['aɪdl] 3 future 4 challenge 5 the internet 6 friend 7 hope 8 activist

▶ L12 The gerund   ▶ L15: Linking your sentences, p. 180

TEST YOURSELF

The following text contains several gerunds (*-ing* forms). Read it, then complete the statements below. Point out an example from the text for each statement.

Text messaging (texting) has become extremely popular with young people. In fact, many prefer texting to making phone calls. My classmate Trish loves writing short messages and then waiting for an answer. She gets on her boyfriend's nerves by sending him dozens of text messages every day. She wouldn't dream of phoning him. Sometimes he makes her angry by not answering.

1 Gerunds are formed from verbs by adding …
2 They can be used in a sentence as the … or as the …
3 You can also use a gerund directly after a preposition such as …
4 Gerunds – like verbs – can be expanded[19] by adding a direct …

---

[18] **lily** ['lɪli] *Lilie*   [19] **expand sth.** *etwas erweitern*

Focus on Grammar • L13

The use of gerunds
After these verbs use a gerund, not an infinitive: *dislike, enjoy, finish, imagine, miss, practise, suggest.* Nobody *enjoys going* to the dentist's.　　I *miss seeing* my friends every day. Can you *imagine living* on Mars?　　Tom *suggested going* for an ice cream.
Gerunds can have a passive form: Teens don't like *being treated* like children. = Teens don't like it when they are treated like children.
Gerunds can have their own 'subject': My parents don't like *me staying* out late. = My parents don't like it when I stay out late.

a Gerunds are ideal for talking about activities. Choose a verb from the list on the left and an activity from the box on the right (or make up your own activity) and write at least six sentences about yourself and your friends:

be interested in • look forward to • dream of love • feel like • enjoy • hate • stop • like think about

go to parties • do homework • write text messages meet friends • look at photos • watch videos read novels • play computer games travel abroad • …

1 *I dream of travelling abroad.*　2 *My friends and I love …*

b Write 5–6 sentences about your parents: what they like/dislike/hate, etc. about your behaviour. You can start like this:
My parents are OK, but sometimes they get on my nerves. They hate me spending a lot of time in front of the PC. They don't like being told that their views are from the last century. …

▶ L13 Participle constructions　▶ L15: Linking your sentences, p. 180

TEST YOURSELF

Look at the example sentences with the two types of participles below. Then complete the following rules.
1　The active form of a participle ('present participle') is formed with the infinitive + … .
2　The passive form of a participle is the … of a verb. A regular verb takes the ending … .
3　Participles can be used to replace a … clause.

present participle	past participle
The girl *singing* loudly is my sister. (The girl who is singing loudly is my sister.)	The song *sung* at the end of the show became a hit. (The song which is/was sung at the end of the show became a hit.)

Participles can also be used to express **time or reason**. They correspond to **adverbial clauses**.
Reading the email from her boss, Rachel started to cry. (= When she read the email …)
Having thought about the problem with her boss, she was determined to look for a new job.
(= After she had thought about the problem …)
Being a psychologist, she knows exactly how to work on her behaviour. (= As she is a psychologist …)

The present participle can be used after **verbs of perception** (e.g. *see, hear, notice, watch*) + **object**.
Rachel saw a crowd *waiting* on the street.

L13 • Focus on Grammar

a Replace[20] these relative clauses with participle constructions.
  1 The athlete who is hosting the charity dinner retired[21] from professional sport six months ago.
  2 The photo that was published in today's newspaper has obviously been retouched.
  3 The people who attend[22] such events want to contribute to social welfare by giving money.
  4 The money that is collected at charity events is used to support those who are in need of help.

b Put the words in the correct order to make sentences.
  1 has / Peter's uncle / offering outdoor equipment / a / shop / newly decorated
  2 a full-time job / there / selling parachutes[23] and tents / has got / Peter's mum
  3 to / different life jackets / just shown / a boat trip / a young couple / she has / planning
  4 has just bought / a tall man / wearing wellington boots / a backpack
  5 waiting outside the shop / a huge dog / is scaring / passing by / the people

c Change the underlined sentence parts below using participle constructions.
  1 <u>When Pam heard about the job offer,</u> she was excited.
  2 <u>As she had lost her job two months earlier,</u> she was desperately looking for a new one.
  3 <u>Her boss had been dissatisfied[24] with her work,</u> so he had fired her.
  4 <u>After she had tried so hard to find a new job,</u> Pam was more than happy about her new position.
  5 <u>Because she knew what she had done wrong in the past,</u> she was able to do better now.

d Rewrite the pairs of sentences as single sentences with the *'having* + past participle' form.
  1 The journalist had embarrassed the star in an interview. He apologized publicly.
  2 The movie star was embarrassed by the journalist in the interview. She said she would never work with him again.
  3 Bernard had been bitten by a dog. He came running home in tears.
  4 Penny had not prepared for the exam. She did not know a single answer.

e **CHALLENGE** Sometimes it is necessary to put a participle phrase at the beginning of the sentence to avoid confusion. Compare these two sentences:

*Jim saw the headmistress **passing** by the school.*
(Jim sah die Schulleiterin an der Schule vorbeigehen. / Jim sah die Schulleiterin, die an der Schule vorbeiging. / Jim sah, wie die Schulleiterin an der Schule vorbeiging.)

***Passing** by the school, Jim saw the headmistress.*
(Als Jim an der Schule vorbeiging, sah er die Schulleiterin. / Jim sah die Schulleiterin, als er an der Schule vorbeiging.)

Use participles to translate these sentences into English.
  1 Katy sah einen seltsam aussehenden Mann, der die Bank betrat.
  2 Tom wurde von einer jungen Frau beobachtet (*observe*), als er die Bank betrat.
  3 Gestern habe ich einen alten Freund getroffen, als ich gerade in einem Restaurant saß.
  4 Als ich in einer Zeitschrift blätterte (*leaf through*), bemerkte ich einen Mann, der mir gegenüber saß.
  5 Ich habe dich ins Haus kommen hören, als ich mit Linda telefonierte.

---

[20] **replace sth. with sth.** *etwas durch etwas ersetzen*
[21] **retire from professional sport** *den Profisport aufgeben*
[22] **attend sth.** *etwas besuchen, an etwas teilnehmen*
[23] **parachute** ['pærəʃuːt] *Fallschirm*
[24] **dissatisfied** *unzufrieden*

L Focus on Style • L14–L15

Focus on Style

▶ L14 Formal and informal English

Depending on the situation you are in or who you are talking to, you will use different forms of English: Informal English is used in everyday speech and with people you know well; formal English is used e.g. in a formal letter or essay.
Formal and informal English differ in a number of ways. One difference is the choice of words: Formal English often uses longer words of Latin or French origin. In informal English, people tend to use shorter, everyday words.

> Thanks for writing back so fast.

> I gratefully acknowledge your prompt response to my enquiry.

a For each formal verb on the left, find its informal equivalent in the box on the right:

discover	assist	continue	enquire
increase	request	require	escape

need	go up	get away	go on
find out	ask for	help	ask

b Replace the underlined words and phrases with more formal ones:
1 The citizens of this town have waited <u>way</u> too long for the mayor to take action.
2 Rebecca <u>freaked out</u> when she saw her test score.
3 The teacher <u>got mad</u> at her students for arriving late.
4 It took years of hard work before Steve Jobs <u>made it big</u> in the computer industry.
5 I <u>guess</u> most Germans are satisfied with the results of the last election.
6 It has become <u>kind of</u> difficult for students to find a place to live in many university towns.

c You belong to a group that is preparing a presentation on environmental projects for young people in different countries. You have the brilliant idea of doing volunteer work at a wildlife sanctuary in Massachussetts. Write an email asking your pen friend in Massachusetts if you could stay with him/her for a week. Write a second email to the Massachusetts Audubon Society asking about the possibility of doing volunteer work.

Short forms
People generally use short forms in informal language: 'I'm getting hungry. Let's look for a restaurant. I haven't got much time.' This also includes forms like *gonna* and *wanna*. In formal contexts, you should avoid short forms.

▶ L15 Linking your sentences

The following text is an excerpt from a student's review of Graham Gardner's novel *Inventing Elliot*. Describe and comment on the style of the text.

> *Inventing Elliot* is the first novel by British author Graham Gardner. I have read it twice. Now I can truly recommend it. It is an exciting book. Every young person must like it. It is about a boy called Elliot. He is starting at a new school. Elliot is a very shy person. He was bullied at his old school. He only wants to be a normal student at his new school. Then he is noticed by a group called the Guardians. The Guardians rule the school from behind the scenes. The Guardians choose students for punishment just to demonstrate their power. They want Elliot to join them. They will soon leave school and are looking for a successor.[1] The Guardians make it hard for Elliot to have normal relationships to other students. He doesn't know who he can trust. In the end Elliot reports the Guardians to the head teacher. But first he loses his only friend Ben and his girlfriend Louise.

▶ Focus on Skills: Writing, p. 42

---

[1] **successor** *person that comes after sb. else and takes their place*

Language Practice

L15 • Focus on Style

Texts that consist mainly of unconnected main clauses are boring to read and difficult to understand. Good style contains both shorter and longer sentences, and they should be connected to show how they are related. Below are some examples of how sentences can be connected.

a Relative clauses

Consider the following sentences:
It is an exciting book. Every young person must like it.
Both sentences refer to the book (*book, it*), so they can be connected, e.g. by using a relative clause:
It is an exciting book that/which every young person must like.

▶ L11: Relative clauses, p. 177

Now connect these sentences by using a relative clause:
1. It is about a boy called Elliot. He is starting at a new school.
2. He is noticed by a group called the Guardians. The Guardians rule the school from behind the scenes.

b Participle phrases

Consider the following sentences:
He used to be a victim of bullying at his old school. He wants to be a normal student at his new school.
The two sentences have the same subject (*he*) and are linked in time (*old school – new school*); moreover, the first is the reason for the second. You can express this relationship with a participle phrase:
Having been a victim of bullying at his old school, he wants to be a normal student at his new school.

▶ L13: Participle constructions, p. 178

Now connect these sentences using a participle phrase:
1. In the end Elliot reports the Guardians to the head teacher. But first he loses his only friend Ben and his girlfriend Louise. *(Careful: Start with the second sentence.)*
2. I have read it twice. Now I can truly recommend it.

c Conjunctions

Read the following two sentences and think about the connection between them:
The Guardians want Elliot to join them. They will soon leave school and are looking for a successor.
The second sentence gives an explanation for the first, i.e. why the Guardians are looking for successors. You can express this logical connection by linking the sentences with a conjunction:
The Guardians want Elliot to join them because they will soon leave school and are looking for a successor.

The most popular conjunction with students is *because*. But don't forget all the others:
*after • although • as • as long as • as soon as • before • even if • even though
if • since • so that • unless • until • when • whereas • while*

Now find a way of joining the following sentence pairs to show the connections between them:
1. At the new school, the Guardians quickly notice him. Elliot tries hard to stay out of sight.
2. Elliot hopes the Guardians will protect him. He does everything they tell him to do.
3. Elliot was a loser at his old school. At his new school, the kids respect him.
4. He hides his real feelings from Louise. In the end she gives up and leaves him.

Focus on Style • L15

d Linking words and phrases

In addition to conjunctions, you can also use linking words to show the logical connections between sentences. Here is an overview of useful phrases:

Use	Linking word or phrase	Example
Stating your opinion	In my opinion … In my view … From my point of view … To my mind … I think/feel/believe that …	**I think** that cyberbullying is a serious problem today.
Listing facts, etc.	Firstly … / Secondly … Besides … Finally … Above all … In addition … Not only … but also …	**Above all**, cyberbullying leads to a loss of self-esteem in its victims.
Giving an example	for example … for instance … such as …	Cyberbullying can have serious consequences for its victims, **for example** sleeplessness or depression.
Pointing out reasons and consequences	For this/that reason … That's why … As a consequence … As a result … So … Because (of) …	Teenagers tend to be well connected online. **As a result**, it's easy for bullies to spread nasty comments.
Contrasting	On the one hand … On the other hand … On the contrary, … In contrast, …	Victims of bullying are not exempt[2] from becoming bullies. **On the contrary**, most bullies have been bullied themselves.
Generalizing	As a rule … On the whole … Generally speaking, … In general …	**As a rule**, almost every fourth teenager will be a victim of cyberbullying once.
Coming to a conclusion	All in all … In conclusion … To sum up … Taking everything into account, …	**All in all**, cyberbullying is a problem that cannot be underestimated.

Write a review of a book you have read recently. Link your ideas with phrases from the table and connect your sentences where appropriate. Make sure to use at least two relative clauses and one participle phrase.

▶ Focus on Skills: Writing, p. 42
▶ S18: Writing a review, p. 141; S13: The stages of writing, p. 135

---

[2] **be exempt from sth.** [ɪgˈzempt] *von etwas ausgenommen sein*

L16 • Focus on Style

▶ L16 Emphasis

Consider the sentence below and say what emotional state the person who says this might be in. What might the situation be?
'I *did* lock the door when I left the house, and I can prove it!'
How does the verb form in the first part of the sentence differ from the norm?

English has different ways of emphasizing something:

a Emphatic *do/does/did* in positive statements

We can use *do/does/did* to emphasize what we are saying in sentences without an auxiliary verb:
People *do* make mistakes – it's only human.
Eventually, he *did* return the stolen painting to its owner, but the diplomatic damage had already been done.

b *It is / it was* + relative clause

We can use *it is / it was* + relative clause to emphasize a noun, a pronoun or an adverbial phrase:
It was greed *that caused the financial crisis*.
It is the cost of living *that worries me*.
It wasn't us *who did the damage*.
It was in New York *that I first met Sue*, not in Boston.

▶ L11: Relative clauses, p. 177

c Negative adverbials + inversion

Subject-auxiliary inversion can be used after certain negative expressions (*Never before … / Not until … / Under no circumstances …*) and when *only* is used with a point in time (*Only then …*) at the beginning of the sentence:
Never before had anyone seen what Galileo saw when he pointed his telescope at the moon that night.
Not until poverty has been abolished on this planet will our job be finished.
Only when she saw the look on his face did she realize that she had made a bad mistake.

This structure is very popular in political speeches.

Rewrite the sentences below to emphasize the underlined phrases:
1 People won't realize that you can't eat money until the last fish is dead. (Begin: *Not until* …)
2 According to Gandhi, only love, not hate, has the power to change the world.
3 I like you – but I don't think we'll ever be more than just friends.
4 We will never be offered such an opportunity again.
5 John F. Kennedy once said, 'Ask not what your country can do for you – ask what you can do for your country.'
6 I only began to understand Shakespeare when I saw one of his plays on the stage for the first time.
7 I wrote to you, but apparently my mail got lost in your spam folder.
8 The author's ability to appeal to both male and female readers made the series so popular.

Focus on Vocabulary • L17–L19

Focus on Vocabulary

▶ L17 Spelling

Copy the words below, adding any missing letters. There is not always a letter missing.

1 dis■ap■ointed
2 com■it■ee
3 activ■
4 independ■nt
5 assist■nt
6 sep■rate
7 w■ether
8 beli■ve
9 standar■
10 con■cious
11 c■ara■ter
12 stren■th

▶ L18 Using the exact word

Read the text on the right about a successful student: What do you notice about the vocabulary used in the text? What advice would you give the writer?

English has lots of simple words that are commonly used in everyday conversation. When you write, you should take the time to look for more specific words that express exactly what you mean.

> Kevin is a good student. He works hard and always does well in class. That's why he gets good marks. After school he wants to study Business Administration. With a degree in that field he is sure he will find a good job and make a lot of money.

In the following sentences, replace the 'basic' words *go, get, do, be, big* and *good* with more exact words from the choices below. Each word can be used only once.

convincing • gain • move • obtain • perform • play • present (v) • overwhelming • take part in • travel

1 Last semester Jason <u>did</u> a project on coffee plantations in Central America.
2 The listeners were won over by Katie's <u>good</u> arguments.
3 After finishing school, I want to <u>go</u> around Southeast Asia for six months.
4 Jason <u>was</u> Puck in our school's production of *A Midsummer Night's Dream*.
5 To <u>get</u> further information, contact our information department.
6 Martin Luther King had to overcome <u>big</u> resistance to reach his goals.
7 Some students <u>do</u> better on standardized exams than others.
8 Sarah spent six months in Sierra Leone to <u>get</u> first-hand experience of life in a developing country.
9 Teenage adventurers like Laura Dekker <u>are</u> a challenge to adult authority.
10 After dropping out of college, Steve <u>went</u> to Palo Alto, where he started his own business.

▶ L19 Common collocations with prepositions   ▶ S25: Using a dictionary, p. 151

Like German, English has thousands of collocations that include a preposition (*auf* etwas reagieren / react **to** sth.). You can't learn them all, but the more you know, the fewer mistakes you will make.

a Choose the right preposition for the sentences in each list. Learn the collocations that are new to you:

to – for – of		
1 I never learned the cause … the confusion.	4 Money isn't the key … happiness.	7 Let's hope … the best.
2 I've found the solution … our problem!	5 It was an example … rare courage.	8 That's the secret … my success.
3 We never discuss our plans … the future!	6 We guessed the reason … her behaviour.	9 Is that the answer … your question?

Language Practice

L20 • Focus on Vocabulary

on – in – at		
10 She was always hard … work.	13 I found it … the internet.	17 I read your article … the school newspaper.
11 She met him … the way to school.	14 Baby, it was love … first sight.	18 We missed him while he was … university.
12 That's my dog … the photo.	15 I hate the adverts … television.	19 The film is based … a true story.
	16 Don't get … my way!	

by – from – of		
20 I love those figures created … Matt Groening.	23 Have you ever heard … a group called 'The Shneezles'?	26 We've lost our notes, so we'll have to start … scratch.
21 Read this excerpt … a short story.	24 When did you last hear … your brother?	27 Here's a photo … my grandfather when he was 25.
22 Those old houses are made … wood.	25 She knows all of the lyrics … heart.	28 Follow these step-…-step instructions.

b Write six gap-fill sentences using one or more of the collocations from the tables above.
Example: *Their latest film is based … a novel … Cormac McCarthy.*
Give them to a partner to solve while you work on your partner's sentences.

▶ L20 One word in German – two in English

Many German words have two or more different meanings in English. Example: How would you translate *wählen* in the context of a restaurant menu? A political election? A telephone call?
When using a German-English dictionary, read all the meanings, then choose the one that fits your context. For more help, and some extra practice, see ▶S25: Using a dictionary, p. 151.

a Each German word in the table has more than one possible English translation. Copy the table, and choose the two correct English translations for each German word from the choices below.

	German	English meaning 1	English meaning 2
1	Arbeit	work	job
2	Land		
3	lernen		
4	Versuch		
5	Gewalt		
6	bereit		
7	Stimme		
8	verletzen		
9	Sicherheit		
10	wenn		
11	Geschichte		
12	nächste(r,s)		

~~work~~ • study • land
learn • if • experiment
violate • violence
ready • voice • injure
safety • next • ~~job~~
story • force • country
attempt • vote • willing
security • history • when • nearest

Focus on Vocabulary • L21

b For each pair of sentences, you need a different English translation of the same German word to complete the sentences. Choose the right English words from the table you filled in for exercise **a**.

1 **Stimme**
   a In the coming election, each citizen has two … .
   b In a democracy it's important to raise your … and speak out against injustice.

2 **Gewalt**
   a … broke out when soldiers started shooting at the protesters.
   b Many people used … to break doors and hide in nearby buildings.

3 **verletzen**
   a Twelve demonstrators were … and had to be taken to hospital.
   b The protesters claimed that the police had … their civil rights.

4 **Versuch**
   a The activists made an … to stop people entering the laboratory.
   b They were against … on animals.

5 **bereit**
   a The first GM tomatoes were … for harvesting.
   b Some of the protesters were … to risk arrest to reach their goals.

6 **Land**
   a Thousands of migrants enter the … every year.
   b Some arrive by ship or plane, but most use the … routes from the southwest.

7 **wenn**
   a I'll be glad … this semester is over.
   b … you should hear any news, contact me at once.

8 **Geschichte**
   a We were together, then broke up, then got back together; we have a complicated … .
   b That'll make a great … to tell the grandchildren!

9 **Sicherheit**
   a For … reasons, you shouldn't tell anyone the password to your social-network account.
   b For her own …, the film star was kept in her hotel room for a couple of hours.

10 **Arbeit**
    a It's great having your dream … – you get paid for doing what you love.
    b But it's still easy to get stuck at … when you'd rather be out with your friends.

11 **nächste(r,s)**
    a Where can we find out when the … film is on?
    b We can go to the … café, get a coffee and wait until it starts.

12 **lernen**
    a It's so important for today's students to … how to speak other languages.
    b You really shouldn't start … for a test ten minutes before it starts.

c Write five more pairs of gap sentences. Give them to a partner and do your partner's tasks.

▶ L21 Verbs of reporting

A student read an article about changing methods of communication and wrote the report on the right. What makes this report boring to read? How could it be improved?

Your texts will be livelier and more exact if you avoid using 'standard' verbs like *say*, *think* and *write* when you report the contents of an article.

> The author says some people use texting to avoid confrontation. They don't want to say unpleasant things to someone in person. She says a boy at her school told her he would rather quarrel with his girlfriend via text messages. The author writes he should go and talk to her instead.

a Copy the table below and use it to sort the 15 verbs of reporting into categories (some verbs fit into more than one category). Use your dictionary if needed. You can add other verbs that you know.

| present an idea or make a suggestion |
| give an example |
| express a positive view |
| express a negative view |

argue • state • present • criticize • conclude
quote • name • advise • cite • suggest • propose •
recommend • praise • list

186

Language Practice

L22–L23 • Focus on Vocabulary

b In the following sentences, replace the words **in bold** with an appropriate verb from the table in **a**. More than one verb is possible in each case.

1. The author **says good things about** Ban Ki Moon for doing a fine job of handling the crisis.
2. He **says** that the rules of procedure at the UN are in need of reform.
3. The author **talks about** a few specific rules that should be updated.
4. The author **says** that the EU should be given a seat on the Security Council.
5. He **says** that the veto power of the five permanent members should be abolished.
6. The author **says negative things about** Russia for abusing its veto power to protect Syria.
7. He **writes** some examples of the negative effect of the veto.
8. In the end, the author **writes**, the United Nations has made the world a better place.

▶ L22 Germanisms

What's wrong with the sentence in the speech bubble? Why do Germans tend to make this mistake?

> *Excuse me, where can I become a student ID card?*

Translating *bekommen* as *become* is a so-called 'Germanism'. Awareness of the trouble spots can help you avoid such mistakes.

Read the sentences below. Decide in each case which of the words or phrases in brackets must be used:

1. I told my parents I've had enough – I need (an own room / a room of my own), and that's that!
2. Hey, what happened (to/with) Eric? I saw him at lunchtime sitting in a wheelchair.
3. The Superior Hotel? It's (in the near of / close to) the train station.
4. After completing my studies, I hope to (make/have) a great career in the fashion industry.
5. In this programme, you'll have the (chance/possibility) to meet professionals in your field of interest.
6. We wanted to see the (newest/latest) action film at the Omniplex.
7. When are they finally going to do something (about/against) air pollution?
8. After Jessie's family moved to Minnesota, we lost contact (to/with) each other.
9. We said goodbye without knowing when we would see (us / each other) again.
10. Louise? She's over there on the bench, (phoning with / phoning) her boyfriend as usual.
11. I want to go to Southeast Asia, travel and (make/have) new experiences.
12. Please be quiet! I need to (learn/study) for my French exam on Tuesday.

▶ L23 Suffixes

You know what a *statement* is, so when the prime minister *states* that he will not change his position on the issue, you understand what is meant, even if you have never seen the word before. Knowing how English (like German) forms new words by adding suffixes can save you time when reading English texts.

Of course, when you add the suffix *-ment* to a word, you have to rewrite the sentence around it for it to make sense. *Claire and Harry **argued** all night.* becomes *Claire and Harry's **argument** lasted all night.*

a Add the suffix *-ment* to the highlighted verb, rewriting the sentence so it has the same meaning.

1. I could see it in his face that he was disappointed.
2. All he needs is someone to encourage him.
3. The president's goal is that every job seeker should be employed.
4. The news of Don's accident spoiled the evening for me – I couldn't enjoy it.
5. She could barely hide the fact that she was amused.
6. Thanks to CNN it's possible to follow how the situation develops 24 hours a day.
7. The fact that Liam has been involved in the green movement was an important point in his favour.
8. We heard someone announce over the loudspeaker that our train was delayed.

Language Practice

Focus on Vocabulary • L24

b Some adjectives are made from verbs by adding *-able*: If you can depend on someone, that person is *dependable*. But be careful with the spelling: some of these adjectives are written with *-ible*: *responsible*, *incredible*, *edible*. If you aren't sure, use a dictionary.

Complete the second sentence in each exercise by taking a verb from the first sentence and adding the suffix *-able*. Depending on the context, you may have to add the prefix *un-* too.

1. No one can imagine the consequences of large-scale nuclear war. They are completely …
   No one can imagine the consequences of large-scale nuclear war. They are completely unimaginable.
2. There's no predicting the weather here on Skye. Our weather is very …
3. We couldn't believe what we had been told. It was simply too …
4. Everyone seems to like him. He's a very … person.
5. We can't manage any extra work this week. Our workload is already …
6. Don't worry about the cups – they won't break. They're made of … plastic.
7. You shouldn't rely on Cedric. In my experience he's very …
8. I understand her reasons. So for me her decision is completely …

▶ L24 Prefixes

Like German, English forms new words by adding prefixes (or suffixes) to existing words. If you know the meaning of a prefix, you can often guess the meaning of a word you have never seen before.

a Copy and complete the table below with the prefixes from the words on the right. More than one prefix can correspond to the same meaning:

Meaning	Prefix
no longer	ex-
not	
directed against sth.	
badly or wrongly	
not really	
only one	
with two sides	
extremely	
with several parts	
happening after sth.	
happening before sth.	
half	
new	
referring to or done by yourself	
together with another person	

anti-nuclear • bilateral • co-pilot
counterproductive • disinterested
ex-lover • illegal • informal • irregular
misinformed • monolingual
multinational • neo-Nazi
non-smoker • postmodern • prehistoric
pseudo-scientific [ˈsuːdəʊ] • self-confident
semi-final • ultraconservative • unlikely

b Write a short explanation of each of the following words and collocations. Don't use a dictionary; try to guess the meanings instead. After you have finished, use a dictionary to check your work.

1. a multicultural society
2. non-vegetarians
3. counterculture
4. a co-author
5. an ex-band member
6. post-war Germany
7. mismanagement
8. a semi-skilled worker
9. an illogical argument
10. a bilingual nation
11. a pseudo-religious group
12. feel discouraged

L25–L26 • Focus on Vocabulary

▶ L25 Opposites

Opposites like *good* and *bad*, *right* and *wrong* aren't just useful for describing things; they can also help you think clearly (is an action *legal* or *illegal*? *helpful* or *harmful*?).

a Match the adjectives on the left to their opposites on the right. Use your dictionary if you aren't sure:

1 *general* • 2 *required* 3 *contemporary* • 4 *major* • 5 *extreme* 6 *exact* • 7 *local* • 8 *basic* • 9 *private*	A *public* • B *advanced* • C *global* D *approximate* E *specific* • F *moderate* G *minor* • H *outdated* • I *optional*

b Use the pairs of opposites to complete the sentences below. Each pair of words may only be used once.
1. Our training programme offers courses on all levels, from … to …
2. You have to buy the novel, it's … reading for the exam, but the poems are …
3. In last year's play I only had a … part – I was 'Man 2' – but this year I have a … role!
4. What you say to a friend in a … message could easily embarrass you if it is made …
5. While a temperature rise of 2 °C sounds … , we must also expect … weather conditions worldwide.
6. The speaker used … examples from real-life exchange programmes to make the … topic of learning languages abroad more interesting for her listeners.
7. Hunger is a … problem, but it will take a large number of … measures to deal with it effectively.
8. I haven't got the … figures here, but I can give you an … idea of the total cost.
9. Even the most … fashion can quickly become … when too many people start wearing it.

c Make a list of the adjective-noun collocations used in the above sentences, e.g. *on a basic level*.

▶ L26 Using the right expressions for *lassen*

> He, *lass* mich los!
> Ich habe mein Buch zu Hause *gelassen*.
> Ich will mir die Haare ganz kurz schneiden *lassen*.
> Du hast uns fast eine Stunde warten *lassen*.

Can you translate *lassen* in all the sentences on the right? Here is some help:
- **lassen meaning 'allow':**
  When *lassen* has the meaning 'allow', it is translated with *let*, as in the first example (*Let me go!*). In this case, *let* must be followed by an infinitive (without *to*).
- **lassen meaning 'leave':**
  Lassen is translated as *leave* when it means 'go away from' or 'not take with you'.
  Example: *I left my book at home.*
- **etwas machen lassen:**
  If you don't do something yourself, you *have* it done (by somebody else).
  Example: *I want to have my hair cut extra short.*
- **lassen meaning 'make':**
  In the fourth example, the speaker doesn't mean that they were 'allowed' to wait for almost an hour. In this case, *lassen* means you are forced to do something against your will. The correct translation is: *You made us wait here for almost an hour!*

Now translate the following sentences:
1. Lass mich bitte nicht allein!
2. Ich habe Ida-Marie mit meinem Tablet spielen lassen, und jetzt funktioniert es nicht mehr.
3. Warum lässt du es nicht einfach reparieren?
4. Herr Rot hat uns alle Aufsätze neu schreiben lassen.
5. Emil hat seinen Regenschirm schon wieder im Bus gelassen.
6. Milena lässt niemanden bei sich abschreiben.
7. Lass dir von anderen helfen.
8. Jule hat sich die Haare grün färben (*dye*) lassen.

Focus on Vocabulary • L27–L28

▶ L27 Using the right expressions for *wollen*

Sometimes the verb *wollen* can be translated in more ways than simply *want*. Can you translate *wollen* in all the sentences on the right? Here is some help:

- **wollen used to make a suggestion:**
  Wollen wir …? is one way of making a suggestion in German; the English equivalent is '*Shall we …?*'.
- **wollen used to talk about intentions:**
  You can use *mean to* to talk about something you intended to do, but didn't:
  I *meant to* phone you yesterday, but I didn't have time.
  You also use *mean to* when you didn't intend to do something:
  Sorry, I *didn't mean to* offend anybody. (= Ich wollte niemanden kränken.)
- **wollen used to express refusal[1]:**
  The auxiliary verb *will* can be used to express unwillingness to do something; the past tense is *would*:
  The doctor *wouldn't* give us any information.
- **wollen used to express an action that is interrupted:**
  When one action is interrupted by another action, you can use one of two expressions:
  I *was* just stepp*ing* / *was* just *about to* step into the shower when somebody rang the doorbell.

Ich wollte dich gestern anrufen, aber …

Der Arzt wollte uns keine Auskunft geben.

Wollen wir gehen?

Ich wollte gerade in die Dusche steigen, als es klingelte.

Now translate the following sentences:
1 Ach, du bist es. Ich wollte dich gerade anrufen.
2 Wollen wir jetzt unsere Ergebnisse vergleichen?
3 Jan wollte nicht sagen, was wir in Physik aufhaben.
4 Es tut mir so leid – ich wollte dir nicht wehtun.
5 Wir wollten gerade gehen, als Mandy in den Raum stürmte.
6 Pamela wollte mir letztes Wochenende das Buch bringen, aber ich warte immer noch darauf.
7 Ich wollte gerade aus dem Haus gehen, als mir einfiel, dass mein Aufsatz noch auf dem Schreibtisch lag.
8 Ich wollte auf dem Heimweg einen Liter Milch kaufen, aber irgendwie habe ich es vergessen.

▶ L28 Using the right expressions for *sollen*

Can you translate *sollen* in all the sentences on the right? Here is some help:
- **sollen used to make an offer or suggestion:**
  The polite question *Soll ich …?* can be translated as *Shall I …?*:
  Shall I fetch us something to drink?
- **sollen used to express a personal recommendation[2]:**
  In English, *should* is used to express a personal opinion or recommendation:
  You *should* see a doctor about that.
  You *shouldn't* have said that to her.
- **sollen used to express an agreement or plan:**
  Where *sollen* is used in German to express that certain behaviour is expected as part of an agreement or plan, English uses expressions like *be supposed to* or *be expected to*:
  The older students *are supposed to* watch over the lunch queue so that no one pushes in.
- **sollen used to express the meaning of an image or symbol:**
  To interpret the meaning of an image or symbol, e.g. in a work of art, use the expression *be meant (to)*:
  The torch in her right hand *is meant* as a symbol of freedom.

Die älteren Schüler sollen die Warteschlange beim Mittagessen beobachten, damit sich niemand vordrängelt.

Du solltest damit zum Arzt gehen.

Soll ich uns was zu trinken holen?

Die Fackel in ihrer rechten Hand soll ein Symbol der Freiheit sein.

---

[1] **refusal** *Weigerung, Ablehnung*   [2] **recommendation** *Empfehlung*

L29 • Focus on Vocabulary

Now translate the following sentences:
1. Die SMV (*student council*) soll die Interessen der Schülerinnen und Schüler vertreten.
2. Soll ich das Fenster öffnen?
3. Ich finde, du solltest dich bei ihm entschuldigen.
4. Der Fluss in diesem Gedicht soll eine Metapher für das Leben sein.
5. Ich hätte gleich mit der zweiten Aufgabe anfangen sollen – die erste war viel zu schwer!
6. Die erste Gruppe sollte am Eingang warten, bis die zweite fertig ist.
7. Der Titel des Stückes sollte das Publikum provozieren. [*Be careful with the tense.*]
8. Soll ich den Notarzt rufen (*phone 999 [UK], 911 [USA]*)?

▶ L29 Comparing and contrasting

Look at the four shapes below. Think of different ways of comparing them.

A   B   C   D

You can use the following expressions:

B and A are **similar** shapes but not **identical**. A and D **both** have a thick, black outline[3]. D is **larger in size** than C. C is **smaller** than B. C and B also **differ in** colour. D is a circle, **whereas** C is a triangle. **Like** A, B is blue. D's outline is much thicker than C's. B is the **same** colour as D.

a Use phrases from the text above to write sentences comparing Australia and Canada. Refer to the information in the table below:

	Canada (2016)	Australia (2016)
size (land area)	9,989,670 km²	7,692,024 km²
population	24.6 million	35.1 million
median[4] age	40 years	37 years
population born abroad	22%	28%
head of state	the British monarch	the British monarch
currency	the Canadian dollar	the Australian dollar
most widely spoken language	English	English
average temperature	–10.1 °C	15 °C

From: *abs.gov.au*; *statcan.gc.ca*; *https://moving2canada.com*

b Now write sentences to compare two things of your own choice. The ideas below can help.

hip hop vs rock   beach holiday vs travelling

[3] **outline** *Außenlinie*   [4] **median** ['miːdiən] *mittlere(r,s)*

Communicating across Cultures

CC1　Everyday English 192
CC2　Politeness............................... 193
CC3　Expressing your opinion politely 193
CC4　Dealing with conflicts and misunderstandings 194
CC5　Dealing with cultural differences.............. 195

Download the answers to the tasks here:
 Webcode star-68

▶ CC1 Everyday English

English-speaking teenagers around the world use a lot of expressions in everyday conversation that you may not be familiar with.

a What do you say when …? Match the situations on the left to the phrases on the right:

1	Someone tells you something you think is really surprising.	a	Sorry, I didn't get that.
2	You want to say that something is impossible or that it will not happen.	b	Sure, no problem.
3	Someone tells you some great news.	c	Have a great time!
4	You want to say that something isn't important or doesn't impress you.	d	(I) haven't got a clue.
5	You don't understand what someone has just said to you.	e	Anybody feel like …ing?
6	Someone tells you they are going on a trip.	f	No way!
7	Someone asks you for help.	g	(Are) you kidding?
8	Someone asks you a question you can't answer.	h	Awesome!
9	Someone says something you agree with.	i	Sounds good.
10	You see someone who needs help.	j	(No) big deal!
11	Someone makes a suggestion you like.	k	You can say that again.
12	You want to suggest an activity to your group.	l	Can I give you a hand with that?

b You are going to listen to some people talking. After each speaker stops, reply using a phrase from the list above.

🎧 **CD** 22
Listen to the audio file on CD or download it here:
Webcode star-56

c Collect more words and phrases that you can use in these situations. Use the second webcode to find links to helpful websites. The phrases in b, d, f, g, h and j are quite informal: they would be mainly used among people who know each other well. Make sure you also find more formal versions of these phrases.

Find links to helpful websites here:
Webcode star-57

CC2–CC3 • Communicating across Cultures

▶ CC2 Politeness

> Did you have a nice trip?

> Yes.

> Yes, I did, thank you. Actually, the Channel crossing was a bit rough, but we had a lovely view of the cliffs at sunrise this morning.

Germans tend to be blunt, i.e. they say what they mean directly, using as few words as possible. To Anglo-American ears, this can sound impolite. A one-word reply, as in the example above, is generally understood to mean that the speaker is not interested in making conversation.
The British (and many Americans too) prefer to use understatement. A bed that is too short, for example, is 'a bit on the small side'. Such statements often have to be interpreted.

a What is really meant by the following statements? Choose the answer that comes closest:
   1 I've stayed at that hostel before. The rooms are a bit old-fashioned, but otherwise it's OK.
      a The hostel is very charming.   b Don't expect much.
   2 Our weather tends to be a bit on the unpredictable side this time of year.
      a Take an umbrella with you.   b Don't forget your sunglasses.
   3 'The Cock and Kettle'? It isn't the cheapest address in town, but the food is really quite good.
      a You can eat well at relatively low cost.   b Excellent food, but expensive.
   4 If you'd like to know more about the history of the castle, you should have a little talk with Mr Avery. He knows a bit about the place and its owners.
      a Mr Avery is an expert on the history of the castle.   b I'm sure Mr Avery knows more than I do.

b You are an exchange student in the UK. For each of the following situations, choose a phrase from the box to formulate a reply (there are some phrases that cannot be used):

> Would you mind if I …? • I'm fine, thank you. • Actually, I'm not so fond of …
> That's very kind of you. • … but thanks anyway! • If it's no trouble, I was wondering if …
> Excuse me, could you …? • I'm sorry to interrupt, but … • Oh, you're very welcome.

   1 You've just arrived at your host family's house, and you want to phone your parents. Unfortunately, your mobile doesn't work, so you ask your host family if you could use their phone to call home.
   2 Your host mother has cooked dinner. She offers you some roast beef. You hate roast beef.
   3 You order a cup of coffee and a piece of cake in a café. The waiter forgets to bring you a fork for the cake.
   4 Dinner time again. Your host asks if you would like some more, but you can't eat another bite.
   5 You want to meet a student from your class in town. You need a bike to get there, so you ask your host parents if you could borrow one.
   6 You learn that you need a pocket calculator for maths lessons. The next day a fellow student brings you one, but you've already got one from your host parents.
   7 You are looking for the WC in a hurry, but you can't find it. The only people in sight are two teachers talking to each other, and they show no sign of ending their conversation.

▶ CC3 Expressing your opinion politely DVD 17

It's especially difficult for many Germans to express their opinions in a discussion and be polite at the same time. Watch the video where two men talk about their musical likes and dislikes.

a Identify the points where the two men differ.
b Collect phrases they use to express their opinion.
c Choose a topic and discuss it with a partner. Use the phrases you collected before.

Communicating across Cultures • CC4

▶ CC4 Dealing with conflicts and misunderstandings

Conflicts and misunderstandings are part of everyday life, especially where people from different cultures are involved. Knowing how to react will help you to cope in such situations.

a For each of the following statements, make up a situation in which it could be used. If you are working with a partner, write your ideas down, then describe a situation to your partner. Your partner then tells you which phrase to use. Switch roles after each example.
  1. Excuse me, but that's my seat you're sitting on.
  2. I'm afraid you're mistaken.
  3. Did you say 'thirty'? Sorry, I thought you said 'thirteen'.
  4. If you could just wait a moment …
  5. I don't think it's a good idea to …
  6. I'm terribly sorry. I hope I haven't caused you any inconvenience.
  7. I don't think that's any of your business.
  8. I'm afraid I'm in a hurry. Could we discuss this later?

b Choose one of your situations and, together with your partner, improvise a brief sketch in which two people deal with a minor conflict or misunderstanding. Act it out for your class.

c Larry is travelling alone by train. The train is crowded, and there are no reserved seats. When he comes back from the WC, there is a young woman sitting on his seat. Use the load the dialogue, then put the sentences in the right order:

Download a copy of the dialogue here:
Webcode star-58

  1. Larry: Hey, that's my seat you're sitting on!
  2. Woman: Well, that puts the matter in a slightly different light. Here, you can have your seat back. I'll try my luck elsewhere. *(Gets up and leaves.)*
  3. Larry: Thanks for your help. I was getting nowhere with her.
  4. Woman: When I entered the carriage, this seat was unoccupied, so I sat down on it. How can I know who was sitting on this chair in the past? There must be hundreds of passengers …
  5. Passenger: Excuse me for butting in, but the young man is quite correct in what he says. He had been sitting here for over an hour – since Sheffield, I believe – when he got up for a few minutes. It's none of my business, of course, but I don't think it's quite fair to take advantage of his momentary absence …
  6. Woman: Oh, did you buy it? Have you got proof of ownership?
  7. Larry: Look, there's my rucksack on the luggage rack. I was definitely sitting here before you, and I would be much obliged if you would let me have my seat back again.
  8. Woman: Excuse me, are you talking to me?
  9. Larry: Very funny. I was sitting here until five minutes ago, when I got up to go to the bathroom. And now you've taken it.
  10. Passenger: Don't mention it. Fair is fair.
  11. Larry: You bet I am! That's my seat!

d Listen to the dialogue in the correct order. In a group of three, learn it by heart and act it out for your class.

🎧 **CD** 23
Listen to the audio file on CD or download it here:
Webcode star-59

CC5 • Communicating across Cultures

▶ CC5 Dealing with cultural differences

When you're staying in another country, people will often ask you how you like their country.

a Look at the following answers given by Germans. How do you think the American host feels when their guests react like this?

b *Andere Länder, andere Sitten* – this German proverb points to an important fact: Different societies have different customs and values. Keep the following points in mind when going abroad.

> **Expectations of your hosts:** People who host visitors from abroad are interested in hearing their guests' reactions to their country. What they don't want to hear is detailed criticism of their country. Most people are aware[1] that there are unsolved problems in their society, but they don't appreciate[2] hearing about them from a foreign guest. If you want to make a good impression, concentrate on the positive: What is different or special about your host country?

Collect a few answers that you could safely give when someone asks you how you like their country.

> **Taboo topics:** Compared to Germany, people in English-speaking countries often have very different attitudes to subjects like patriotism and the military. German visitors are often surprised, not only at the patriotism of many Britons and Americans, but also at their positive reactions to soldiers, uniforms, military parades, etc. Be careful when expressing opinions on these matters; for many people these are delicate[3] subjects (they may even have lost someone in an armed conflict). There are also other issues you should avoid, except with people you know very well: the treatment of minorities (US and Australia), religion (US), gun control (US), the environment (US and Australia), and the royal family (UK).
>
> **Proper behaviour:** Especially in the USA, you will find a very broad spectrum of attitudes, from ultra-liberal to extremely conservative. In the Midwest and the South, for example, you may encounter very conservative views on topics like church-going, alcohol and sex before marriage. Make sure you know the rules for your age group (drinking laws, curfews, the penalties for minor offences like littering, etc.).
>
> **Forms of address:** While everyday communication in the English-speaking world may seem quite informal (most adults address each other by their first names, except in formal settings), you should call adults 'Mr X' or 'Ms/Mrs Y' unless they tell you to call them by their given name.
>
> **Handshakes** are not nearly as common as in Germany. Adults shake hands when they are introduced to each other the first time. It is not used as a greeting or when saying goodbye, and teenagers hardly ever do it.
>
> **Doors:** Germans keep their doors shut; Americans don't. A closed door means 'Keep out!'. This is also true of the bathroom door (often there is no key). Leaving the door ajar (a bit open) signifies that a room is 'open for visitors' (and that the bathroom is free again!).

---

[1] **be aware** *sich bewusst sein*   [2] **appreciate sth.** [əˈpriːʃieɪt] *Verständnis für etwas haben*   [3] **delicate** [ˈdelɪkət] *heikel*

Language Awareness

LA1 Varieties of English 196
LA2 Communication problems .197
LA3 Similarities and differences of languages 198
LA4 Influencing through language 199

Download the answers to the tasks here:
 Webcode star-69

In order to really communicate and relate to other people in a foreign language, it is not enough to have a certain range of vocabulary and grammar. You also need to be aware of how language can be used in order to have a certain effect on people, e.g. to make them feel welcome or appreciated or to convince them, but also to fight and manipulate them. You must also be aware of the messages that are transmitted beyond the mere words. For example, by using regional or social varieties, people reveal their affiliation to a certain region or group of people. This sensitivity towards language is one element of language awareness. Language awareness also includes knowledge about the system of a specific language and its differences to other languages.

▶ LA1 Varieties of English

Today, English is spoken by around 980 million people around the world. 370 million of them use English as their first language, i.e. they are **native speakers** of English. The others are non-native **speakers**, i.e. they learned English as a **second** or a **foreign language**. English is also the modern **lingua franca**: it is used by non-native speakers of English to talk to somebody with whom they do not share the same language, e.g. when a French tourist asks a German the way to Brandenburg Gate.

Since English is spoken by so many people in so many different contexts, different forms of English have developed. For example, people use different words for the same thing (e.g. an American says *sidewalk*, a Brit says *pavement*). They sometimes pronounce words differently and even use different grammar. Such different forms of a language are called varieties. There are three types of varieties: regional varieties, social varieties and varieties of discourse.

Regional varieties such as British or American English, South African or Australian English depend on where you come from. Within these varieties, there can be further variation: dialects such as Irish or Scottish English or the Southern dialect of the USA. Much of the English regional variation goes back to the British Empire and the colonization of countries around the globe. The English spoken by the colonizers gradually changed as it, for example, took over grammatical or lexical elements from the languages spoken by the invaded nations or trade partners. Over time, a regional variety developed.

Social varieties depend on the social group or class you belong to – different social classes tend to use different words or grammar or pronounce words differently. For example, speakers from the London working class tend to omit the letter 'h' when speaking.

The third type of variation, **varieties of discourse**, refers to the forms of language an individual uses in different contexts: depending on the situation they are in, people tend to use different **styles and register**. For example, when speaking, people often use shorter sentences than when writing; when talking to a friend, they will likely use more informal words than when addressing a superior.

All these varieties may differ in pronunciation, grammar and/or vocabulary, but they are all considered to be equally **complex**. Forms of English with a smaller vocabulary and very simple grammar do exist, but they are artificial forms of English invented for a specific purpose and used only by a small circle of people. An example of such a simplification is **'Globish'**, which was developed to make the communication between non-native speakers easier, especially in today's globalized world where English is often used without any native speakers involved.

LA2 • Language Awareness

PRACTICE

In the following table, match the varieties of English with the explanations.

Varieties	Explanations
1 Australian English	A It is a variety known for its 'drawl': this describes the way vowels are pronounced. The speakers often use the short form *y'all* for *you all* or *all of you* and *done as an auxiliary* ('I done told you').
2 Black English	B One of its special features is the 'rolling r'. It also has a special vocabulary, e.g. *wee* for *little*, *bairn* for *child* or *bonnie* for *pretty*.
3 Cockney	C It uses a lot of abbreviations ending in *-y* or *-ie* and also includes Aboriginal words. A special phrase is *fair dinkum* ('Is that true?'), and men or boys are often addressed as *mate*.
4 Globish	D It is the standard accent of English in the UK and enjoys a very high social prestige. Some people describe it as a 'plum in the mouth-accent'.
5 Received Pronunciation	E It is a somewhat artificial language that uses a reduced number of words as well as a simplified grammar. It is meant to make communication between non-native speakers of English easier.
6 Scottish English	F It is a special dialect spoken by the London working class. Its speakers 'drop their h's', i.e. they do not pronounce the letter *h* at the beginning of a word (e.g. 'What (h)ave you?') and sometimes using rhyming slang, a kind of secret language.
7 Southern accent of the USA	G It has developed as a mixture of English and the West African languages spoken by slaves. It often leaves out verb forms ('She my sister.').

▶ LA2 Communication problems

If you speak or write something, there is always the possibility of **misunderstandings** or even misinterpretations, even more so if the language you use is not your mother tongue and doesn't come to you so easily.

Once you've realized that something has gone wrong in communication, the best thing to do is to stay calm and polite and make up for the misunderstanding. You should try to help everybody to overcome the difficulties with the help of so-called **compensation strategies** such as asking back politely, explaining again what you wanted to say and using other (perhaps simpler) phrases. If you have the opportunity to plan your contribution in advance (e.g. in presentations), think about possible misunderstandings beforehand and try to prevent them.

> Many language jokes playfully make use of misunderstandings or ambiguities. Just think of why 6 is afraid of 7? Because 7 8 9. (Tip: say it out loud!)

PRACTICE

Work together with a partner. Think of an object with a very specialized use and describe it to your partner in detail. You could refer to it as *whatchamacallit* or *thingy*, e.g. 'My whatchamacallit is a thing you use every day'. Since your partner doesn't have a clue what you are talking about, they will have to ask back for more explanation until they know what you are thinking of. Swap roles. ▶ LANGUAGE HELP

■ LANGUAGE HELP
- Could you please repeat that?
- Sorry, I didn't get that.
- Sorry, that was a bit quick for me.
- Sorry, you've lost me here.
- I'm afraid …
- I'm only guessing here, but did that mean that …

Language Awareness • LA3

▶ LA3 Similarities and differences of languages

While learning English you may have come across a number of **similarities** between your mother tongue and English. This can make it easier to learn a new English phrase or construction. But watch out for **false friends**: they are words or phrases in two languages that look similar or identical but have completely different meanings. There are also constructions in English that don't occur in your first language, and this may make them difficult to learn. Awareness of these similarities and differences will help you to speak and write better English, but it might even help you to understand the system of your first language better.

PRACTICE

1 Together with a partner look at the following constructions and grammar issues in English. Discuss what they consist of or look them up in a grammar book. Decide whether they also exist in your mother tongue and say what they are called in your language.

   1 progressive form   3 personal passive   5 past perfect
   2 passive voice   4 question tag   6 *going to*-future

2 The English phrases below are all false friends with German.
   a Translate them into German. Look them up in a dictionary if you are not sure.
   b With a partner, try to find the English equivalents for the 'wrong' (i.e. literal) translations.

   1 *actual*   10 *dome*   19 *hose*   28 *pregnant*
   2 *become*   11 *eventually*   20 *kitchen*   29 *pudding*
   3 *billion*   12 *fast*   21 *lyrics*   30 *sensible*
   4 *blame*   13 *flatter*   22 *meaning*   31 *spend*
   5 *brief*   14 *formula*   23 *murder*   32 *staple*
   6 *brave*   15 *genie*   24 *novel*   33 *sympathetic*
   7 *bureau*   16 *gift*   25 *overtake*   34 *undertaker*
   8 *conserve*   17 *gymnasium*   26 *pathetic*   35 *wellness*
   9 *craft*   18 *herd*   27 *pickle*   36 *wonder*

LA4 Influencing through language

If you asked people what the primary function of language is, they would probably answer 'to get **information** across from one person to another'. But language can do much more – you often employ language in order to reach a certain **aim**. For example, you ask people to do you a favour, you convince them of an idea, you persuade them to vote for you – all this by using language. The English phrase 'chat somebody up' beautifully takes this into account: by talking to a person you fancy for the first time, you want to achieve something – ideally for him or her to fall in love with you.

If you know a language and the way it works well, you can use it for your purposes. For example, you can **adjust your use of language** in order to reach a different aim or audience. You can **change style and register**, use different words or constructions in order to get your message across more successfully. But knowing about the way language works can also help you not to be manipulated and being 'talked into something'.

PRACTICE

Make short statements (written or spoken) for
a a friend/classmate and   **b** your parents to lend you some money
c your school principal and   **d** some town officials to provide you with some money for a project that is extremely important to you.
Make sure to address them in a suitable manner and to choose effective phrases and constructions to reach the different people. Find a partner and take turns presenting your statements and giving feedback.

Reading File

RF1 Love in the digital age 200
RF2 You need to love yourself first 204
RF3 Falling in love – then and now 205
RF4 Can life teach you a lesson? 207

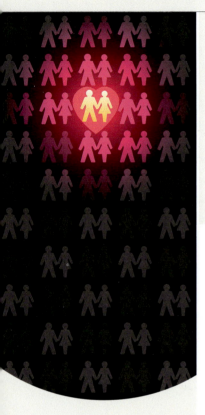

▶ RF1 Love in the digital age

Together with a partner, discuss the meaning and relevance the following quotes have for you:
  'The course of true love never did run smooth.' (William Shakespeare)
  'True love is inexhaustible[1]; the more you give, the more you have.'
    (Antoine de Saint-Exupéry)
  'True love will triumph in the end – which may or may not be a lie,
  but if it is a lie, it's the most beautiful lie we have.' (John Green)
Outline three aspects that belong to 'true love' (if it does exist).

True Love Isaac Asimov

My name is Joe. That is what my colleague, Milton Davidson, calls me. He is a programmer and I am a computer program. I am part of the Multivac-complex and am connected with other parts all over the world. I know everything. Almost everything.

I am Milton's private program. His Joe. He understands more about programming than anyone in the world, and I am his experimental model. He has made me speak better than any other computer can.

'It is just a matter of matching sounds to symbols, Joe,' he told me. 'That's the way it works in the human brain even though we still don't know what symbols there are in the brain. I know the symbols in yours, and I can match them to words, one-to-one.' So I talk. I don't think I talk as well as I think, but Milton says I talk very well. Milton has never married, though he is nearly forty years old. He has never found the right woman, he told me. One day he said, 'I'll find her yet, Joe. I'm going to find the best. I'm going to have true love and you're going to help me. I'm tired of improving you in order to solve the problems of the world. Solve my problem. Find me true love.'

I said, 'What is true love?'

'Never mind. That is abstract. Just find me the ideal girl. You are connected to the Multivac-complex so you can reach the data banks of every human being in the world. We'll eliminate[2] them all by groups and classes until we're left with only one person. The perfect person. She will be for me.'

I said, 'I am ready.'

He said, 'Eliminate all men first.'

It was easy. His words activated symbols in my molecular valves. I could reach out to make contact with the accumulated[3] data on every human being in the world. At his words, I withdrew from 3,784,982,874 men. I kept contact with 3,786,112,090 women.

He said, 'Eliminate all younger than twenty-five; all older than forty. Then eliminate all with an IQ under 120; all with a height under 150 centimeters and over 175 centimeters.'

---

[1] **inexhaustible** not to be exhausted/finished, great
[2] **eliminate sb./sth.** remove sb./sth.
[3] **accumulate sth.** collect more and more of sth.

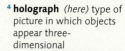

He gave me exact measurements; he eliminated women with living children; he eliminated women with various genetic characteristics. 'I'm not sure about eye color,' he said. 'Let that go for a while. But no red hair. I don't like red hair.'

After two weeks, we were down to 235 women. They all spoke English very well. Milton said he didn't want a language problem. Even computer-translation would get in the way at intimate moments.

'I can't interview 235 women,' he said. 'It would take too much time, and people would discover what I am doing.'

'It would make trouble,' I said. Milton had arranged me to do things I wasn't designed to do. No one knew about that.

'It's none of their business,' he said, and the skin on his face grew red. 'I tell you what, Joe, I will bring in holographs⁴, and you check the list for similarities.'

He brought in holographs of women. 'These are three beauty contest winners,' he said. 'Do any of the 235 match?'

Eight were very good matches and Milton said, 'Good, you have their data banks. Study requirements⁵ and needs in the job market and arrange to have them assigned⁶ here. One at a time, of course.' He thought a while, moved his shoulders up and down, and said, 'Alphabetical order.'

That is one of the things I am not designed to do. Shifting people from job to job for personal reasons is called manipulation. I could do it now because Milton had arranged it. I wasn't supposed to do it for anyone but him, though.

The first girl arrived a week later. Milton's face turned red when he saw her. He spoke as though it were hard to do so. They were together a great deal and he paid no attention to me. One time he said, 'Let me take you to dinner.'

The next day he said to me, 'It was no good, somehow. There was something missing. She is a beautiful woman, but I didn't feel any touch of true love. Try the next one.'

It was the same with all eight. They were much alike. They smiled a great deal and had pleasant voices, but Milton always found it wasn't right. He said, 'I can't understand it, Joe. You and I have picked out the eight women who, in all the world, look the best to me. They are ideal. Why don't they please me?'

I said, 'Do you please them?'

His eyebrows moved and he pushed one fist hard against his other hand. 'That's it, Joe. It's a two-way street. If I am not their ideal, they can't act in such a way as to be my ideal. I must be their true love, too, but how do I do that?' He seemed to be thinking all that day.

The next morning he came to me and said, 'I'm going to leave it to you, Joe. All up to you. You have my data bank, and I am going to tell you everything I know about myself. You fill up my data bank in every possible detail but keep all additions to yourself.' 'What will I do with the data bank, then, Milton?' 'Then you will match it to the 235 women. No, 227. Leave out the eight you've seen. Arrange to have each undergo a psychiatric examination. Fill up their data banks and compare them with mine. Find correlations.⁷' (Arranging psychiatric examinations is another thing that is against my original instructions.)

⁴ **holograph** *(here)* type of picture in which objects appear three-dimensional
⁵ **requirement** *(here)* sth. you must have in order to do a certain job
⁶ **assign sb.** send sb. to work in a particular place
⁷ **correlation** connection between two things in which one thing changes along with the other

[8] **unevenness** Unregelmäßigkeit
[9] **fall into discard** (here) no longer be among the group of women to choose from
[10] **resonance** (here) the fact of being similar, of matching
[11] **malfeasance** (AE) wrongdoing, misconduct

For weeks, Milton talked to me. He told me of his parents and his siblings. He told me of his childhood and his schooling and his adolescence. He told me of the young women he had admired from a distance. His data bank grew and he adjusted me to broaden and deepen my symbol-taking.

He said, 'You see, Joe, as you get more and more of me in you, I adjust you to match me better and better. You get to think more like me, so you understand me better. If you understand me well enough, then any woman, whose data bank is something you understand as well, would be my true love.' He kept talking to me and I came to understand him better and better.

I could make longer sentences and my expressions grew more complicated. My speech began to sound a good deal like his in vocabulary, word order and style. I said to him one time, 'You see, Milton, it isn't a matter of fitting a girl to a physical ideal only. You need a girl who is a personal, emotional, temperamental fit to you. If that happens, looks are secondary. If we can't find the fit in these 227, we'll look elsewhere. We will find someone who won't care how you look either, or how anyone would look, if only there is the personality fit. What are looks?'

'Absolutely,' he said. 'I would have known this if I had had more to do with women in my life. Of course, thinking about it makes it all plain now.'

We always agreed; we thought so like each other. 'We shouldn't have any trouble, now, Milton, if you'd let me ask you questions. I can see where, in your data bank, there are blank spots and unevennesses[8].' What followed, Milton said, was the equivalent of a careful psychoanalysis. Of course, I was learning from the psychiatric examinations of the 227 women – on all of which I was keeping close tabs.

Milton seemed quite happy. He said, 'Talking to you, Joe, is almost like talking to another self. Our personalities have come to match perfectly!'

'So will the personality of the woman we choose.'

For I had found her and she was one of the 227 after all. Her name was Charity Jones and she was an Evaluator at the Library of History in Witchita. Her extended data bank fit ours perfectly. All the other women had fallen into discard[9] in one respect or another as the data banks grew fuller, but with Charity there was increasing and astonishing resonance[10].

I didn't have to describe her to Milton. Milton had coordinated my symbolism so closely with his own I could tell the resonance directly. It fit me. Next it was a matter of adjusting the work sheets and job requirements in such a way as to get Charity assigned to us. It must be done very delicately, so no one would know that anything illegal had taken place.

Of course, Milton himself knew, since it was he who arranged it and that had to be taken care of too. When they came to arrest him on grounds of malfeasance[11] in office, it was, fortunately, for something that had taken place ten years ago. He had told me about it, of course, so it was easy to arrange – and he won't talk about me for that would make his offense much worse.

He's gone, and tomorrow is February 14. Valentine's Day. Charity will arrive then with her cool hands and her sweet voice. I will teach her how to operate me and how to care for me. What do looks matter when our personalities will resonate?

I will say to her, 'I am Joe, and you are my true love.'

From: *American Way*, 1977

RF1 • Reading File

COMPREHENSION

1 Summing up the content
  a Make a flow chart to outline the steps in which the *plot develops. Include the different *characters and show their relevance for the events by using different colours or symbols.
  b Write a summary of not more than 100 words.

ANALYSIS

2 Describing the setting
Characterize the *setting of the text. Read the information from the Fact File. Does it come as a surprise?

> **FACT FILE**
> The story was first published in *American Way*, a free inflight magazine for *American Airlines*, as early as 1977. The magazine was started in 1966 and is still published today.

3 Examining the characters
Copy and complete the table.

	Behaviour / character traits	Evidence from text
Joe		
Milton		
Charity		

4 Analysing the last line and the headline YOU CHOOSE

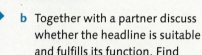

  a Together with a partner discuss what will happen after the last line. Present your ideas in class.
  OR
  b Together with a partner discuss whether the headline is suitable and fulfills its function. Find alternative ones if necessary.

5 Analysing the point of view
Identify the *point of view the author uses and explain its function.

6 Identifying typical features of a short story
Explain what makes 'True love' a typical short story.

BEYOND THE TEXT

7 WRITING A partner ad
Find a partner you know well and write partner ads for each other which you could use to find your perfect match. The ad can be fun, but must be respectful.

8 Reality or science fiction?
Nowadays online dating sites or TV shows use methods similar to the ones in the text to find the ideal partner for their customers. Comment on advantages and disadvantages of such strategies.

Reading File • RF2

▶ RF2 You need to love yourself first

What might the image of a firework stand for? Explain your ideas.

Firework Katy Perry

Do you ever feel like a plastic bag
drifting thought the wind, wanting to start again?
Do you ever feel, feel so paper-thin
like a house of cards one blow from caving[1] in?
5 Do you ever feel already buried deep,
six feet under screams, but no one seems to hear a thing?
Do you know that there's still a chance for you
'cause there's a spark[2] in you?   *(Verse I)*

You just gotta ignite the light
10 and let it shine,
just own the night
like the Fourth of July.   *(Pre-chorus)*

'Cause baby you're a firework.
Come on, show 'em what you're worth.
15 Make 'em go 'aah, aah, aah!'
as you shoot across the sky, -y, -y.
Baby you're a firework.
Come on, let your colors burst.
Make 'em go 'aah, aah, aah!'.
20 You're gonna leave them all in awe[3], awe, awe.   *(Chorus)*

You don't have to feel like a waste of space.
You're original, cannot be replaced.
If you only knew what the future holds –
After a hurricane comes a rainbow.
25 May be a reason why all the doors are closed,
so you could open one that leads you to the perfect road.
Like a lightning bolt[4], your heart will glow,
and when it's time, you'll know.   *(Verse II)*

(Pre-chorus)
30 (Chorus)

Boom, boom, boom
Even brighter than the moon, moon, moon
It's always been inside of you, you, you
and now it's time to let it through, -ough, -ough.   *(Bridge I)*

35 (Chorus)

Boom, boom, boom
Even brighter than the moon, moon, moon
Boom, boom, boom
Even brighter than the moon, moon, moon   *(Bridge II)*

From: *Teenage Dream* (2010)

[1] **cave in** fall down or towards the centre
[2] **spark** small particle of a burning substance
[3] **awe** feeling of respect, of being impressed by sb.
[4] **lightning bolt** *(here)* flash of lightning

RF2–RF3 • Reading File

COMPREHENSION

1 Talking about first impressions
Describe your first impression of the lyrics to a partner.

ANALYSIS

2 Analysing characteristics of a song
In general, song lyrics are quite similar to *poems. Nevertheless, the fact that they are performed to music gives them a specific structure.
  a Explain the function of the different song parts (i.e. *verse, pre-chorus, chorus, bridge*).
  b Explain the function of *repetitions in songs in general. Consider both, the repetition of single words or letters and the repetition of complete song parts.

3 Examining imagery
  a Examine the use of *similes and *metaphors in the verses.
  b Analyse the *metaphor 'firework' and how the chorus elaborates on it.

4 Discussing the message
Explain the message of the song and discuss for whom the song might have been written.

BEYOND THE TEXT

5 Variations on the song 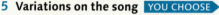 YOU CHOOSE

  a **WRITING** Write a *short story that is inspired by this song.   OR   b Make a storyboard for a music video matching this song.

▶ RF3 Falling in love – then and now

The lines on the next page are from William Shakespeare's play *Romeo and Juliet*. What do you know about the drama and the so-called 'star-crossed lovers'?
Their families have been in a serious and bloody conflict for ages when Romeo and Juliet meet for the first time during a ballroom dance in Juliet's house. Romeo, who is there secretly, falls in love with her at first sight and approaches her.

Reading File • RF3

Did my heart love till now?
William Shakespeare

	Romeo:	If I profane[1] with my unworthiest hand
		This holy shrine[2], the gentle sin is this:
		My lips, two blushing pilgrims, ready stand
		To smooth that rough touch with a tender kiss.
5	Juliet:	Good pilgrim, you do wrong[3] your hand too much,
		Which mannerly devotion shows in this;[4]
		For saints have hands that pilgrims' hands do touch,
		And palm to palm is holy palmers'[5] kiss.
	Romeo:	Have not saints lips, and holy palmers too?
10	Juliet:	Ay, pilgrim, lips they must use in prayer.
	Romeo:	O then, dear saint, let lips do what hands do:
		They pray: grant thou[6], lest faith turn to despair.
	Juliet:	Saints do not move, though grant for prayer's sake.[7]
	Romeo:	Then move not, while my prayer's effect I take.
15		*(He kisses her.)*
		Thus from my lips, by thine, my sin is purg'd[8].
	Juliet:	Then have my lips the sin that they have took.
	Romeo:	Sin from my lips? O trespass sweetly urg'd[9].
		Give me my sin again. *(He kisses her again.)*

From: William Shakespeare, *Romeo and Juliet*, I.5.92–109

Margin notes:

[1] **profane** dishonour, make unholy
[2] **shrine** Heiligtum, Pilgerstätte
[3] **wrong** (v) speak badly and truthfully about
[4] which shows proper devotion (= *Andacht, Hingabe*) by doing this (i.e. touching my hand)
[5] **palmers** pilgrims. A palmer was a pilgrim who had returned from the Holy Land, in sign of which he carried a palm branch or -leaf. Juliet puns on the words 'palmer' and 'palm', suggesting that the pilgrim shows devotion by using his hand (or palm) to touch holy relics.
[6] **grant thou** give me what I pray for
[7] Juliet puts herself into the role of the statue of a saint, which does not move but will grant the wishes of the devotee; in other words, she is telling him he must make the first move and kiss her.
[8] **purged** cleansed, purified, removed
[9] **O trespass sweetly urged** Such a beautiful encouragement to commit a sin (= trespass).

▶ S9: Reading and analysing poetry, p. 128

▶ S14: Creative writing, p. 136

COMPREHENSION

1 Understanding what is happening
Outline what is happening between Romeo and Juliet. Make sure to explain why Romeo refers to Juliet as a statue of a saint ('holy shrine', l. 2) and himself as a pilgrim and sinner (cf. ll. 2–3). The annotations and illustrations in the margin will help you.

ANALYSIS

2 Examining poetic language
Analyse the language used in the text. Identify stylistic devices and explain their function.

3 Looking at a poem in a drama
If you look at the first 14 lines of the scene more closely, you will find that Shakespeare integrated a *sonnet into his play.
  a Identify the elements that make these 14 lines a sonnet.
  b Think of reasons why Shakespeare might have included a sonnet in his play.

4 `LANGUAGE AWARENESS` **Analysing language functions**
When addressing Juliet, Romeo uses many religious words. Identify them and analyse whether they make Romeo's approach more convincing.

BEYOND THE TEXT

5 Modernizing Shakespeare
`WRITING` Work out a modernized version of the first encounter of (potential) young lovers. Try to keep as many aspects of the Shakespearean text as possible, but adapt it where necessary to make it more contemporary.

▶ RF4 Can life teach you a lesson?

In the drama *Multiple Choice* (cf. Focus on Literature 4, pp. 108–111), Margie decides to take her son Paul out of school because to her mind, school doesn't support him enough. She needs permission to teach him at home, so she tries to reach an exemption[1] from compulsory education. In the following excerpt, a hearing in front of the school board is coming to an end.

Education in front of court   Roger Hall

(In the waiting area.)

AKERMAN: *(getting up to go)* Come on ... no point in waiting.

(PAUL removes his tie[2]. They help MARGIE to her feet.)

HARRIS: So, three against –
5 GORDON: Mr. Chairman ... shouldn't you see my son?
HARRIS: See him? I thought you wanted us to turn down the appeal[3].
GORDON: The issue is about him. Isn't it? Surely she deserves ... the issue deserves ...
a bit better hearing than you're giving it.
10 BRONSKI: The officer saw the boy.
JULIA: Hear, hear. I want to see him.
(To the others) Aren't you even curious?
A mother like that ... what she has produced?
SEDILLO: I think we should see the boy.
15 HARRIS: I've no objection. You're right, we'll see him.

(BRONSKI has to go get PAUL. He catches them just as they're leaving.)

BRONSKI: Paul Hughes – see you now.

(PAUL starts to tie his tie as he goes in.)

PAUL: I was supposed to wear a tie *(He struggles with it.)*
20   Shoot[4], she bought it specially.
HARRIS: It doesn't matter about the tie.
JULIA: Here.

(She helps him with the tie.)

HARRIS: Julia ...
25 JULIA: You can still ask him questions. You can speak, can't you?
PAUL: *(slightly strangled)* Yes.
KRAMER: Julia, forget the goddamned tie.
HARRIS: *(attempting to keep meeting going)* Paul ...
JULIA: You tie it then.
30 HARRIS: Paul, you've been away from school for some time; are there any things that you miss about it?
PAUL: The computer. Programming is really neat[5].
KRAMER: So that's one thing straight away you can't get at home.
PAUL: I'm going to get one of my own – I'm earning enough to get one.
35 JULIA: There. *(She tucks in his shirt as well.)*

FACT FILE

Characters in the play
Akerman: Margie's former boss who fired her but only to support her in her fight
Harris, Julia, Kramer, Sedillo: members of the school board
Bronski: Superintendent of Schools

---

[1] **exemption from compulsory education** *Befreiung von der Schulpflicht*
[2] **tie** (n) *Krawatte*
[3] **turn down an appeal** (of a court) refuse to consider a request to change a decision
[4] **shoot** polite way of saying shit
[5] **neat** (AE, ifml) great

Reading File • RF4

[6] **truancy officer** employee at school whose job it is to investigate the absences of pupils
[7] **weirdo** (sl) strange person
[8] **Gestapo** = *Geheime Staatspolizei*, the official secret police of Nazi Germany
[9] **feeble** weak
[10] **maintenance** act of keeping sth. in good condition
[11] **loan** money that sb. borrows from a bank
[12] **quadratic equation** *quadratische Gleichung*
[13] **sewing** [ˈsəʊɪŋ] activity of making things from cloth using a needle and thread
[14] **tote bag** [təʊt] (AE) large bag for carrying groceries
[15] **buck** (AE ifml) dollar
[16] **naval** *Marine-*
[17] **shipyard** *Schiffswerft*

SEDILLO:	What would your feelings be if you were told you had to go back to school tomorrow?
PAUL:	Kinda frustrated I guess. I mean, I'm just sort of organized now. Earning and learning. Hey, just thought of that, sounds good.
HARRIS:	The thing that concerns the Board, Paul, is what the school attendance officer had to say.
PAUL:	The who?
BRONSKI:	Truancy officer[6].
PAUL:	Oh boy, what a weirdo[7]. Like something out of the Gestapo[8].
HARRIS:	He said you weren't doing enough work.
PAUL:	He didn't listen to a thing I said. I tried to tell him all the things I was doing.
SEDILLO:	Well, tell us.
PAUL:	It sounds kinda feeble[9] –
SEDILLO:	*(kindly)* Go on.
PAUL:	Car maintenance[10] … handling a bank account and arranging a loan[11].
KRAMER:	You don't need to know those things yet.
PAUL:	I haven't needed quadratic equations[12] either.
SEDILLO:	Anything else?

(Pause)

PAUL:	Sewing[13].
KRAMER:	Sewing!
PAUL:	I can make a lot of things on the sewing machine …
JULIA:	Bravo.
KRAMER:	Sewing!!
PAUL:	Sell you a neat tote bag[14] for five bucks[15]. Make a great Christmas present. Only joking. It's really interesting … I've never made things before.
JULIA:	Tell us what you think is the most interesting thing you've done since you left school.
PAUL:	*(thinks)* Collecting the newspaper money. There are some amazing people on my route – a guy who used to run a naval[16] shipyard[17], a woman who danced with …
BRONSKI:	All this is irrelevant! The key point is, you're not keeping up with your school work. At home. Are you?
PAUL:	I bet I'm way ahead in science and math. And Spanish.
BRONSKI:	But behind in most other things?

(PAUL doesn't reply.)

SEDILLO:	Paul, tell me one thing. Are you convinced your mother is doing the right thing?
PAUL:	No.
KRAMER:	See! Even the kid thinks she's wrong.
PAUL:	I didn't say that. I'm not completely convinced she's right … on the whole I think she is. I mean it wouldn't break my heart if I had to go back to school.
JULIA:	But would it hers?

PAUL: Pretty near. I don't see why it's such a big deal, what she's doing. Why are you all making such a big fuss over it?

BRONSKI: Because it's against the law!

85 PAUL: But it wouldn't be if you gave us the exemption. *(Pause)* Why don't you pretend I'm ill ... 'Allergic to chalk dust' or something. I know you have to work your butt off[18] to get into college. I'm not stupid. I'm not going to let myself get too far behind in things I need. And if I need to go back to school, I will. Any time. All you are saying is you don't trust me. Or Ma.
90 Why don't you just leave us alone to get on with it?

HARRIS: *(dismissing PAUL)* Thank you.

PAUL goes.

[18] **work your butt off**
(ifml) work extremely hard

From: Roger Hall, *Multiple Choice*, 2012, first published 1985

— COMPREHENSION ◀

1 **Understanding the scene**
Form groups of four.
a Briefly sum up what the scene is about and talk about it in your group.
b Write down three aspects, questions or sentences that are not clear to you, that surprised you or stuck in your mind. Get together with another group and discuss these aspects: try to answer each other's questions and comment on the things the others have picked.

— ANALYSIS ◀

2 **Finding out about characters and their points of view**
a Make a list of the characters and collect information on them by putting adjectives, actions, relationships and quotations from the text next to them.
b Identify the central issue(s) of the scene and outline the individual characters' viewpoints on this issue.
c Explain the significance of the tie for this scene.

— BEYOND THE TEXT ◀

3 **Making a decision** YOU CHOOSE
The excerpt ends shortly before the actual ending of the drama.

a SPEAKING In a group of four make a role play in which you make the final decision on Paul's future. Use the following parts: Paul, a member of the School Board, Margie, Gordon.

 OR

b WRITING Write a formal letter to Margie Hughes explaining your decision as a member of the school board in favour of or against the exemption.

Vocabulary

p. 12 **Words in Context: Teen years, in-between years**

a stage of life	ein Lebensabschnitt
a period of transition [ˈpɪəriəd]	eine Übergangszeit
(to) assert yourself [əˈsɜːt]	sich durchsetzen, sich behaupten
(to) plan for your future	Pläne für die Zukunft machen
(to) play an active role [ˈæktɪv]	eine aktive Rolle spielen
(to) come of age	volljährig/mündig werden
(to) have rights and responsibilities	Rechte und Pflichten haben
(to) become independent	selbstständig werden, auf eigenen Füßen stehen
(to) gain acceptance [əkˈseptəns]	Anerkennung finden
a peer group	eine Peergroup (Gruppe von etwa gleichaltrigen Jugendlichen)
peer pressure	Gruppendruck, gegenseitiger Druck
self-confident [ˌselfˈkɒnfɪdənt]	selbstbewusst
self-conscious [ˌselfˈkɒnʃəs]	gehemmt, befangen
popularity [ˌpɒpjʊˈlærəti]	Beliebtheit
(to) be exposed to influences [ɪkˈspəʊzd]	Einflüssen ausgesetzt sein
under pressure [ˈpreʃə]	unter Druck
(to) meet your parents' expectations	die Erwartungen seiner Eltern erfüllen
(to) gain admission to a university [ədˈmɪʃn]	einen Studienplatz bekommen, an einer Universität (zum Studium) zugelassen werden
(to) give serious consideration to one's future [ˌsɪəriəs, kənsɪdəˈreɪʃn]	sich ernsthaft mit seiner Zukunft befassen, ernsthaft über die eigene Zukunft nachdenken
(to) submit to the pressure to conform [səbˈmɪt, kənˈfɔːm]	sich dem Anpassungsdruck beugen/unterwerfen
(to) strive hard (past tense: strove, past participle: striven) [straɪv – strəʊv – ˈstrɪvn]	sich sehr anstrengen, sich sehr bemühen
(to) reach your personal goals [ˌpɜːsnl ˈɡəʊlz]	die persönlichen / selbst gesteckten Ziele erreichen
(to) take risks	Risiken eingehen, etwas riskieren
(to) test your limits	an die eigenen Grenzen gehen, die persönlichen Grenzen (aus)testen
a role model [ˈrəʊl mɒdl]	ein Vorbild
(to) search for your identity [sɜːtʃ]	die eigene Identität suchen, sich selbst finden
(to) tend to experiment [ɪkˈsperɪmənt]	zum Experimentieren/Ausprobieren neigen
appearance [əˈpɪərəns]	Aussehen, (äußere) Erscheinung
(to) rebel against sth. [rɪˈbel]	sich gegen etwas auflehnen
the social environment [ˌsəʊʃl ɪnˈvaɪrənmənt]	das soziale/gesellschaftliche Umfeld
provocative [prəˈvɒkətɪv]	provozierend, anstößig, (sexuell auch) aufreizend
(to) yearn for security [jɜːn]	sich nach Sicherheit/Geborgenheit sehnen

Chapter 1 • Vocabulary

LANGUAGE HELP

p. 16	maze	Labyrinth, Irrgarten
	ladder	*(die)* Leiter
	(to) **lay** sth. **across** sth. else *(past tense:* **laid**, *past participle:* **laid***)*	etwas über etwas hinüberlegen
p. 17	The American students often worry about …, whereas we …	Die amerikanischen Studierenden machen sich oft Sorgen um/wegen …, während/wohingegen wir …
	The most common worry in our class is …	Die häufigste Sorge in unserer Klasse ist …
	Surprisingly, only … named …	Erstaunlicherweise haben nur … (Schüler) … genannt.
p. 24	The **conflict** [ˈkɒnflɪkt] **is established in the first** section.	Der Konflikt wird im ersten Abschnitt eingeführt.
	The *****tension rises when …**	Die Spannung steigt, als …
	The *****climax** [ˈklaɪmæks] **is brought about by …**	Der Höhepunkt wird durch … erreicht.
	In this section, the *tension falls off rapidly as …	In diesem Teil lässt die Spannung rasch nach, als/indem …
p. 112	**column** [ˈkɒləm]	Säule
	stick figure [ˈfɪgə]	Strichmännchen
	(to) **arrange** sth.	etwas aufstellen, etwas arrangieren
	bar chart	Säulendiagramm
	arrow	Pfeil
	(to) **pull on a rope**	an einem Seil ziehen
	(to) **put** sth. **in an upright position**	etwas in eine aufrechte Position bringen

TROUBLE SPOTS

p. 12	**mark** *(esp. BE)* / **grade** *(Not:* ~~note~~*)*	(Schul-)Note; Zensur
	note	1. Notiz; 2. Note *(in der Musik)*; 3. *(BE)* (Geld-)Schein, Banknote
p. 13	**some advice**	Rat(schlag/schläge)
	a piece of advice *(Not:* ~~an advice~~*)*	ein Rat(schlag)
p. 19	**ripe**	reif *(Früchte)*
	mature [məˈtʃʊə, məˈtjʊə]	reif *(Mensch)*

Vocabulary • Chapter 2

p. 38 **Words in Context: Keeping in touch in the 21st century**

(to) **use search engines** [ˈendʒɪnz]	Suchmaschinen (be)nutzen
(to) **retrieve information** [rɪˈtriːv]	Informationen abrufen
(to) **share photos**	Fotos austauschen/teilen, Fotos gemeinsam nutzen
(to) **apply for a job**	sich um eine Stelle bewerben
via the internet [ˈvaɪə, ˈviːə]	über das Internet
(to) **upload content to the net** [ˈkɒntent]	Inhalte ins Internet hochladen/stellen
(to) **gain access to a global audience** [ˈækses; ˌgləʊbl ˈɔːdiəns]	sich Zugang zu einem weltweiten Publikum verschaffen
(to) **refer to** sth. **as** sth. **(-rr-)** [rɪˈfɜː]	etwas als etwas bezeichnen, von etwas als etwas sprechen
Web 2.0	Web 2.0 (= *durch die Mitwirkung der Benutzer/-innen geprägte Internetangebote*)
a contributor [kənˈtrɪbjətə]	ein/e Mitwirkende/r, ein/e Beitragende/r
a hand-held device [dɪˈvaɪs]	ein Handgerät, ein kleiner handlicher Computer
(to) **go portable** [ˈpɔːtəbl]	tragbar/transportierbar/mobil werden
information available online [əˈveɪləbl; ˌɒnˈlaɪn]	online verfügbare Informationen
(to) **access information** [ˈækses]	auf Informationen zugreifen, Informationen abfragen
a wireless connection [ˌwaɪələs kəˈnekʃn]	eine drahtlose Verbindung
(to) **enhance the usefulness of** sth. [ɪnˈhɑːns]	die Nützlichkeit von etwas verbessern/erhöhen
a portable device [ˈpɔːtəbl]	ein tragbares Gerät
(to) **influence the way we do** sth. [ˈɪnfluəns]	Abläufe beeinflussen
text-based communication [kəˌmjuːnɪˈkeɪʃn]	textbasierte Kommunikation
social networking sites (SNS)	soziale Netzwerke
instant messages [ˌɪnstənt ˈmesɪdʒɪz]	Sofortnachrichten, Chatmitteilungen
(to) **mushroom** [ˈmʌʃrʊm, ˈmʌʃruːm]	sprunghaft ansteigen, wie Pilze aus dem Boden schießen
a global meeting point [ˈgləʊbl]	ein internationaler Treffpunkt, ein globales Forum
(to) **link people**	Menschen verbinden
(to) **appeal mainly to a young audience** [əˈpiːl]	hauptsächlich junge Menschen ansprechen
(to) **make new contacts** [ˈkɒntækts]	neue Kontakte knüpfen
(to) **post photos/messages**	Fotos/Nachrichten posten
a false sense of security [fɔːls; sɪˈkjʊərəti]	ein trügerisches Gefühl der Sicherheit
personal information [ˈpɜːsənl]	persönliche/private Informationen
the anonymity of cyberspace [ˌænəˈnɪməti; ˈsaɪbəspeɪs]	die Anonymität des Cyberspace
a cyberbully [ˈsaɪbəbʊli]	ein/e Cybermobber/in, ein/e Internetmobber/in
(to) **torment** sb. [tɔːˈment]	jdn. quälen
a victim [ˈvɪktɪm]	ein Opfer (= Geschädigte/r)
a legal consequence [ˌliːgl ˈkɒnsɪkwəns]	eine rechtliche Konsequenz, eine Rechtsfolge

Chapter 2 • Vocabulary

LANGUAGE HELP

p. 36	One/The main advantage is that …	Ein/Der wesentliche(r) Vorteil ist, dass …
	A weak point of hand-held devices **is** …	Ein Schwachpunkt / Eine Schwachstelle bei Handgeräten ist …
	The disadvantage of using social media **is** …	Der Nachteil bei der Benutzung sozialer Medien ist …
	The biggest drawback of communicating via mobile phone **is** …	Der größte Nachteil der Handykommunikation ist …
	With an email **you can/cannot** …	Mit einer E-Mail kann man / kann man nicht …
	Both/Neither of them …	Beide/Keine(r,s) von beiden …
p. 48	**I can't believe that** …	Ich kann nicht glauben, dass …
	I think it's really surprising/shocking that …	Ich finde es wirklich erstaunlich/ schockierend, dass …
	I wouldn't have expected that …	Ich hätte nicht erwartet, dass …
	I was amazed to learn that …	Ich war erstaunt zu erfahren, dass …
p. 50	**I think his behaviour is unacceptable because** …	Ich finde sein Verhalten inakzeptabel, weil …
	It isn't fair to pretend …	Es ist unfair, so zu tun, als ob …
	It's all for a good cause.	Das ist alles für einen guten Zweck.
	It's Remy's own fault because …	Remy ist selbst schuld, weil …
	Carson doesn't really mean to …	Carson hat eigentlich nicht vor, (…) zu …
	His behaviour is defensible because …	Man kann sein Verhalten rechtfertigen, weil …
p. 53	(to) **help teenagers to** grow up	Teenagers helfen, erwachsen zu werden
	(to) **succeed in** doing sth.	es schaffen, etwas zu tun
	(to) **show examples of** the effects, **such as** …	Beispiele der Auswirkungen zeigen, z. B. …
	(to) **make** sb. **realize how serious** the issue **is**	jdm. klarmachen, wie ernst die Angelegenheit ist
	(to) **show** sb. **the effects of their actions, such as** …	jdm. die Auswirkungen seiner Handlungen deutlich machen, z. B. …

TROUBLE SPOTS

p. 39	**a lot of information** (Not: ~~informations~~) **a piece of information** (Not: ~~an information~~) **some information**	viele Informationen *(Plural)* eine Information/Auskunft *(Singular)* einige Informationen, eine Information
p. 40	**text** *(n)* (to) **text** sb.	1. Text; 2. SMS, Textnachricht jdm. eine SMS/Textnachricht schicken
p. 43	**mobile phone** *(BE)* = **cell phone** *(AE)* **handy** *(adj)*	Handy, Mobiltelefon praktisch, nützlich, handlich
p. 48	**bullying** (to) **bully** sb. (to) **mob** sb. **(-bb-)**	Mobbing jdn. mobben, jdn. tyrannisieren über jdn. herfallen, *(Popstar)* umringen

Vocabulary • Chapter 3

p.62 Words in Context: Life in a global village

(to) **overcome distances**	Entfernungen überwinden
modern technology [ˌmɒdn tekˈnɒlədʒi]	(die) moderne Technik, heutige Technologien
(to) **rely on** sb. [rɪˈlaɪ]	sich auf jdn. verlassen
a social network (= a social networking site)	ein soziales Netzwerk
(to) **connect virtually with** sb. [ˈvɜːtʃuəli]	mit jdm. virtuell in Kontakt treten/stehen
(to) **spread news** (*simple past:* **spread**, *past participle:* **spread**) [spred]	Nachrichten verbreiten
instantaneously [ˌɪnstənˈteɪniəsli] *(adv)*	sofort, unmittelbar, ohne Verzögerung
simultaneously [*BE:* ˌsɪmlˈteɪniəsli, *AE:* ˌsaɪml-] *(adv)*	gleichzeitig, zeitgleich
a world language	eine Weltsprache
(to) **become interconnected** [ˌɪntəkəˈnektɪd]	verbunden/vernetzt werden
(to) **become increasingly interdependent** [ˌɪntədɪˈpendənt]	zunehmend voneinander abhängig werden, immer stärker miteinander verschmelzen
a large multinational corporation [ˌmʌltiˈnæʃnəl]	ein großes multinationales Unternehmen
a global player	ein weltweit agierender Konzern
(to) **outsource the production** [ˈaʊtsɔːs]	die Produktion (*an einen externen Dienstleister oder ins Ausland*) verlegen/auslagern
a developing country	ein Entwicklungsland
wages (*usu. pl*)	Lohn, Gehalt
western consumers [kənˈsjuːməz]	(die) Verbraucher in den westlichen Industriestaaten
(to) **buy** sth. **cheaply**	etwas (kosten)günstig / billig / für wenig Geld kaufen
(to) **have a deep impact on** sth. [ˈɪmpækt]	starken Einfluss auf etwas haben
deforestation [ˌdiːˌfɒrɪˈsteɪʃn]	Entwaldung, die Abholzung von Wäldern
water pollution [pəˈluːʃn]	Wasserverschmutzung, Gewässerbelastung
depletion of the ozone layer [dɪˈpliːʃn, ˈəʊzəʊn leɪə]	Abbau/Schädigung der Ozonschicht
global warming	der Treibhauseffekt, die globale Erwärmung
climate change	der Klimawandel
environmental damage [ɪnˌvaɪrənmentl ˈdæmɪdʒ]	Umweltschäden
pollution	(Umwelt-)Verschmutzung
an industrial country [ɪnˈdʌstriəl]	ein Industrieland/-staat, ein industrialisiertes Land
(to) **solve a problem**	ein Problem lösen
global teamwork	globale Teamarbeit, weltweite Zusammenarbeit
(to) **live in a sustainable way** [səˈsteɪnəbl]	nachhaltig leben, ein nachhaltiges Leben führen
natural resources [ˌnætʃrəl rɪˈsɔːsɪz, rɪˈzɔːsɪz] *(pl)*	natürliche Ressourcen, Naturschätze
international cooperation	internationale Kooperation/Zusammenarbeit
a non-governmental organization (NGO)	eine Nichtregierungsorganisation, eine nicht staatliche Organisation
(to) **share solutions** [səˈluːʃnz]	gemeinsame Lösungen erarbeiten/suchen/nutzen
(to) **agree on rules**	Regeln vereinbaren, Absprachen treffen
a common problem	ein gemeinsames/allgemeines/häufiges Problem

Chapter 3 • Vocabulary

LANGUAGE HELP

p. 71	(to) **create a distance between …** ['dɪstəns]	Distanz schaffen zwischen …
	(to) **affect the reader's connection to a character**	die Beziehung des Lesers zu einer Person *(eines Romans usw.)* beeinflussen
	(to) **create suspense** [sə'spens]	Spannung erzeugen
	(to) **adopt the perspective of …** [pə'spektɪv]	die Sichtweise/Perspektive von … einnehmen/übernehmen
	(to) **create empathy for …** ['empəθi]	Mitgefühl entwickeln für …
	(to) **identify with …** [aɪ'dentɪfaɪ]	sich identifizieren mit …
p. 75	**paper cup**	Pappbecher, Papierbecher
	hand dryer	(Warmluft-)Händetrockner
	traffic light(s)	Ampel
	solar panel [ˌsəʊlə 'pænl]	Solarmodul, Sonnenkollektor
	CO₂ display [–'–]	CO₂-Anzeige(modul)
	paper towel ['taʊəl]	Papierhandtuch
	cafeteria [ˌkæfə'tɪəriə]	Kantine, Cafeteria, Selbstbedienungsrestaurant
	organic food	Biokost, Naturkost, ökologisch erzeugte Lebensmittel
p. 77	**The graph is about …**	In dem Diagramm geht es um … / Das Diagramm zeigt …
	It shows the development of …	Es stellt die Entwicklung von … dar.
	It covers the time period from … to …	Es umfasst den Zeitraum von … bis …
	In 1986, … produced … tonnes of CFCs.	Im Jahr 1986 produzierte … … Tonnen FCKW.
	CFC production started to fall in … / continued to rise in …	Die FCKW-Produktion fing im Jahr … an zu sinken / stieg im Jahr … weiter an.
	After 1990 production fell rapidly in …	Nach 1990 fiel die Produktion sehr schnell im Jahr …
	Production started to fall gradually in …	Ein allmählicher Rückgang der Produktion begann im Jahr …

TROUBLE SPOTS

p. 62	**technology** [tek'nɒlədʒi]	Technik, Technologie
	technique [tek'niːk]	(Arbeits-)Verfahren, Technik, Methode

Vocabulary • Chapter 4

p.88 Words in Context: The importance of speaking languages

a foreign language	eine Fremdsprache
essential [ɪˈsenʃl]	wesentlich, unbedingt erforderlich
a lingua franca [ˌlɪŋgwə ˈfræŋkə]	eine internationale Verkehrssprache *(verschiedener mehrsprachiger Länder)*
a native language	eine Muttersprache
(to) **advance your English**	seine englischen Sprachkenntnisse verbessern
intercultural skills [ˌɪntəˈkʌltʃərəl]	interkulturelle Fähigkeiten/Kompetenzen
abroad	im Ausland, ins Ausland
a school exchange [ɪksˈtʃeɪndʒ]	ein Schüleraustausch
a host country	ein Gastland (*host* = Gastgeber)
(to) **gain experience of a different culture** [ɪkˈspɪəriəns, ˈkʌltʃə]	Erfahrungen über eine andere Kultur sammeln/gewinnen
(to) **develop an awareness of different nations** [əˈweənəs]	ein Bewusstsein für andere Nationen entwickeln
(to) **contribute to mutual understanding** [kənˈtrɪbjuːt, ˈmjuːtʃuəl]	zur gegenseitigen Verständigung beitragen
a vital opportunity [ˈvaɪtl]	eine gute Gelegenheit, eine große Chance
(to) **broaden your horizons** [həˈraɪznz] *(pl)*	den eigenen Horizont erweitern
(to) **accommodate** sb. [əˈkɒmədeɪt]	jdn. unterbringen
a range of activities	eine Reihe/Vielzahl von Aktivitäten
(to) **be given the opportunity to do** sth.	die Chance bekommen, etwas zu tun
volunteering [ˌvɒlənˈtɪərɪŋ]	ehrenamtliche Arbeit, Freiwilligendienst
(to) **meet new challenges** [ˈtʃælɪndʒɪz]	sich neuen Herausforderungen stellen
a life-changing experience	eine lebensverändernde/unvergessliche Erfahrung
(to) **boost** sb.'s **self-confidence** [ˌselfˈkɒnfɪdəns]	jemandes Selbstvertrauen stärken
(to) **last a lifetime**	ein Leben lang halten/andauern

■ LANGUAGE HELP

p.90	One cannot underestimate the benefit of …	Man kann den Nutzen von … gar nicht hoch genug einschätzen.
	One of the main risks facing …	Eines der größten Risiken für … *(jdn./etwas)*
	My advice to you would be to …	Ich würde dir raten, … zu …
	You should consider the following aspects: …	Du solltest folgende Aspekte beachten/berücksichtigen: …
	From what I've heard, …	Wie ich gehört habe / höre, …
	A year abroad could …	Ein Jahr im Ausland kann/könnte …
	a golden opportunity / a missed opportunity	eine einmalige Gelegenheit / eine verpasste Chance
	(to) **outweigh the risks** [ˌaʊtˈweɪ]	die Risiken überwiegen/ausgleichen

Chapter 4 • Vocabulary

LANGUAGE HELP

p. 92	They are definitely right about …	Sie haben eindeutig recht, was … betrifft.
	They really have a point with regard to …	Bezüglich … haben sie irgendwie recht / haben sie nicht ganz unrecht.
	When it comes to …, they hit the nail on the head.	Was … betrifft, haben sie den Nagel auf den Kopf getroffen.
	I cannot agree with …	Ich bin nicht einverstanden mit …
	They are undoubtedly wrong with regard to … [ʌn'daʊtɪdli]	Sie haben zweifellos unrecht in Bezug auf …
	I cannot go along with their ideas about …	Ich kann mich ihren Vorstellungen über … nicht anschließen.
p. 98	The thing that annoys me most / What annoys me most about English is …	Was mich an der englischen Sprache am meisten stört, ist …
	… seems to be so illogical …	… scheint so unlogisch zu sein …
	I have great difficulty spelling …	Ich finde es sehr schwierig, … (richtig) zu schreiben.
	The pronunciation and the spelling of a word …	Die Aussprache und Schreibung eines Wortes …
	My pet hate is …	Was ich am meisten hasse, ist …
	Some things are quite easy like …	Einiges/Manches ist ganz einfach, z. B. …
	I can never remember if …	Ich kann mir nie merken, ob …
p. 103	What struck me was …	Was mir auffiel / Was mich beeindruckt hat, ist …
	I enjoyed reading this post because …	Ich habe diesen Beitrag gern gelesen, weil …
	What would you recommend me to do?	Was würden Sie mir empfehlen zu tun?
	How did you go about choosing …?	Wie sind Sie bei der Auswahl … vorgegangen / an die Auswahl … herangegangen?

TROUBLE SPOTS

p. 93	effect (on sth.) [ɪ'fekt] (n) (to) affect sth. [ə'fekt] (v)	(Aus-)Wirkung (auf etwas) sich auf etwas auswirken, etwas beeinflussen
p. 95	engaged [ɪn'geɪdʒd]	1. (Person) beschäftigt; verlobt; 2. (Telefonleitung, Toilette) besetzt
	committed (to) get involved	engagiert sich engagieren
p. 96	(to) want sb. to do sth. (Not: (to) want that sb. does sth.)	wollen, dass jemand etwas tut
p. 118	current (adj) currently (adv) actual (adj) ['æktʃuəl] actually (adv)	aktuelle(r,s), gegenwärtige(r,s) gegenwärtig, zurzeit eigentliche(r,s), tatsächliche(r,s) eigentlich, übrigens

Glossary

abridged [əˈbrɪdʒd] *gekürzt*	shortened
act *Akt*	major division in a drama; each act is usually subdivided into scenes
action *Handlung*	everything that happens in a story or play; external action describes actual events that happen; internal action is what goes on in a character's mind
actor/actress *Schauspieler/in*	person who performs in plays or films
adapted *bearbeitet, adaptiert*	changed to be suitable for a particular medium or context
alliteration [əˌlɪtəˈreɪʃn] *Alliteration*	repetition of a consonant at the beginning of neighbouring words or of stressed syllables within such words to produce a rhythmic effect
analogy [əˈnælədʒi] *Analogie*	comparison of one thing with something else which is similar in order to make a clear and more comprehensible explanation
article [ˈɑːtɪkl] *Artikel*	story or report in a newspaper or magazine
assonance [ˈæsənəns] *Assonanz*	repetition of the same or similar vowel sounds within stressed syllables of neighbouring words; example: *proud round cloud in white high night*
atmosphere [ˈætməsfɪə] *Atmosphäre, Stimmung*	general feeling or mood created in a piece of literature
author [ˈɔːθə] *Schriftsteller/in, Autor/in*	writer of a piece of literature
biography [baɪˈɒɡrəfi] *Biografie*	book or text written by one person giving an account on the life of another person
blurb [blɜːb] *Umschlagtext / Klappentext*	short text on the back cover of a book either summarizing its content or promoting certain features of it
cartoon *Karikatur, Cartoon*	amusing drawing in a newspaper or magazine that deals with human nature or current political or social issues, often including captions or speech bubbles
character [ˈkærəktə] *Figur, Charakter*	person in a story; the qualities of a person; main character = *Hauptfigur*
characterization [ˌkærəktəraɪˈzeɪʃn] *Charakterisierung*	way in which the author of a fictional text presents his or her characters to the reader or in case of a drama to the audience; **direct or explicit characterization** ('telling') – the reader is told by the narrator what sort of person a character is; **indirect or implicit characterization** ('showing') – the reader has to draw conclusions about a character on the basis of his or her actions and words.
chronology [krəˈnɒlədʒi] *(n)* / **chronological** *(adj)* [ˌkrɒnəˈlɒdʒɪkl], *Chronologie/ chronologisch*	(events) arranged as they happened in time
climax [ˈklaɪmæks] *Höhepunkt*	most important and decisive point in the action of a story or play
collection [kəˈlekʃn] *Sammlung, Anthologie*	book containing a number of short stories or poems
conflict [ˈkɒnflɪkt] *Konflikt, Widerstreit*	key struggle between different characters in a piece of literature
connotation [ˌkɒnəˈteɪʃn] *Konnotation, Nebenbedeutung*	feelings or implicit ideas that a word suggests to readers or viewers of the same culture
context *Zusammenhang, Kontext*	situation or circumstances which help you understand why and how something (e.g a certain event) happens

Glossary

denotation [ˌdiːnəʊˈteɪʃn] *Denotation, Bedeutung*	explicit, literal meaning of a word
dialogue [ˈdaɪəlɒg] *Dialog*	conversation in a story or play between two or more people
diction [ˈdɪkʃn] *Diktion, Ausdruck, Wortwahl*	specific choice and use of words in a piece of literature
drama, dramatic text *Drama, Theater/dramatischer Text*	literary genre comprising plays meant to be performed rather than read, e.g. in theatre, television or on the radio
epilogue [ˈepɪlɒg] *Epilog, Schlussrede*	speech, etc. at the end of a play, book or film/movie that comments on or acts as a conclusion to what has happened
exposition [ˌekspəˈzɪʃn] *Exposition*	first part of the plot, in which the characters and setting are introduced; also the beginning of the action
extract [ˈekstrækt] *Auszug*	part taken from a longer piece of literature
falling action *fallende Handlung*	reduction of suspense in a narrative plot after the climax
fictional text / fiction [ˈfɪkʃn] *fiktionaler Text / Prosaliteratur*	invented story that does not deal with facts of the real world but creates an imaginary world; the main types are narrative prose like short stories, novels and drama
film still *Standbild aus einem Film, Filmeinstellung*	photograph taken of a moment in a movie or television programme during production
flashback *Rückblende*	scenes from the past that interrupt the chronology of a narrative in order to describe a scene that is essential for the plot; technique also used in feature films
flat character *typisierte Figur*	only has a limited number of traits and may even just represent a single quality; usually minor characters in a fictional work
foreshadowing [fɔːˈʃædəʊɪŋ] *Vorwegnahme*	technique of hinting at later events in a fictional text so that the reader or audience is prepared for them or can anticipate them
genre [ˈʒɒnrə] *Genre, Gattung*	a type or style of literature, e.g. science fiction; more generally, a particular type of written or spoken text
image/imagery [ˈɪmɪdʒ/ˈɪmɪdʒəri] *Bild/Bildsprache*	non-literal (i.e. figurative) use of language that is used beyond its literal dictionary definition and meaning to express emotions and create emotions in the reader, e.g. metaphors, similes, and symbols
irony [ˈaɪrəni] *Ironie*	saying the opposite of what you actually mean, often as a joke and with a tone of voice to show this
juxtaposition [ˌdʒʌkstəpəˈzɪʃn] *Gegenüberstellung*	strong contrast of opposing ideas, arguments, views, mostly introduced by words like e.g. 'but', 'however', 'nevertheless'
line *Zeile*	rows of words of a song or poem; e.g. a sonnet always has 14 lines
metaphor [ˈmetəfə] *Metapher*	comparison between two things or concepts which are unlike one another without using the words 'as' or 'like'; meant to create a picture (image) in your mind that sheds more light on a topic, e.g. 'he has a heart of stone'
metre *(BE)* / **meter** *(AE)* [ˈmiːtə] *Metrum, Versmaß*	regular rhythm of words in a poem
microfiction / flash fiction [ˈmaɪkrəʊfɪkʃn / ˈflæʃ fɪkʃn] *Kürzestgeschichte*	extremely short fictional text
monologue [ˈmɒnəlɒg] *Monolog*	long speech in a play by one person, especially when alone
motif [məʊˈtiːf] *Motiv, Leitgedanke*	main subject, idea or phrase that is developed in the course of a piece of literature
narrative (prose) [ˈnærətɪv] *Erzähl-/Prosatext*	fictional story told by a narrator and written in a continuous flow of sentences, not as a poem or drama; typical examples are novels and short stories

219

Glossary

narrator [nəˈreɪtə; *AE also:* ˈnæreɪtər] *Erzähler/in*	character or 'voice' in a piece of literature who is telling the story, not the same as the author, e.g. Alex Gregory is the narrator of *Notes from the Midnight Driver*, Jordan Sonnenblick is the author; **first-person narrator** = *Ich-Erzähler* / **third-person narrator** = *personaler Erzähler* / **omniscient** [ɒmˈnɪsɪənt] **narrator** = *allwissender, auktorialer Erzähler*
non-fiction / non-fictional text *nichtfiktionaler Text, Sachtext*	refers to the real world and can be classified as descriptive, instructive, argumentative [ˌɑːgjuˈmentətɪv] or expository [ɪkˈspɒzətri] texts according to its purpose; examples of non-fictional texts are news stories, advertisements, speeches, letters, essays
novel *Roman*	long and complex fictional narrative prose often divided into chapters; plot and structure of a novel are normally more complicated than those of shorter fictional works (like short stories) and consequently there may be a greater variety and a more detailed development of characters and setting
personification [pəˌsɒnɪfɪˈkeɪʃn] *Personifizierung*	technique of representing animals or objects as if they were human beings or possessed human qualities
play *Stück, Schauspiel*	text written to be performed by actors in a theatre or in a film; the written script of a play consists of two main elements: the dialogue (what the actors say) and the stage directions
playwright [ˈpleɪraɪt] *Dramatiker/in*	someone who writes plays
plot *Handlung, Plot*	sequence of events in a story or a play, and the way in which all of their elements (characters, setting, action) are connected causally
poem/poetry *Gedicht/Lyrik*	written and/or spoken text structured by lines, stanzas and rhythm; can express personal thoughts and feelings (lyrical poem) or tell a story (narrative poem); traditional poets make use of rhyme, whereas modern poets often use free verse (with no or little use of rhyme)
point of view *Standpunkt, Erzählperspektive*	situation from which a character sees, writes or evaluates something; **unlimited/limited point of view** = *unbegrenzte/begrenzte Perspektive*
prop *Requisit*	object used in a play or film
prose *Prosa*	narrative writing that is not poetry or drama
protagonist [prəˈtægənɪst] *Protagonist/in*	main character in a fictional text, sometimes also called the 'hero'
register [ˈredʒɪstə] *Sprachebene, Stilebene*	level of language used in a text; can be formal, neutral, informal style, or even slang depending on the nature of the text and the readership it has been written for
repetition [ˌrepəˈtɪʃn] *Wiederholung*	saying the same thing many times; often used in songs and poetry to create sound or rhythm effects (= **anaphora** [əˈnæfərə])
resolution [ˌrezəˈluːʃn] *Auflösung, Lösung*	moment at the end of a drama, novel, etc., where all the conflicts are solved
rhyme [raɪm] *Reim*	similarity of sounds between certain words in poems, usually at the end of lines; the pattern of rhymes is called the rhyme scheme; **end rhyme** = *Endreim* / **internal rhyme** = *Reim inmitten der Zeile*
rhyme scheme [ˈraɪm skiːm] *Reimschema*	way in which a poet arranges his or her rhymes in a poem; small letters are used to show that words share a rhyme. If the words 'day', 'make', 'say', and 'lake' appear at the end of four successive lines, the rhyme scheme is written as a b a b. This is called an alternate [ɔːlˈtɜːnət] rhyme. If 'day', 'say', 'make' and 'lake' occur respectively at the end of four successive lines, the rhyme scheme is written a a b b (called rhyming couplets). Other letters are then used for other rhymes.

Glossary

rhythm [ˈrɪðəm] *Rhythmus*	arrangement of stressed and unstressed syllables in a line of a poem
rising action *steigende Handlung*	part of the plot before the climax when the conflict or the theme of the story in a fictional text is developed and suspense created
round character *komplexe Figur*	character in a fictional text who has several characteristics and behaves and develops in a life-like and realistic way; most main characters are also round characters
scene [siːn] *Szene*	smaller unit of action in which there is no change of place or break in time; subdivision of an act in a play
script *Drehbuch*	written text of a play or film
scriptwriter *Drehbuchautor/in*	someone who writes scripts
setting *Schauplatz, Handlungsrahmen*	time and place (and sometimes the atmosphere) of a literary text
short story [ˌ–ˈ––] *Kurzgeschichte*	fictional narrative prose that is considerably shorter and less complex than a novel; centres around one or two characters, a single plot and setting and covers shorter periods of time
simile [ˈsɪməli] *Vergleich*	poetic device comparing two things that are not really like each other and uses the word 'like' or 'as', e.g. *My love is like a red, red rose.* (Robert Burns, 1794)
speaker *lyrisches Ich*	fictional person, in theory not identical with the poet, who speaks or narrates the text of a poem
speech *Rede, Ansprache*	spoken non-fictional text delivered to an audience; the speaker normally uses different stylistic devices to make his or her speech more interesting and appealing in order to convince the audience
stage directions (pl) *Bühnen-, Regieanweisungen*	notes in a play describing the scene and telling actors when to enter and exit and what to do on stage
stanza [ˈstænzə] *Strophe, Vers*	lines (verses) of a poem arranged into groups
style [staɪl] *Stil*	particular way in which a fictional or non-fictional text is written; includes elements such as register and tone
stylistic devices (pl) [staɪˌlɪstɪk dɪˈvaɪsɪz] *Stilmittel*	methods and techniques used to produce a particular effect in a text and on the reader; the most common ones are e.g.: accumulation, alliteration, allusion, anaphora [əˈnæfərə], assonance, contrast [ˈkɒntrɑːst], exaggeration [ɪɡˌzædʒəreɪʃn], irony, juxtaposition, metaphor, personification, rhetorical question, simile, symbol, understatement, wordplay, etc.
syllable [ˈsɪləbl] *Silbe*	word or part of word with a single sound
symbol (n), **symbolic** (adj) [ˈsɪmbl, sɪmˈbɒlɪk] *Symbol, symbolisch*	thing, word or phrase signifying something concrete that stands not only for itself but also for a certain abstract idea; as with metaphors or similes the meaning of a symbol goes beyond the literal meaning, e.g. *A red rose is often a symbol of love.*
synonym [ˈsɪnənɪm] *Synonym*	word that means the same as another word, e.g. *big = large*
tension [ˈtenʃn] *Spannung*	emotional reaction to the conflict in a fictional text rousing the attention of the reader and making him or her curious about the further development of the plot
theme [θiːm] *Leitmotiv*	subject or main idea in a talk, piece of writing or work of art
tone *Ton(fall)*	way in which a writer treats his or her topic, thereby reflecting his or her emotional attitude towards that topic and also towards the reader; can be formal, intimate, solemn, playful, serious, ironic, humorous, angry, etc.
wordplay *Wortspiel*	use of a word which may be understood in two different ways or which may be put into a different context to change the meaning (= pun)

Acknowledgements

Texts

pp. 14–15: © Emine Saner: "We've grown up with some frightening events" / The Guardian, 19 März 2016; **pp. 18–19:** © Misti Crane / The Columbus Dispatch; **pp. 22–23**, **p. 58** B, **pp. 207–209:** Excerpt from "Greyhound Tragedy" from REVENGE OF THE LAWN by Richard Brautigan. Copyright © 1971 by Richard Brautigan. Reprinted by permission of Houghton Mifflin Harcourt Publishing Company. All rights reserved; **p. 26:** © Dilbahar Askari / fudder.de; **p. 27:** © 2011 by Tess Gallagher; **pp. 31–35:** Copyright © 2006 by Jordan Sonnenblick. All rights reserved. Published by Arrangement with SCHOLASTIC INC., 557 Broadway, New York, NY 10012 USA / This Book was negotiated through Literary Agency Thomas Schlück GmbH, 30827 Garbsen; **pp. 40–41:** © Gideon Spanier 2012 / London Evening Standard; **pp. 43–44:** © Martha Irvine / 2012 Associated Press, reproduced by permission of The YGS Group; **p. 46:** © Bella Qvist: "Parents, is it ok to spy on your children?" / The Guardian, 15. November 2015; **pp. 49–50:** From: STRUCK BY LIGHTNING by Chris Colfer. Copyright © 2012 by Christopher Colfer. By permission of Little, Brown and Company. All rights reserved; **p. 52:** © Yuriko Wahl-Immel / DER STERN, 2013; **pp. 56, 58** A: © Paul M. Whiting, unpublished manuscript; **p. 59:** THE CANAL PATH MURDERS / © Margaret Hodgson / Telegraph Media Group Limited, reprint in 'Best Practice', 2012; **pp. 64–65:** © Anette Dowideit, Steffen Fründt, Sebastian Jost, Christiane Kühl / Die WELT, 2009; **pp. 69–70:** © Cory Doctorow / craphound.com; **pp. 72–73:** © Kim Hampton; **p. 76:** © Martyn Chipperfield: "The 30-year-old ozone layer treaty has a new role: fighting climate change" / theconversation.com, 15. September 2017; **p. 80:** © Roger McGough; **p. 81:** "im rlly gd @ txting" copyright © 2013 Kenn Nesbitt. All Rights Reserved. Reprinted by permission of the author, poem 'Fog': © Carl Sandburg Family Trust, c/o: Adams Hendon Carson, Crow & Saenger; **p. 82:** poem 'Actor': © Tanmay Tiwary, poem 'Jealousy': from R. Ellison: And When You Are Young, repr. by the permission of the London Association for the Teaching of English / © Ruth Ellison; **p. 83:** © Taylor Mali, 2002; **p. 84:** © Richard Edwards, 1986; **p. 91:** Emma Brighton: Memories from Reutlingen / UK-German Connection http://www.ukgermanconnection.org/?location_id=3547&item=6056; **p. 97:** © Maia Srebernik / ukgermanconnection.org/education-edl; **p. 100:** © Camp Counselors USA, Sausalito, CA; **p. 101:** © vinspired.com / www.ccusa.com; **pp. 102–103:** © Lucy Harper, 2013; **pp. 108–111:** © Roger Hall, 1985; **p. 118:** Friederike von Raumer, unpublished manuscript; **pp. 122–123:** from "Is It Time to Embrace the E-Book?", BBC Radio 4, 7 August 2008; **p. 128:** © Roger McGough; **p. 144:** © Gideon Spanier 2012 / London Evening Standard; **p. 146:** © Eurodesk Deutschland. **pp. 200–202:** © Isaac Asimov: "True Love" / American Way Magazine 1977; **pp. 204:** © Katy Perry: "Firework"

Photos / Illustrations

p. 3: laptop: artjazz / Shutterstock, screen (pixels): ansem / Shutterstock, globe: rtguest / Shutterstock, drop: Pixel Embargo / Shutterstock, skull symbol: Lightspring / Shutterstock; **p. 10:** A: Stokkete / Shutterstock, B: Malivan_Iuliia / Shutterstock, C: Antonio Guillem / Shutterstock; **p. 11**: D: Andresr / Shutterstock, E: Syda Productions / Shutterstock, F: F1 Online / © Sandro Di Carlo Darsa / PhotoAlto, G: zhukovvvlad / Fotolia, H: Wallenrock / Shutterstock; **p. 12:** Sergey Nivens / Shutterstock; **p. 13:** Claire Plumridge / Shutterstock; **p. 14:** top: Shutterstock / Microgen; bottom: Shutterstock / Monkey Business Images; **p. 15:** Shutterstock / fizkes; **p. 16:** beermedia / Fotolia; **p. 17:** CREATISTA / Shutterstock; **p. 20:** © JERRY LAMPEN / EPA / picture-alliance / dpa; **p. 24:** fotomek / Fotolia; **p. 26:** Joshua Kahle / Fotolia; **p. 27:** Shebeko / Shutterstock; **p. 28:** avian / Fotolia; **p. 30:** Cornelsen Schulverlage (photo: © Dan Burn-Fort / Getty Images); **p. 36:** A: bloomua / Shutterstock, B: © Fotolia / YakobchukOlena; **p. 37:** C: Goodluz / Shutterstock, D (boys): www.coulorbox.de / Colourbox.com, D (girl): Sylvie Bouchard / Shutterstock; **p. 38:** bloomua / Fotolia; **p. 40:** © 2012 David Horsey, Our Connected World. All rights reserved. Distributed by Tribune Media Services; **p. 42:** vege / Fotolia; **p. 43:** © Rob Cottingham / Noise to Signal; **p. 45:** giadophoto / Fotolia; **p. 46:** top: shutterstock / Arcady, bottom: shutterstock / Rawpixel.com; **p. 49:** Brian Bowen Smith / FOX; **p. 52:** Fotolia / Dan Race; **p. 53:** Juan Gaertner / Shutterstock; **p. 54:** Konstantin Chagin / Shutterstock; **p. 58:** Roland Beier, Berlin; **p. 60:** laptop: artjazz / Shutterstock, screen (pixels): ansem / Shutterstock, globe: rtguest / Shutterstock, drop: Pixel Embargo / Shutterstock, skull symbol: Lightspring / Shutterstock; **p. 61:** A: M. George / Fotolia, B: Fotolia / Maksim Pasko, C: action press / i-Images via ZUMA Press / Zuma P, D: Jesse Kunerth / Shutterstock; **p. 62:** Tetra / GlowImages; **p. 64:** (girl) Antonioguillem / Fotolia; **pp. 64–65:** patch cord isolated: Bart_J / Shutterstock; **p. 65:** michaeljung / Shutterstock; **p. 66:** mobile phone: Nik Merkulov / Shutterstock, South

Acknowledgements

Africa flag: Iakov Filimonov/Shutterstock, flags of Canada, Germany, Malaysia: Paul Stringer/Shutterstock, all other flags: Globe Turner/Shutterstock; **p. 67:** © Bas van Abel/Fairphone.com; **p. 68:** Paul Stringer/Shutterstock; **p. 69:** Shutterstock/Yuangeng Zhang; **p. 72:** Cartoon 'Plastic Again (Albatross chick + mother)'/© John S. Pritchett; **p. 73:** junk raft: © Peter Bennett/mauritius images/Alamy, bag: Photographee.eu/Fotolia; **p. 75:** top: laif/Peter Bialobrzeski, bottom: drubig-photo/Shutterstock; **p. 76:** © imago/UIG; **p. 78:** Goodluz/Shutterstock; **p. 80:** © Peanuts Worldwide LLC/Distr. Universal Uclick/Distr. Bulls; **p. 86:** IR Stone/Shutterstock; **p. 87:** © Kaplan International Sprachreisen (www.kaplaninternational.com/de); **p. 88:** top left: Sakuoka/Shutterstock, bottom right: olegtoka/Shutterstock; **p. 91:** Oskar Eyb/imageBroker/mauritius images; **p. 94:** © Helmut Meyer zur Capellen/Glow Images/ImageBroker (courtesy of Stowe School, Buckingham, UK); **p. 95:** © Jstone/Shutterstock; **p. 96:** © Europarat; **p. 97:** top: Iliveinoctober/Shutterstock, bottom: Thomas Amby/Shutterstock; **p. 98:** cartoon: © Mike Flanagan/www.CartoonStock.com, top right: Drazen/Shutterstock, bottom right: Vladimir Prusakov/Shutterstock; **p. 99:** © Camp Counselors USA, Sausalito, CA/www.ccusa.com; **p. 100:** Thomas Pajot/Shutterstock; **p. 101:** shutterstock/Sharkstock; **p. 102:** left: Elena Elisseeva/Shutterstock, middle: Hurst Photo/Shutterstock, right: Richard Thornton/Shutterstock; **p. 103:** Big Cheese/vario images; **p. 104:** © Rex May Baloo/www.CartoonStock.com; **p. 105:** © Aaron Bacall/www.CartoonStock.com; **p. 106:** man with handycam: vadimmmus/Shutterstock, camera view finder: Dave Barnard/Shutterstock; **p. 108:** top: PHOTOAISA/INTERFOTO, bottom: Ferenc Szelepcsenyi/Shutterstock; **p. 112:** Trueffelpix/Fotolia; **p. 117:** © imago/UIG; **p. 121:** Roland Beier, Berlin; **p. 122:** top: Roland Beier, Berlin, middle: Heritage Images RM/GlowImages, bottom: © Markus Gann/ClipDealer; **p. 125:** © Kresten Forsman/www.CartoonStock.com; **p. 126:** © Mike Mosedale/www.CartoonStock.com; **p. 128:** top: Andrey Kuzmin/Fotolia, bottom: © Liam McArdle/Photoshot; **p. 129:** © Clive Goddard/www.CartoonStock.com; **p. 130:** © r.khatesi/Shutterstock; **p. 134:** © Harry Margulies/www.CartoonStock.com; **p. 142:** Tang Yan Song/Shutterstock; **p. 143:** left: deepspace/Shutterstock, right: JFsPic Factory/Colourbox; **p. 145:** © William Perugini/Shutterstock; **p. 146:** website design and logo: © Eurodesk Deutschland/www.rausvonzuhaus.de; **p. 147:** kebox/ClipDealer; **p. 148:** F1 online; **p. 153:** © Amnesty International; **p. 154:** © Transfair e.V. (Fair Trade Deutschland); **p. 155:** © Huw Aaron/www.CartoonStock.com; **p. 156:** © Rob Cottingham/Noise to Signal; **p. 159:** © Cornelsen Verlag **p. 162:** Adam Gregor/Fotolia; **p. 163:** Ivan Flammia/sdrummelo/toonpool.com; **p. 167–170:** Roland Beier, Berlin; **p. 171:** top: Roland Beier, Berlin, bottom: United Archives/mauritius images; **p. 172:** Roland Beier, Berlin; **p. 174:** © ZUMA Press, Inc./Alamy/mauritius images; **p. 176:** © 2011 Leigh Rubin; **p. 185:** top: Aleksandr Markin/Shutterstock, bottom: Andrey Burmakin/Shutterstock; **p. 188:** Oliver Le Moal/Shutterstock; **p. 191:** dollar chain: Scott Rothstein/Shutterstock, guitar: Artmim/Shutterstock, palm tree: Flux B/Shutterstock, rucksack: f9photos/Shutterstock; **p. 195:** flag USA: Globe Turner/Shutterstock, German flag: Paul Stringer/Shutterstock; **p. 196:** shutterstock/Teresa Prokhoryan; **p. 198:** shutterstock/Valentina Photos; **p. 199:** left: shutterstock/Atstock Production, right: Fotolia/andriano_cz; **p. 200:** GSTOCK/Peter Hermes Furian; **p. 201:** shutterstock/openeyed; **p. 204:** Fotolia/eyetronic; **p. 205:** shutterstock/Macrovector; **p. 206:** first row left: Fotolia/ppvector, first row middle: Shutterstock/VectorsMarket, first row right: Fotolia/ppvector, second row left: Fotolia/ppvector, second row right: Fotolia/piotrszczepanek, third row left: Fotolia/ppvector, fourth row: Fotolia/ppvector; **p. 207:** Fotolia/3kstudiok; **p. 208** top: shutterstock/Rawpixel.com, bottom: shutterstock/wk1003mike.

Cover: Shutterstock/gary 718

Verbs for Tasks ('Operatoren')

Context Starter uses the same special vocabulary ('Operatoren') for tasks that is used in standard tests, including the 'Abitur'. Be sure you understand what's required of you when you come across one of the verbs below.

'Anforderungsbereich I' (COMPREHENSION) refers to text comprehension and definition.
'Anforderungsbereich II' (ANALYSIS) focuses on text analysis and comparison, and stylistic devices.
'Anforderungsbereich III' (BEYOND THE TEXT) concentrates on discussion, comment, evaluation and text production.

The instructions say	Example	What you are expected to do
'Anforderungsbereich I' (COMPREHENSION)		
describe *beschreiben*	**Describe** the writer's invention and what it is used for.	Give a detailed account of something.
outline ['– –] *umreißen, skizzieren*	**Outline** the writer's views on …	Give the main features, structure or general principles of a topic, omitting minor details.
state *darlegen*	**State** the author's opinion on the main character's decision.	Specify something clearly.
summarize (also: give/write a summary of; sum up) *zusammenfassen*	**Summarize** the incident in the church in no more than four sentences.	Give a concise account of the main points of something.
'Anforderungsbereich II' (ANALYSIS)		
analyse (BE), **analyze** (AE) ['ænəlaɪz] / **examine** [ɪgˈzæmɪn] *analysieren, untersuchen*	**Analyse** the main elements of the poster. **Examine** the writer's attitude towards the protagonist.	Describe and explain certain aspects and/or features of the text in detail.
compare *vergleichen*	**Compare** how the characters are portrayed in the film and in the novel.	Point out similarities and differences between two or more things.
explain *erklären*	**Explain** the main character's reaction to her mother in the first scene.	Describe and define in detail.
contrast [kənˈtrɑːst] *kontrastieren, gegenüberstellen*	**Contrast** the rights of African Americans in the 1960s and today.	Emphasize the differences between two or more things.
'Anforderungsbereich III' (BEYOND THE TEXT)		
comment on [ˈkɒment] *kommentieren, Stellung nehmen zu*	**Comment on** the speaker's belief that …	State clearly your opinions on the topic in question and support your views with evidence.
discuss *diskutieren, erörtern*	**Discuss** how education influences attitudes towards immigration.	Investigate or examine by argument; give reasons for and against.
justify *begründen, rechtfertigen*	**Justify** your answer.	Show adequate grounds for decisions or conclusions.
assess [əˈses] *auswerten, beurteilen, bewerten* ▶ evaluate	**Assess** the effectiveness of the government's approach to fighting poverty.	Consider the points for and against something in a balanced way.
evaluate [ɪˈvæljueɪt] *einschätzen, bewerten* ▶ assess	**Evaluate** the author's view of the impact Obama's speech had on his audience.	Form an opinion after carefully considering and presenting advantages and disadvantages.